THE PLEIADIAN MISSION

A Time of Awareness

Randolph Winters

Published by

The Pleiades Project, Inc.

P.O. Box 386

Atwood, CA 92601

The Pleiadian Mission

ISBN   1-885757-07-7

Printed in the United States of America

Special Acknowledgments

It took me three years to finally get this information
out of my head and into a book.   I would like to acknowledge the
encouragement and friendship of the Pleiadian study
groups in both Los Angeles and Orange county
for their support and friendship,
and to Armanda for always
being there.

Edited by Ann Tremaine

Cover art by David Dees

Table of Contents

Introduction

1   *A Prophet Comes to Earth*
The Pleiadians watch over Earth - An old spirit comes to Earth

8   *The Pleiadian Mission to Earth*
A mission to Earth from the Pleiades - The Pleiadians come to Earth in 1685 - The importance of the New Age - The meaning of our lives, religion, science, social development, history and spiritual understanding - Interfering with history to cause certain inventions and inspirations - A woman is chosen as the first physical contactee

20   *Contact from the Pleiades*
Eduard Meier is born - His first contacts with the Pleiades - A ride in a pear-shaped ship - Meeting Semjase, a lady cosmonaut

36   *History of Man*
Our Ancestors from Lyra - 22 million years of human history - The founding of the Pleiades - Earth, Mars, and Milona are colonized - The Great Plan to colonize Earth - Pelegon, the first God of Earth - The founding of Atlantis - The origin of life on Earth - The beginning of our current civilization - The Codex, 144,207 Lyrian spirits come to Earth

62   *Life in the Pleiades*
The planets of the Pleiades - The founding father of the Pleiades - Born in the Pleiades - How they raise children - Economics - Their government - The High Council - Love & Marriage - Landing on the White House lawn

77   *The Beamships*
The Pleiadians travel in spacecraft called Beamships - The science behind the propulsion - A trip to the Pleiades in a Beamship, a fantasy ride - The metal of the Beamship - Gravity is explained - Life on the mothership - Time travel - Touching eternity

Table of Contents

96   How the Universe Was Created
Pleiadian science - The Absolutum, the beginning of our universe - The energy spiral of life - Creating matter - Time begins - Moving in time - The planets form - The logic of how the universe is evolving

112   The Evolution of Human Life
The Logic of Creation - Man's development is dictated by the Creation - The 7 steps of evolution of human life - Evolving into being one with the Creation - The Laws of Creation - The equality of man

127   Spiritual Growth
The process of spiritual growth - How the mind works - How we can gain control of our evolution - Understanding how we add information to our spirit - How our minds work with thought forming a thought - How our 5 senses gather information and process it - What is wrong with the thinking of Earthman - Psychic illness - Our connection to Creation - The akashic records - Heaven, the other side - Telepathy, how the Pleiadians contact people on Earth - Channeling - Reincarnation - How spiritual wisdom is carried to the next life

152   Learning Meditation
What is meditation and why we should use it - Negative and Positive thinking - The spiritual powers - Concentration - A simple meditation - Observation - Pausing - Flashing - Using colors - Clarity of vision - How health is controlled by thinking - Peace on Earth

179   The Story of Jmmanuel
Jesus lived in India - The life story of Jmmanuel (Jesus Christ) - The Antichrist - The Talmud Jmmanuel, the original writings - The Crucifixion - The confusion of Saul - The original Lord's Prayer

191   The Mysteries of Earth
What is the mystery of the Bermuda Triangle - Who was Quetzalcoatl - The ancient city of Agharta - Mount Shasta - What is an Ice Age - The ozone problem - Easter Island - The Greek gods - The Great Pyramids - The Bafath - Adolph Hitler - Ashtar Sheran - The blue-skin race - The Destroyer Comet - The origin of the moon - Earth people in contact with the Pleiadians - The closest planet with human life - When will Earth have open contact with ET's - The story of St. Germain - ET's in our government - Earth-made Beamships - Life forms in our universe

209   *Future Visions and Pleiadian Prophecy*
Future movies - The last Pope - Floods - War with aliens - Ancient cities - The end of New York - The Federal system falls - Antichrist - Natural disasters

223   *The Death of Semjase*
Semjase has an accident - Billy sees her dead - The men of Sona return her life - The FIGU is on probation - The contacts end

233   *A New Vision for Earth*
A vision for the future of our planet - The Lightworker's role - Who speaks for Earth - The Constitution of The People of Earth

248   *Epilog*

249   *Glossary*

260   *References and Suggested Reading*

Introduction

Our civilization has gone through many important changes such as the discovery of fire, the development of the wheel, languages, religion, the industrial revolution, and technology; now we are moving into a New Age of mind and spirit.

The next major event in history will be open contact with life forms from other worlds and taking our position in the family of man in the universe. This event has already started, but as in many historic changes, it is first known only to a few before it becomes known to the masses. The timing of this event is particularly important since our current civilization is in the beginnings of a transformation into a state of higher consciousness that will forever change the way we live on Earth.

We have been contacted by humans from a small cluster of stars called the Pleiades. The inhabitants, the Pleiadians, are a race of people not unlike ourselves who have advanced thousands of years beyond us in technology and spiritual understanding. They are stimulating our consciousness through the dissemination of information so that we can make the necessary changes to create a new world based on *Saalome*, a Pleiadian word meaning "peace in wisdom," for the coming New Age on Earth.

We are fortunate that these visitors from the Pleiades have chosen to gently awaken us to the knowledge of their existence. If they suddenly filled the skies with their spacecraft or landed on the White House lawn, the majority of the people of Earth would probably fall into panic and confusion. Others would worship them or expect them to bring us the long-awaited peace. Governments might fall or lose control as people began to think of themselves as citizens of Earth rather than any particular country. Reactions would vary, but one thing is for sure: the Earth would never be the same, for the knowledge that they bring about science, life, and philosophy could have a devastating effect on our social, economic, religious, and political structures. Too much information too fast could overwhelm a world that is used to making changes slowly.

As our neighbors from another world come to visit, it can also be a wonderful time of discovery. There is the possibility to learn from them, change the way we live on Earth, and create real peace among men. Their knowledge can be used to enlighten our world so that we can resolve the differences that separate us here on Earth and prepare us to fit in with the universal family of man on other worlds. Up to now, the many different races on Earth have been unsuccessfully trying to learn to live together and come to terms with their many different ideologies and social customs. Through contact with the Pleiadians, we are forced to examine ourselves through the revelations of a higher intelligence and hopefully move to a new level of awareness that can facilitate the peaceful coming together of the many nations on Earth.

As we move out into the cosmos, we will come in contact with other races who live differently than we live; they may have mannerisms and customs we will not even understand. How exciting it would be to peer into the future fifty years from now and see all of the wonderful changes Earth will go through as we come into contact with beings from other worlds. The biggest event in our history is unfolding before us right now.

When I became aware of our extraterrestrial visitors from the Pleiades, I traveled to Switzerland to the home of a Swiss farmer named Billy Meier, who was in contact with these off-world visitors. Over a three year period I made several trips to Switzerland to learn all I could about these contacts with extraterrestrial life. After becoming friends with Billy, he appointed me his representative to speak at lecture halls in America and Europe on what I had learned. This gave me the opportunity to share the important messages of heightened spiritual awareness, our connection to the Universal Family of Man, the science of space travel, and the true origin of man on Earth through our connection to the Pleiades.

After several years and hundreds of lectures, I am no longer his representative, but I would like to share with you what I have learned through studying the notes that Billy made of his contacts with the Pleiadians, as well as my own insights gained from private conversations with both Billy and other members of his group. Also included are my own ideas on how we can create a new future for our planet by using the knowledge of higher consciousness. This is not a book of UFO stories or fantasy, but a book of information based on the true life experiences of

Introduction

Billy Meier and the information passed on to him by the Pleiadians for the planet Earth. My intention is to educate, provide stimulating ideas, and raise awareness in order to help us adapt to the changes that are being instigated by our contacts with other forms of life.

Each day it is necessary that we feed our bodies with food to nourish ourselves. It is also important that we feed the mind and spirit as well. Here I offer you food for your mind and spirit in the hope that we can all come together and create peace on Earth in the New Age. It is time for us to come together through education, not the force of legislation.

UFO's....

It is no longer a question of whether or not it is real, but a question of whether or not you know about it.

A Prophet Comes to Earth

Earth: 9500 B.C.

Earth was suffering from the most difficult of times. The great societies of Atlantis and Mu had lived in peace for over 20,000 years, and now treachery and deceit pitted brother against brother. Everywhere were the cries of war and hatred. Soon the oceans would boil with blood as the great scientists readied their weapons of destruction and violence. The peace that had long been their friend was just a memory as history was about to erase all traces of these two great civilizations.

Far away on the home planets of the Pleiades, the great spiritual leaders watched and listened as their younger brothers on Earth quarreled. The highly developed sense of Pleiadian consciousness moved across time and space and felt the coming tides of death and destruction. Earth would be falling into a dark time which would last for many thousands of years - a time of despair, destruction, and degeneration - as those who would survive would be living on a planet with no spiritual guidance. It would be thousands of years before another civilization would again grow out of this hard and difficult period.

A decision was made to help the people of Earth by sending them a special being of higher consciousness to serve as a prophet. This being would be much older and wiser than the people of Earth, and would have already lived through the difficult times of material evolution that provided the great insights of life that would be needed to nourish the souls of men. The spirit, or soul, of this prophet had to possess the integrity and strength of character to teach the truth in the face of all opposition, hate, anger, and doubt that would be directed at it since the truth can sometimes be hard for people to accept. Not an easy task for a normal person, so the Pleiadian spiritual leaders had to choose a very special spirit who could see beyond the cries of anger and ignorance of the uneducated Earthman and still be able to offer love and guidance.

In order to find this special spirit, the wise High Council of the Pleiades knew it would be necessary to search for a spirit that had evolved beyond the bounds of material life and existed in pure spiritual,

1

nonmaterial form. It was known to the Pleiadians that the spirit, or soul, of all human beings eventually evolves beyond the material and becomes a purely spiritual form that no longer requires a material body to survive. Having accumulated vast knowledge of the material life, the human spirit is then well-suited to helping younger and less educated spirits who are still in material form. Even at this point evolution will continue, and the spiritual form will continue to learn and evolve until it becomes part of a larger, more highly evolved form of spirit called a collective consciousness. (To the Pleiadians the word *spirit*, or *spirit-form*, means the same as our use of the word *soul*, and refers to the eternal life force energy that lives forever.) The home planets of the Pleiades were not inhabited by such highly evolved beings, so the search began on other worlds.

Human life is a spirit-form that has
emerged from the Eternal Creational Spirit
and has developed its own consciousness.
It is still connected to the Creational
Source and progresses through a series
of material lives in order
to evolve.

A ship was sent to a remote area of the galaxy to a small planet called Lahson. Here on this quiet world lived a race of beings who through millions of years of evolution had evolved into a spiritual race, no longer having any need for the material bodies they once knew. Their knowledge of the material existence was complete and had freed them from the boundaries of the life and death cycle, for they now existed in the state of development common to higher life forms called a *collective consciousness*. Each one of these collective groups was comprised of seven different spirit-forms. Each of these spirit-forms still retained some measure of memory of their individual personalities, but they could think and exist as a single unit while sharing their collective wisdom.

Here, on this peaceful and tranquil world, the Pleiadians made contact with one of these collective consciousness' who was sympathetic to the problems of man. As the wise, old spiritual collective consciousnesses listened, one of its seven spirit-forms volunteered to degenerate back into material life and help the people of Earth. This was a very serious decision, for once the spirit returned to material life, it would lose contact with its memories and the accumulated wisdom that it had earned over billions of years of evolution. Once back in the material realm, it would

2

be up to the Pleiadians to educate and help the old spirit reconnect with its vast knowledge in order to perform its important role in this special Mission.

In order to get the old spirit to Earth, it was necessary to move it into a material body for the trip. The Pleiadians had brought with them a small child, who had been born especially for this Mission, to serve as host for the old spirit's journey. Since material bodies can be inhabited by more than one spirit at a time, it was easy for the highly advanced, old spirit to move itself into the Pleiadian child and once again feel the sensation of interacting with the world through physical means. Now separated from the highly evolved collective consciousness, the old spirit was ready to begin a mission on Earth that would last for 12,000 years; then, through the aid of the Pleiadians, it would return to Lahson and to the life it once knew. Once the Mission was over, it would have to relive many lifetimes in order to evolve back to the level of evolution it was leaving behind. Many of the lessons of life that had been painstakingly learned would have to be learned all over again.

The Pleiadian ship quickly left for Earth with the small child carrying the ancient and highly developed spirit. Having more than one spirit in a body at a time normally causes confusion, but the child was very young and would only have to support the visiting spirit for a short trip. Once on Earth the old spirit removed itself from the child and prepared itself for its first incarnation into a material life. The small Pleiadian child passed over to the *other side,* or heaven as we call it, so its spirit-form could then incarnate into life on Earth. The wise, old spirit was also on the other side and prepared for its mission on Earth.

The Pleiadian's spiritual knowledge makes it possible for them to contact the other side, the place where sleeping spirit-forms cogitate the experiences of the past material life and prepare for a new material existence. Once they are ready to reenter the material world and continue their path of growth and learning, Creation, the Eternal Spiritual Energy, provides an opportunity to return to the material realm through the process we call birth. Normally this is a natural occurrence involving both the spirit-form, who signals its readiness to return, and Creation, which makes it possible. When we are born, we begin to create the material body that we will live in. This material matter is called *coarse-matter* (energy in a solid state) by the Pleiadians and is created in relation to the spiritual evolution of the spirit-form that is creating it. The evolution of the mother and the father that begins the process of creating the body is most important. Since the spirit-form does not enter the body until it is already started by the mother, it is important to the incoming spirit-form to find a body to enter that is as close as possible to the same level of evolution as itself. This is one of the prime laws of Creation, which controls this process.

In the case of the old spirit-form this would be impossible, for the level of evolution on Earth was far too underdeveloped compared to its own evolution. This first lifetime would be most difficult and awkward, for there would be a great loss in memory and intelligence as it degenerated into a material body not capable of holding its vast knowledge. This new Earth body would not have enough brain connectors and sensors to hold all of the incoming experience and wisdom; much would be lost. There would be no turning back once it entered this material body since its connection to the vast wisdom of the collective consciousness on Lahson would no longer be available. Here on Earth it would be disconnected from much of its own evolution and would need the help of the Pleiadian spiritual leaders for guidance on this Mission.

After preparation and observation, the first material life of the great spirit-form began on Earth. During this physical life it would be known as a prophet in a world that was spiritually stagnant. Even though disconnected from the memories and knowledge of the previous lives on Lahson, the high evolution of the spiritual self that would remain intact would enable it to quickly adjust and learn the knowledge needed to help the people of Earth. Once born into its new material body, the spiritual memories would have to be opened up by the Pleiadian spiritual leaders in order to allow access to the knowledge of Creation and to some of the memories of its former lives. The knowledge of how to access spiritual wisdom was known to only a few on Earth, so it was up to the Pleiadians to help the old spirit-form. In each lifetime it would once again be made aware of its spiritual identity and role in the Pleiadian Mission. The old spirit-form would be awakened to the wisdom that rested within its spiritual self, so it could be used during the material life. This being would also be given the opportunity to return to Lahson at any time, if it so desired. This would be the process through all of its lifetimes on Earth for the next 12,000 years.

Lifetime after lifetime the Pleiadians helped the old spirit-form through various material lives in order to bring truth to the people of Earth. The life of a prophet is always difficult, for he bears the burden of upholding the words of truth to those who are usually afraid to hear it. To the Pleiadians, the people of Earth were learning the lessons of life very slowly and making their lives unnecessarily difficult. This seemed to be happening because of misleading information about the meaning of life that caused people to live a very material and unrewarding existence.

Thousands of years passed as man continued on his slow path of evolution. The old spirit-form was procreated by the Pleiadians on several occasions to lead the life of a prophet, while very slowly the people of Earth were responding and learning the lessons of life. In some incarnations the old spirit-form would dedicate the entire lifetime to teaching just one message which would have such an impact that the world would change forever. Such was the case during the 16th century when the old spirit-form came into life for the sole purpose of educating the world about Earth's place in the universe. It was a time when the church dominated the thinking of man and interpreted the Bible as saying the Earth was the center of the universe; it was God's chosen planet and the sun and all of the other planets revolved around it. The church leaders also believed that the stars in the heavens were made of different materials than the Earth. They had created a position of power for themselves which was enslaving the minds of men.

The Time of Galileo

The Pleiadian spiritual leaders concentrated their highly skilled consciousness into the other side and the sleeping spirit-form was again pulled into life. The year was 1564 in the town of Pisa, Italy, where on February 15th a new lifetime began in the name of Galileo Galilei. His father, Vincenzio Galilei, taught music and wrote books speaking out against the prevailing numerical theories of harmony.

Galileo became educated in medicine and mathematics and became a university professor. He was well-known in the scientific community of Italy and was on speaking terms with the highest minds of the day, including a friendship with the Pope. His position in the community and his status as a learned man prepared him for the role he would play in the changing of history.

It was in the year 1597 that Galileo read a book on the Copernican theory of Astronomy that removed the Earth from its traditional stationary position at the center of the universe, and treated it as a planet that rotated on its axis daily. Copernicus also went on to postulate that the Earth revolved around the sun. This was in direct opposition to the church, who insisted that the Earth was the center of the universe and was made up of different material than the heavens that revolved around it.

Galileo agreed with Copernicus, that the Earth was revolving, because it helped him explain ideas he was working on, such as the tides and other phenomena on Earth. In 1615 he went to Rome and argued publicly for the ideas of Copernicus. This action angered the Pope, who immediately appointed a commission to examine the theory of the Earth's motion. The findings of the commission were that the Copernican theory was contrary to the Bible and possibly heretical. The Pope was very

5

angry at this attempt to undermine the authority and power of the church and ordered Galileo to never speak or write on the Copernican theory again. He was also forbidden to speak of it or teach it to anyone else.

Galileo returned to Florence and turned his work toward astronomy and the telescope. He had made his voice felt to the public and the seeds were planted. Although the Pope had crushed his efforts to enlighten the scientific community, he had opened up the minds of those who had listened to him and started the slow breakup of church domination over science.

In 1624 Galileo visited Rome again because his old friend Maffeo Barberini was elected Pope and had taken the name Urban VIII. He asked the Pope to rescind the edict of 1616 which banned the work of Copernicus. Urban would not do this, but did give Galileo permission to write a new book comparing the old and new astronomy's, providing the information in the book would be treated hypothetically.

Encouraged by this small breakthrough, Galileo returned home and began work on the new book, which he called *The Dialogue Concerning The Two Chief World Systems*. It took several years to finish the work, and it was published in 1632. The book became another attack on the church's idea that the Earth is composed of a totally different kind of matter from that of the heavens. Galileo reconciled the Earth's motion with man's experience in everyday life. He set forth the concept of the relativity of motion, inertia, and the notion of composition of independent motions. *The Dialogue* basically rejected current astronomy and physics and most of the prevailing philosophy.

The book was printed with the church's authority, and Galileo felt he had truly made some progress against the old world thinking. However, within 5 months time the church changed its position on his book and called Galileo to Rome to explain himself. His old friend, the Pope, was no longer friendly and became outraged that Galileo was continuing to undermine the authority of the church and trying to change the thinking that they had postulated.

Galileo was ordered to stand trial, and although he fought gallantly, he lost to the unreasoning Pope who would not listen to his arguments and sentenced him to life imprisonment. All copies of *The Dialogue* were ordered to be burned, and all universities were forbidden to read or sell any of Galileo's books. The church was outraged and was not ready to release its hold over the minds of men.

Galileo's sentence was quickly commuted to house arrest, and he was put under the responsibility of the Archbishop of Sierna. He was later allowed to return to his home at Arcetri in the hills above Florence. At first he was crushed and did not know what to do with himself. But he soon found solace in being allowed to write on noncontroversial physics. Not willing to give up and give in to the church, Galileo smuggled *The Dialogue* out of Italy, and it was eventually printed in Latin and English. The book was retitled and called *Discourses and Mathematical Demonstrations Relating to Two New Sciences*.

Galileo died at home on January 8th, 1642. His life's work of defending the right of science and breaking down the unreasonable attitudes of the church had been successful. History would be forever changed, and his bravery gave hope to others who began to challenge the close-minded authority of the church and discover for themselves the truth about man's position in the universe. The old spirit-form had done well.

The Long Struggle of Mankind

Just as the Pleiadian spiritual leaders had foreseen, it had taken thousands of years for the people of Earth to once again rebuild their great civilization and regain their technology. Years of extraterrestrial intervention by many visiting races had created a world mixed with spirit-forms from many different worlds. Most planets that develop human life have, by nature, only one race that evolves at much the same pace, so the process of developing a peaceful society comes easily. But here on Earth normal evolution has been interrupted by human beings (spirit-forms) that have come from many parts of the galaxy, creating a planet of mixed colors, sizes, and levels of evolution. It is not surprising that we have so many problems here on Earth since our world is such a mixture of people of different spiritual ages. Instead of being a planet where most people are of the same approximate spiritual age and are learning the same lessons of life at about the same time, we are a world mixed with young and old spirits who all need different knowledge and have diverse backgrounds and spiritual memories. Most of the population of Earth came from the constellation Lyra, while others have come from the Vega section of the sky, the Barnard star, and some from star systems called Sirius and Orion. This has created a spiritual imbalance that has made Earth a world dominated by prejudice, hate, and anger.

More than 11,000 years have passed since the inception of the Pleiadian Mission and the arrival of the old spirit-form from Lahson. He has lived many lifetimes in order to gently guide us towards a better understanding of ourselves. The Pleiadians have watched over their younger brothers on Earth and are still with us, hoping that we can overcome the problems of our mixed heritage, and instead, use this rich diversity to our advantage.

The Pleiadian Mission

Even though the Mission to Earth had begun many years before, it was in the late 1600's when more than 250 Pleiadians came to Earth to observe our growth. They built an underground base in Switzerland to conceal their presence. Often they would walk among us, but in most cases they would observe us from the safety of their underground facility or gather information from their sophisticated flying *Beamships*. Unmanned craft called *telemeter ships* were used to monitor our languages and thought patterns. There were many lessons to be learned about the diverse cultures that were evolving here on Earth.

The Pleiadians and their ancient ancestors, called Lyrians, have been aware of our planet for over 22 million years, but this was the first time that they had come to Earth to observe and become involved with us, their younger brothers. They could have come at any time, but it was clear to them that our civilization was beginning to develop, and that an important time was coming which would lead to great change here on Earth.

Having much greater knowledge of the universe than we do, the Pleiadians are aware that our planet is physically moving into a position where it will be greatly influenced by energies from the huge central sun of the galaxy. This happens because our solar system moves in a large orbit which brings us into this position every 25,860 years. This position that we are moving into causes our planet to pass through fields of energies generated by this powerful central sun; the effect is felt by the planet Earth and all life forms on it. Since few Earth scientists or religious leaders have any idea how these energies affect our thinking, it is fortunate our Pleiadian brothers have decided to educate us.

The Age of Aquarius is the Spiritual Era, the Era of effective truth, enlightenment, love of knowledge, freedom, wisdom, and harmony. Unfortunately, all of these lessons will be earned through very difficult struggles. The Age of Aquarius will last 2,155 years, the same as the other constellations, and is repeated every 25,860 Earth years. As we move into this new time, we will have a window of opportunity for 800 years to achieve peace through spiritual growth and the understanding of Creation. If we miss this opportunity to bring a more peaceful and spiritual way of life to our civilization, then the probability rapidly increases that we will fall into a deep and dark period controlled by illogical thinking and negativity. Historically, civilizations typically last for around 10,000 years. Ours is about 8,000 years old and moving into its most difficult phase.

This time of change, or New Age, will be seen by spiritual people as a significant time of clarity, growth, and opportunity. However, the great mass of humanity is so caught up in the material struggle for life that they will perceive this as a time of despair, sorrow, and misery as the mind-set of the industrial age fails to provide the wisdom necessary to lead Earth into a New Age of mind and spirit.

A wonderful opportunity awaits those who have the vision to see the possibilities for peace and love on Earth

The beginning of the Age of Aquarius was on February 3, 1844 at 11:20 a.m. Previously the Earth was in the Age of Pisces, and then moved into the transition period between the two Eras. The complete time for transition from Pisces to Aquarius is 186 years; therefore, at the beginning of the year 1937 the last vibrations of the Age of Pisces were overcome. The Aquarian Era began developing rapidly in its second phase of transition on February 3, 1937 at 11:20 a.m. In the year 2030 the transition time will be complete, and our solar system will be suspended in and bathed with the gold-colored rays of the sign of Aquarius. Then after another 1969 years, the next constellation era of Cosmic Age will arrive. This will be on February 3, 3999 at 11:20 a.m. as our solar system moves into the area of the star sign of Capricorn.

To the Pleiadians, with their vast knowledge of the energies of the universe and the effects they have on the consciousness of man, it was most important that they take this opportunity to lead man towards a new way of life - a path of spiritual understanding and harmony for the future. It is time for us, the people of Earth, to use our higher consciousness to sense the incoming energies and adjust to them, for the effects of these powerful energies cannot be underestimated or taken lightly.

To begin with, it should be made very clear that the Age of Aquarius is not a time heralding the imminent destruction of the world, but the acceleration of spiritual awareness. Some religions and prophets have incorrectly interpreted the Age of Aquarius as the end of the world. This is quite inaccurate, for it will not be the end of the world, but the end of

9

an era of ignorance and the beginning of a new time of enlightenment and awareness. It will also be a wonderful and exciting time of new inventions, the development of mind and spirit, and increasing contact with other life in the universe. The coming rapid changes and discoveries in technology will alter the way we perceive life and the Earth with which we live.

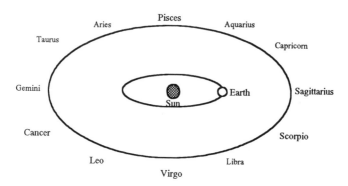

The 12 constellations

Because of the increase in energy from the central sun, the natural rate of development of our society is accelerating rapidly. Think of all of the wonderful inventions and changes we have already been exposed to in the last 100 years. We have come out of the age of the covered wagons, progressed through the industrialization of most of the world, and are moving out into space. Truly, we have made more advancements in the last 100 years than in the past 8,000. It is a most exciting time to be alive.

Spiritual people will see this as a great time of opportunity, for the increase in energy will accelerate personal growth and enlightenment. It is a time for truth and understanding to find their way into our hearts and minds. It is a time for us to discover new ideas and ways of thinking that will lead us into a new period of peace and understanding. We will discover our spiritual connection to Creation and no longer have any need for misleading religious doctrines.

It is a great time for prophets, teachers, and lightworkers. Because of the surge of energy that occurred on February 3, 1937 at 11:20 a.m., the Pleiadians believe that those with the most leadership potential for the New Age were born on the first day of the changeover into the sign of

10

Aquarius. Most of these spirits are among the oldest spirits on the Earth plane and will most likely work in unseen ways as they have no need for public acclaim. Many others were born during that year and will be among the teachers and leaders of this new period for Earth.

This increase in the energies of higher consciousness on Earth is also helpful to the spirit-forms on the other side, for it speeds up the turnaround time for them to return to physical life. Normally, the average turnaround time for a spirit-form to return to material life is 152 years. During this present time of energy increase, the turnaround time can be as short as 15 years. It also facilitates the birth of much more highly evolved spirits to come into material life.

The majority of people will see this as a period of chaos, and will have a very difficult time adjusting to the speed of the changes and to all of the new events that will be happening so quickly. One unfortunate part of these rapidly changing times is that many people will not be able to cope with the turmoil, and they will turn more and more to man-made belief systems and misleading religious doctrines for help instead of seizing the opportunity to take responsibility for themselves. Spiritually conscious leaders will need patience, understanding, and mental balance in order to provide strength, love, and the appropriate role-modeling. The basic teachings of religion, the Ten Commandments, provide the basis for a good, honest life; however, the problem lies with religious leaders who claim to be the mediators of God who provide the passageway to the doorway of heaven. As the coming times become more chaotic, you can expect many new religious sects to spring up that will take advantage of people's fear and lack of knowledge.

Man must face up to being 100% responsible for his actions and his spiritual growth, for there is no God or other divine beings who will do it for him

A friend of mine once mentioned that there is a line being drawn in the sand of awareness. On one side we have the more enlightened and spiritual people who see the coming New Age as a time of opportunity, leadership, and growth. And on the other side, we have the people who are not even aware of what is going on. As you look around and observe, you see that this is true. Most people are consumed with personal problems and live in spiritual ignorance, contributing nothing to the growth of our society or Creation, while others are trying to learn, understand, and grow during this wonderful time.

Knowing the effects that the Age of Aquarius energy will have on us and understanding the difficulties that face us as a civilization, the Pleiadians have chosen to help us, their younger brothers and sisters, with knowledge and understanding that can help us grow and evolve on the right path. Another underground base has been built under Russia in order to become more involved in the development of Earth mankind. After years of careful analysis of our thoughts and studying the actions of our world leaders, they have decided that we need the words of truth in several areas to help us move peacefully into our future.

What Is the Meaning of Our Lives?

The Pleiadians feel that the most important information they can help us with surrounds the meaning and purpose of our lives. Probably no greater question mystifies the people of Earth than this, and at some point in all of our lives we stop to reflect on the purpose of our existence. To those on a spiritual path, it seems almost pointless to be alive if we do not understand why we are living, while those living in a more material world seldom stop to even ask the question.

It is the objective of religions and belief systems to offer an answer to this question. However, if you travel around the world you can find as many answers as there are countries, for almost every religion and belief system has a different explanation of why we are alive. Quite obviously they cannot all be correct. As the world draws closer together through technology and communication, there seems to be an inevitable clash or gridlock approaching whereupon the many answers to this question come face to face and can no longer avoid each other as they have in the past.

From the view of the Pleiadians, they see us as a confused civilization that has turned to death and destruction too many times. In their eyes, the misleading explanations of some religions as to the meaning of our lives has served to keep people in the dark, causing confusion, wars, and bloodshed for thousands of years. There has been no greater loss of life on Earth than that caused by religious wars and persecution. The element of fear has been used all too often to control people and to prevent them from the personal discovery that is possible for anyone – the discovery of Creation and its infinite logic which guides all things in the universe.

The spiritual man who has set aside his ego to travel through the realms of consciousness can find the answer to life for himself. Here Creation can be discovered and the spiritual bonding of all life forms can be felt. The understanding of the infinite spiritual energy can be realized, and the awareness of the purpose of the material consciousness becomes easier to see. For once spiritual existence is understood, the reason for material life becomes clear.

12

We are spiritual beings living through a series of material lives in order to feed our spirits through the wisdom learned from the material existence. It is the process of how spiritual development takes place and how we, as individual spirit-forms, contribute to the whole of Creation and its evolution. The spirit needs the material senses to gather information and to form logic from experience. If the wisdom learned from these experiences is true according to Creation and becomes part of the life of the individual, then it passes into the realm of the spirit and becomes part of the accumulated knowledge of the spirit-form. This is what spiritual evolution is and why we are alive.

Our technical advancements far outweigh our
social development and represent a
clear and present danger to
our future.

Science of the Universe

During the past 300 years of Pleiadian observation, it has become clear that we are not developing fast enough socially to handle our technical growth with responsibility. A lot of scientific effort has been put into the development of war machines, but how about the science of the mind and spirit? Scientists are continually looking for the answers to how things work. Beginning with the simplest question and probing the greatest mysteries, man is always searching for the explanation of how the universe came about and how we fit into it. Seldom does the scientist offer any spiritual conclusions to his quest for knowledge because only the more material or tangible answers are acceptable.

At some point though, the use of formulas and calculations will have to give way to the more spiritual aspect of the universe. To be able to explain the mysteries of the universe, we will need a better understanding of the Creational Spiritual Energy that created it. Man will have to blend together the conclusions learned from questions asked by material science with the knowledge of spirit in order to solve the puzzle, for ultimately the answer to the science of the universe is the explanation of the spiritual power that guides it. Scientists and spiritual leaders, then, are on the same path but approaching on different roads.

Creation is the spiritual power that guides the universe. It is Creation that has the *idea* to create a universe. Once that *idea* is formed, it becomes a reality in the form of a small existence of energy that contains the information on how to begin a universe. That idea is always connected to the Creational power that started it and can never be separated. It is through this connection that Creation serves as a constant guide of how to evolve. A universe can be described as a material life form that is going through its own development and evolution in order to supply wisdom to the Creation that started it.

It is the Creation which lays out the blueprint for the universe to follow. The Creation itself is evolving through a process of discovery learned from experience provided by a material universe. Creation has an awake period during which it creates a material universe for learning and then a sleep period where there is no material existence. It then reawakens and starts the cycle over again at a higher evolution. It is this pattern which permeates all things and provides the explanation of how all life forms evolve. Since all life forms must evolve according to the patterns set by the Creation, it is the understanding of the evolution of Creation through the development of spirit which is most important to the people of Earth.

Spiritual Education

As the Pleiadians lay concealed in their underground laboratories watching the growth of our society, the problem of how they could best be of help to Earth without taking responsibility for us had always been a problem. Trying to find a way to help without interfering with our right of free will was difficult, especially in the area of spiritual education. Finding ways to enlighten us on the use of mind and spirit without being detected or controlling our thoughts challenged the morality by which they live, for the Pleiadians are bound by their own laws of noninterference in our political or power structures and must rely on disseminating information fed through prophets and other enlightened beings.

Nowhere in the Western world is there any public educational process that helps us understand how to use the many different levels of mind and consciousness to control our lives and our evolution. Depending on where you are brought up and what kinds of schools you attend, you will probably be taught nothing more than how to read and write, and then be tossed into the working world to stand in line and fend for yourselves.

Most of the problems of the world are caused by illogical thinking. Misery, depression, heartache, and other forms of emotional illness are all caused by thinking in illogical ways. Imagine how we could change the thinking of the world if we had a logical process by which we could understand how our minds work with information, how it is stored and used by our material consciousness, and how to use the spiritual powers that are in all of us to keep our thoughts in balance. This kind of teaching should be present in our educational system.

14

There is a logical way for anyone to learn about the many different levels of consciousness and how the inner workings of our minds use information. Through meditation we can learn simple exercises to help us understand and control our thinking. We can learn to gain access to powers of spirit that connect us to realms of higher thinking and knowledge. Most importantly, we can learn the balance of mind and spirit that is so necessary to make life enjoyable and fruitful.

It is generally accepted that life is hard and difficult. This is not true. Once the individual learns to control his thinking and use his spirit in day-to-day life, all problems seem to vanish like the rain in sunshine. Luck is a self-inflicted state of mind caused by doing the right thing for the right reason while in a balanced state of mind. The process of maintaining the state of mind that produces luck in life can be learned and used by anyone. Once the balance of spirit and material is understood and the ego is under control, the human can live a rich life of continued happiness.

The History of Man on Earth

Another part of the Pleiadian Mission is to educate us about the history of man on Earth. Our written history is very short and incomplete and provides little information about the origin of our civilization. It seems very unlikely that the many different races of Earth all naturally evolved here, yet we have no practical or scientific explanation of our existence here on Earth. Why are the Asians, Caucasians, Arabs, American Indians, and Africans all so different? It doesn't seem possible that we all could have evolved from the monkeys. The differences between us have provoked prejudice and wars for thousands of years, and now that our weapons are getting more devastating, it's more important than ever that we learn to understand each other and come together as one people, the people of Earth.

The Pleiadians tell us that it has been 626 billion years since the formation of the gas ball that became Earth. Most of that time has been spent evolving spiritual energy into a physical world that can sustain life. However, it has only been during the past 400 to 500 million years that human life on Earth has been detected. Modern science believes that Homo Sapiens (wise man) first appeared around the Mediterranean about 500,000 years ago, and it's only been in the last 6,000 years or so that any kind of details have been recorded. Our current civilization has been but a brief period in the long history of Earth, possibly nothing more than the last second in a yearlong life span.

Anthropologists look for the explanation of our history on Earth through the study of plants, bones, artifacts, and relics left by earlier

15

times. But the discovery of the origin of man is still a mystery left unsolved, for all of the pieces cannot be found. The cutting edge of knowledge continues to change as we learn more and more about our stay here on Earth.

What is missing is the understanding of how life started on Earth and how it has been manipulated, tampered and experimented with for many millions of years. Through the Pleiadians we will discover how ancient travelers from many different worlds have come to Earth and settled here. At last we will know how the many different colors, sizes, and races on Earth can be found in the history of the colonies that have settled on Earth over the past several million years. Most important are the colonizations during the past 100,000 years.

The Pleiadians have studied all the languages ever spoken on Earth for millions of years. They have records of the many different colonies that were founded here and blended together to make the very unique mixture of today's Earthman. We have not been left alone to evolve on our own as most planets have, but instead we are a mixture of many different races that have come here over the millennia. It is this mixture of races who are at different spiritual levels of evolution that has led to the difficult times we are now experiencing. Most planets have only one race and therefore fewer problems. Many war-like races have come here and contributed to our family tree and our bloody history.

The Unsolved Mysteries on Earth

The unrecorded period of the history of Earth has left behind a myriad of unexplained mysteries on our planet, such as the pyramids, Easter Island, the ancient lines of Nazca, and many other unsolved riddles that are connected to our past. The explanations supplied by the Pleiadians of these mysteries will provide an understanding of man and how we came to be here. Once we can see ourselves within the rich history of our past, we will form a new view of our planet as men of Earth, instead of hundreds of independent countries fighting against each other for power and control.

The Pleiadians tell us that their forefathers were our forefathers. We are both descendants of a race of people called Lyrians who have populated Earth on many occasions. It is because of this common ancestry that they see us as their younger brothers and sisters and are trying to help us. Through a better understanding of our origins and how we have all come together, we can put together the pieces of our unique humanity, for we are about to move out into the universe and join up with the family of man that awaits us.

16

Contacting the Minds of Men

It is not clear as to how far the Pleiadians will go to interfere in our growth. They have admitted that about 100 years ago they enlightened some of us Earthlings in order to cause certain inventions to manifest which they felt were needed. As to what these inventions were, we are not certain, but the method they use to transfer ideas is quite interesting.

The Pleiadians see the people of Earth as an insane society, rushing headlong to its own destruction, a destruction that can only be averted by a change in mass consciousness.

They broadcast ideas, visions, thoughts, etc., at levels of consciousness that can be picked up by our subconscious as we sleep. These ideas become part of our dreams, and then we wake up with a great idea, having no awareness of its origin. This way the Pleiadians do not feel they are interfering with our right of free will, for many people may pick up the ideas but only a few will act upon them using their own initiative. In no case do they allow anyone to realize the origin of the thoughts, for that would interfere with our right to create our own future.

They want us to be responsible for our own actions and to make decisions based on our own initiative. They have learned the hard way that it is better to conceal themselves and not let their presence be detected, since in the past when they did this on Earth and on other worlds, it did not work out well. They were sometimes revered as gods, feared as invaders, or found themselves in charge of a planet of helpless people who wanted to be cared for. Since none of these scenarios serve their interests, they have taken a very low profile on Earth at this time and have tried to remain as undetected as possible.

Around the turn of the twentieth century, a decision was made to start physical contact with someone on Earth. This had been tried several times before, but in most cases the person selected lacked sincerity and was not useful to the Mission. The purpose was to see how humanity on Earth would react to the idea that they were not alone in the universe. They had studied the thoughts of people all over the planet but were not sure how most of the population would react to the thought of life on other worlds.

For the most part, very few people at that time had given the idea of life on other worlds much consideration. Life was hard and most of their thoughts and energies were geared toward survival and taking care of themselves and their families. It was quite obvious that with very few exceptions, nothing was known about the real meaning of life or spiritual growth. The decision was made to contact someone on Earth who would carry the message to the world that they were not alone.

We are not told the name of the lady chosen by the Pleiadians for this Mission. This is just as well, as the plan did not work out. She was drawn into several physical contacts with the Pleiadians and educated about other life forms throughout the galaxy and the development of life on Earth. She was asked to go public with the information to let people know what she had learned.

Unfortunately, this did not work out well; her first attempts brought ridicule by her friends and family, and she was considered crazy. She quickly gave up the idea of speaking about her contacts out of fear for her life and her position in the community. People were not ready to open their minds to information that challenged the viewpoints of the powerful religions which so dominated their education. It was quickly learned that the people of Earth were too insecure in their spiritual development to take responsibility for themselves; they found it easier to cling to myths or folk stories of gods that would take care of them and provide an excuse for the many difficulties and problems in life. It seemed to be easier to say, "That's the way God wants it," or "It's God's will," than to take responsibility for one's own decisions, mistakes, achievements, and doubts. The Pleiadians realized we weren't ready, so they stopped the contacts and pulled back again into a position of observation. They didn't understand us as well as they had thought.

The Birth of Eduard Albert Meier

It wasn't until the 1930's that once again the idea of physical contact with Earth was considered. Because of the change that humanity would be going through in the coming New Age of Aquarius, it was becoming even more important that the people of Earth be awakened to the truth about the meaning of life. Earth was spiritually stagnant and controlled by men of power and greed, who caused wars to make money and who placed the attainment of power and control over others above all else. Indeed, mankind was heading toward some hard lessons and not only was not catching on but was becoming more like sheep, with no power to resist the forces of darkness and illogical thinking that ruled the planet.

The time was 1937 and a decision was made to search the other side for a spirit-form that would have the ability to carry the message to Earth, and who would try to break down the barriers of illogical thinking and spiritual darkness that plagued mankind. The great spiritual consciousness of the Pleiadians moved into the realm of the other side and found the old spirit-form from Lahson and brought it back into life to once again serve as a prophet to the people of Earth and provide the knowledge to awaken the spirits of man.

It happened on February 3rd, 1937 at 11:00 a.m. in Bulach, Switzerland. The spirit-form from Lahson was born into the material world and was named Eduard Albert Meier by his parents, who were simple farmers living by the land and the word of God. It had taken the controlled thinking of 7 powerful spiritual leaders of the Pleiades to cause this event. Earth now had a new prophet.

Born at 11:20 a.m., just 20 minutes later, were 3 more spirits who might be helpful with the Mission. They were also born in Europe and would live close to Eduard, so they would be able to help him in his mission if he needed it. The plan was for Eduard to be the physical contact, and the others would be contacted telepathically for the purpose of aiding Eduard through the many difficult times that lie ahead. Once again the Pleiadians would try to assist the people of Earth.

It was hoped that the knowledge the Pleiadians would impart to Earth through the new prophet would help man to better understand himself and rise to new levels of consciousness. The current civilization on Earth had long lived in a self-contained sphere of ignorance, cut off from the knowledge of their ancestry and the spiritual teachings of Creation. This would be the most important time in their history, for Earthlings would be gently awakened to the idea that they were not the only thinking human beings in the universe. It was a time of awakening for the people of Earth because they were about to rejoin the universal family of man after years of darkness, ignorance, and spiritual stagnation. It was a time of *The Pleiadian Mission*.

Contact from the Pleiades

As Creation moved to allow the procreation of the old spirit-form into the world as Eduard Meier, the unseen hand of Pleiadian consciousness gently guided the newborn infant into life. He would be watched over and cared for from that day forward. The importance of this new lifetime could not be understated, for the Pleiadians were aware of the difficult times to come in the New Age. Through this new prophet they would see to it that the wisdom of thousands of years of accumulated lifetimes would find its way into the hearts and minds of the people of Earth.

Of the seven Pleiadians who helped guide the old spirit-form into the world, one, an elderly man named Sfath, decided to take on the task of watching over young Eduard and seeing to his education. In each lifetime that the old spirit-form had served as a prophet, it was necessary in the early years of material life to awaken his sleeping spiritual memories and bring forth the wisdom and abilities that would be needed to perform his mission. In this lifetime it would be Sfath's job to connect with the spirit-form that had become Eduard and prepare him for the tasks ahead.

Sfath began to listen to young Eduard's thoughts, which were just developing, but had no plans to make any contact with him for several years. However, at the age of 6 months Eduard suddenly developed a case of pneumonia that seemed quite serious. For several days Sfath carefully observed Eduard's health which rapidly become very critical. His mother called in the family doctor. After a short examination he informed Mrs. Meier that young Eduard was in a coma and would probably not make it through the night. After the doctor left the house and Eduard was left alone in his room, Sfath decided to take matters into his own hands. Without the knowledge of Eduard's parents, Sfath came into the bedroom and reversed the disease. By morning Eduard's health had returned. Mrs. Meier believed that her prayers had been answered and that a miracle had saved her baby. She would never know her home had been paid a visit by a kindly, old man from another world.

It wasn't until Eduard was 5 years old that Sfath decided to begin contact with the child by stimulating his mind. At first simple thoughts and ideas were telepathically sent to Eduard, challenging him to try to understand their meaning and to respond. This was Sfath's way of getting Eduard to use his mind and wake up his old memories. It was easy enough to contact the spiritual side of Eduard, but the material consciousness was yet not trained in how to use its spiritual self, so the telepathic thoughts went largely unanswered and uncomprehended.

Two years passed as Eduard continued to receive thoughts from Sfath without really understanding their meaning. He did not have the knowledge to comprehend the significance of the strange visions that had been flowing into his head. Sfath had been monitoring Eduard's thoughts and decided that now it was time to open up the spiritual side of Eduard and bring forth the old memories and knowledge that would help him interpret the meaning of his transmissions. To do this, Sfath sent the telepathic command to Eduard to walk out into the forest near his home and to wait for him. Eduard had become accustomed to the telepathic voice by now and was not alarmed or intimidated, so he simply obeyed and went out into the woods and waited.

Sfath was high above the Earth in his spaceship and could sense that Eduard was responding to his request and was now waiting in the forest. The Pleiadian spacecraft was locked in on Eduard's brain patterns and quickly darted down into the atmosphere of Earth and headed for Switzerland. Eduard looked up and saw a small silver dot in the sky. It suddenly streaked toward him like a flash of light and quickly appeared on the ground as a pear-shaped craft. It was unlike anything he had seen before. The craft had arrived quickly without making a sound and gently set down in the meadow where Eduard was waiting. From inside the ship Sfath had carefully scanned the area to make sure that there was no one else around before stepping out of the craft.

Eduard seemed very calm for a young boy of 7 and followed Sfath into his spaceship as he was directed. Within a few seconds the craft left the Earth and was over 40 miles up in orbit. There was no feeling of motion, so Eduard, had no idea where he was until he looked out a window and could see the Earth far below. Sfath was expecting that a short ride in a Pleiadian craft would jar loose some old memories in Eduard's mind and cause him to search himself for their meaning. Sfath wanted him to discover for himself that he had lived many previous lives, during which he had ridden in a similar spacecraft.

Sfath said not a word, but observed Eduard's thoughts as the craft quickly returned to Earth and quietly settled back down on the ground. Eduard was still wordless and seemed to be deep in thought. He had not said a word during the entire trip. Sfath was content with the experience and knew that Eduard's mind would be very busy making some old connections. Billy turned to look at Sfath's ship; it had vanished just as suddenly as it had appeared without making a sound. Eduard was suddenly left alone in the forest to walk home with a lot of new ideas in his head. These ideas would take some time to sort out.

Over the next 2 years Sfath began to send telepathic messages more frequently, and Eduard began to respond and offer answers to the many questions posed to him. He was beginning to remember many things and make some connections, but there was a lot he didn't understand yet. Sfath could tell that Eduard's mind was ready and once again directed him to a meeting place at a remote spot in the forest. This meeting would be different since it was time to open Eduard's mind up and let him know about his mission. He would have to decide for himself if he wished to continue or stop, for Sfath would not coerce him into a stressful lifetime as a prophet. In order for Eduard to make an intelligent decision, Sfath would first have to provide explanations and educate him in many ways.

Once Eduard was aboard the spacecraft and they were safely up in orbit above the Earth where nothing could disturb them, Sfath began to explain to Eduard that he would have to prepare himself for a very serious and extremely important mission. He would have to decide for himself whether or not he would bear the burden of this mission for which he had been born. After many explanations Sfath placed a device on Eduard's head which made a direct contact with his mind and unlocked many old memories and knowledge. More importantly, he brought forward the awareness of the language of spirit that is deep within all of us. This language of spirit is a language of signs and symbols by which one can interpret the meaning of telepathic messages that are sent to the spiritual side of oneself. This immediately allowed Eduard to understand the meaning of some of the transmissions he had received from Sfath. Within minutes his understanding of himself and his mission became much clearer. At this point he made the decision to commit to his part of the Mission.

Happy that Eduard had responded so well, Sfath returned him to Earth. Eduard now had the mental capacity of a 35 year old man and would be able to understand the complex concepts of science and mind that he would now receive telepathically from Sfath. He also possessed spiritual awareness and knowledge far exceeding that of anyone else on Earth. The device that was placed around his head while he had been on the ship had opened up his spiritual self and rekindled much of the old spirit's accumulated wisdom that dwelled deep within his mind. Everything was in place now for Eduard to learn and develop into the prophet of his time.

After several more years of telepathic education from Sfath and other extraterrestrials, Eduard was told he would now be left alone for 11 years to mature and contemplate what he had learned. He would need some time for himself - to travel, to meet his mate, to start a family, and then settle down - before the Pleiadians would revive the contacts.

It was 1965 and the 250 Pleiadians that lived and worked in the vast underground complex under Switzerland had taken relatively little interest in the development of young Eduard; that had been left up to Sfath. They had been busy with their normal duties of monitoring the thoughts of Earth's leaders and studying the effects of the New Age on mass consciousness. Now it was time to choose someone to give Eduard special attention and prepare for the series of physical contacts that would be necessary to educate him as a prophet.

Semjase Prepares for Her Mission

A Pleiadian woman named Semjase volunteered to take on the mission of being Eduard's teacher. She had never been on Earth and was not part of the underground complex team that had been observing Earth for the past 300 years. She was fascinated by the idea of working with the people of Earth. For her it meant that she would have to learn a great deal about the planet, its history, science, languages, its people and, of course, Eduard Meier.

Semjase lived on Erra, the home planet of the Pleiades, where the level of consciousness was quite different than that of Earth, where she would soon be spending so much time. This would pose some problems for her, so she set about her task of preparation slowly. First she studied the German language that was spoken by Eduard. The information storage systems available to her in the Pleiades had on file the King's German that was spoken on Earth during the 16th and 17th century. This was very similar to the Swiss German that was spoken by Eduard and would allow her to understand his thoughts once she began to monitor them.

For the next 10 years she studied the history of Earth and its people over the past several million years so that she could educate Eduard. She would occasionally listen in on his thinking so she would be better prepared to communicate with him when the time came. Throughout all of this time Eduard was unaware that she was listening to this thoughts or that she was studying him.

During this time Eduard had taken on the nickname of "Billy," this was a name he had picked up while watching American movies about Billy the Kid. Very fond of American Westerns, Eduard thought of himself as a cowboy, and thus became "Billy." He wore a cowboy hat and often carried a gun and holster just like his movie heroes, Gene Autry and Roy Rogers.

In order to understand more about his fellow man and to learn about the many philosophies of life, Billy left Switzerland and traveled to the East to continue his education. As the years went by he continued his travels through many countries, including India, Pakistan, and Greece, where he met and married a Greek woman named Kaliope, who went by the nickname of Popi. They returned to Switzerland to the town of Hinwel to start their family. Employed as a night watchman, Billy used his time alone to study the many lessons of life that he had learned over the years in preparation for his mission. He practiced meditation constantly in order to gain access to the spheres of higher consciousness. Sfath had made many references to the previous lives that had been lived by Billy's spirit and had encouraged him to find out about them for himself. Through meditation it was possible for him to connect with his spiritual self, the doorway to the memories of former lifetimes and the lessons learned. Billy was very puzzled by the idea that he had lived previous lives as a prophet serving the Pleiadian Mission, and gave much thought to unraveling this mystery.

Billy's First Contact with Semjase

Semjase was comfortable with her mission and the knowledge she had acquired and felt she was ready to start the contacts. Just before leaving for Earth she spent a few days practicing with a language specialist to brush up on the Kings' German, and then she was ready.

It was on Tuesday, the 28th of January, 1975 at 1:00 p.m. Earth time, when Semjase sent her telepathic message to Billy. He was working at home with his tape recorder, trying to capture the voice of spirits. He had been trying for months with poor results when her thoughts suddenly came into his mind. She was directing him to get his camera and meet her at a remote spot to which she would lead him.

She could tell by his thoughts that he was surprised. They didn't know each other yet, for she had not introduced herself or made her presence known to him during the years she had studied him. Part of his surprise was that he was not expecting contact for another year, but the thoughts in his head made it quite clear he was being led into a remote area for a meeting with a visitor from another world.

As the silver spacecraft floated high above Earth in the clear Swiss sky, she continued to send telepathic messages to Billy guiding him into the remote forest area. He had driven through a small village and within minutes was heading into a local forest. As he rode his small moped along the lonely road, he once again felt the thoughts of Semjase come into his mind and guide him to move on down the road to a more remote location. Looking at his watch, he noticed it was 2:12 p.m. and that he had been driving for a full hour.

From out of the clouds Semjase guided her ship and hurried toward the meeting place in the quiet meadow in the Swiss countryside. Even though the ship was very quiet and flew noiselessly, Billy noticed the rustle of the birds and wildlife that signaled the approach of an alien energy to the forest. He parked his moped by a tree and stood motionless as the sleek, silvery craft set down in the remote meadow.

In her telepathic messages Semjase suggested that Billy bring his camera, for she was going to allow photos to be taken of her spacecraft for proof of her existence. It had been decided by the Pleiadian council that the main purpose of the first visits would be to provide evidence of their existence; it was time to awaken the people of Earth to the idea that they were not alone. In the past they had made contact with other Earth people for the purpose of making their presence known, but had not allowed any photos to be taken. They were concerned that this may be taking the proof of their existence too far and causing mental stress on some people. They had to be careful of the manner in which they exposed themselves to the masses of Earth, and it was clear to them after years of study that the minds of most Earth people at that time were too fragile to handle the idea of visitors from another world.

As soon as the UFO had landed, Billy walked toward it to observe it closer and to get a better photograph. But about 100 meters before reaching the UFO, he was stopped by some unseen force. It felt like he was pushing against the winds of a completely soundless storm. With all his power he tried to fight against the energy field to move forward, but he could only advance a few feet because the counteracting force was simply too great. Billy decided to sit down on the ground, stare at the spaceship and wait for the occupant to come out.

Semjase could tell that Billy was mentally calm and was prepared to greet her, so she opened the hatch to her spacecraft and stepped out onto the ground. As she walked toward him, she could tell his thoughts were all about her appearance. Billy was thinking that her clothes were rather familiar. A cosmic suit, similar in form to some Earthly products, but very pliant and light, he analyzed. Actually, the suit was more like an overall with a peculiar gray color. Very close up it reminded him of the skin of an elephant, which he had seen once in Africa and again in a zoo in Switzerland. The suit fit tightly to the body and appeared to be quite durable. Around her neck was a ring, apparently for the purpose of fastening a helmet of some type. Evidently the Earth's atmosphere was suitable for her, for she never required a helmet during her visits to Billy.

As people tend to do, Billy was quickly looking her over and forming his opinion of her. Her head was exposed and she was easily recognized as being a young woman. The look on her face was free and open with nothing to suggest that she was superhuman or carried a superior attitude. Her manner was that of a normal-looking human being who just happened to be of extraterrestrial origin. Billy could not ignore the fact that she was also very beautiful. Her walk was that of a normal person, only stronger and more self-assured. Her long, red hair shone in the sunlight as she stopped in front of him.

Slowly she extended her hand to Billy, seized him by the arm and pulled him up on his feet. Her grip was strong and sure, but very pleasant and confident. They walked toward Billy's motorbike where they both just sat down in the dry grass. Then she began to speak, not in his home language of Swiss German, but in the older King's German that she had learned. This caused her to have an accent that was peculiar to him, but he had no trouble understanding her.

Semjase introduced herself, explaining that she was from a small cluster of stars called the Pleiades. She told him she had been listening to his thoughts for several years in preparation for this meeting and understood his character very well. She knew that Billy was a fearless man whose integrity could be counted on. For quite some time she and her people had been wanting to come in contact with an Earth human being who was sincere and really wanted to be helpful to their Mission. Many times before, the Pleiadians had tried physical contacts with humans, but the people chosen turned out to be unwilling, and also often lacked loyalty and sincerity. Some of those chosen feared for their safety and kept silent about their contacts or were afraid that they would be thought of as insane by their friends and family.

She told Billy to relax, that today she had information to impart and to only interrupt her if he did not understand something. She promised there would be more meetings in the future where he could ask all the questions that he wanted. Today for their first meeting she simply wanted to introduce herself and let him know what to expect in the future.

To begin with, she and her people were concerned that so many people here on Earth were claiming to be in contact with the Pleiadians and claiming to have ridden in their Beamships as she called them. This simply was not true as they had not conducted physical contacts with any Earth people for some time. The same held true for certain UFO organizations which had been trying to gain knowledge about their Beamships, but they had no photos that were really authentic. There are many photos in existence which appear to be extraterrestrial craft, but are really nothing more than blurred lights. Most of the photos of which she was aware of were nothing more than fabricated deceptions manufactured by dishonest people seeking wealth and fame.

Semjase wanted to make it clear to the people of Earth that her people had been coming to Earth for thousands of years and were not involved directly with the governments or political leaders. Only occasionally do they make contact with a chosen person such as Billy, and then it is only for the purpose of awakening people to the idea that they are not the only thinking rational beings in the universe.

Another point that she wanted to make clear was that she and her people were not superhuman and do not have supernatural powers. Laser beams do not shoot from their eyes, and they do not have the strength of 10 Earthmen. In truth they are human beings just like the people of Earth, but their knowledge and wisdom are very much higher, especially in the technical and spiritual areas. It is their highly developed spiritual knowledge that enables them to use certain powers of spirit which seem like magic to us, such as telepathy, telekinesis, and access to higher realms of consciousness. These abilities also lie within the Earthman, but they are not as well developed.

We should also be made aware, Semjase warned Billy, that there are many deceitful people on Earth who pretend that they are in contact with human beings from other planets in our own solar system and have even flown in their Beamships. This is not true, for the planets they talk about are so desolate that human life is impossible there. Other planets, in contrast, have been lifeless for a long time or are in the first stages of development and do not support life in any form. There is no human life in our solar system except here on Earth and a few scattered bases manned by the Pleiadians and other races.

Other solar systems beyond ours do exist with many forms of life, and not only human. There are also many animal and even plant life forms that have evolved to higher forms of life. It was time for the people of Earth to know that many life forms exist that have reached advanced knowledge and travel through the universe, sometimes visiting Earth. Many of these off-world travelers are malicious and should be considered very dangerous. The people of Earth should be on guard for these types because they often fight and destroy everything that comes their way. Sometimes they will even destroy whole planets or civilizations and force the inhabitants into slavery. Part of her mission was to warn the Earth humans about these creatures because the time rapidly approaches wherein a conflict with some of these beings becomes unavoidable.

Another part of her Mission was directed toward our religions and the

27

consequent subdevelopment of the human spirit. In future meetings she wanted to spend some time in the education of spirit matters, so the people of Earth could learn about the one power that resides over the life and death of each creature. This is the Creation which dictates the logic by which the universe and all life forms exist. This logic is absolute and forms the laws by which man must live. These laws are apparent in nature and reveal the knowledge of life and the direction towards spiritual greatness, which embodies the goal of life. It was time for the Earthman to learn about the true meaning of life and how to live in peace and harmony with nature and the eternal energy of Creation. This would be the subject of many of the future meetings.

By studying the thoughts of Earth, the Pleiadians have also discovered that we are living under the wrong idea that Gods are equal to the Creation itself. We have also misled ourselves into believing that an Earth human being by the name of Jmmanuel was the son of God and the Lord of the Universe. In future contacts Semjase would explain in detail the role of Gods within Creation and provide us with the real truth about the life and teachings of Jmmanuel, whom we call Jesus Christ.

One further point in this area is that the Pleiadians and other extraterrestrial races do not come to Earth on behalf of a God to bring to the Earth the long-awaited peace. Earth humans must learn that never can a god take the role of the Creation or control the destiny or fate of the human being. A God is simply a physical being, a governor and moreover a human being, who has evolved to a level of great understanding and knowledge through millions of life times. Gaining power through this knowledge, these beings usually exercise control over their fellow creatures. Those that are far less developed will believe that these self-styled Gods have power over their lives, but they do not. Creation is the spiritual force that has the knowledge to create a universe, whereas a God is only a material being with knowledge of the human form and is subject to Creation like all other life forms. It is also not true that the Pleiadians came to Earth on behalf of any God because they are no longer governed by Gods or rulers and now live completely free, enjoying their spiritual connection with Creation.

The Creation itself never gives commands or demands worship in any fashion because it is an egoless, nonjudgmental spiritual force. It is eternal knowledge that guides the growth of the universe, and that knowledge is never in need of commands or religions. The Pleiadians would like to bring this truth to the light of the world and make it known to human beings. This is an important part of their Mission. If this does not happen, then it is possible that mankind will slowly destroy itself or fall into complete spiritual darkness.

Semjase then made it clear that there would be many more meetings, and she planned to spend a lot of time with Billy to pass on the information the Pleiadian Council felt was important for Earth. She had prepared for the coming contacts for several years and had great hopes that the information she would provide would be useful in helping the people of Earth create a more peaceful future. Her objective today was only to introduce herself and let Billy know of her plans for the future. This would be all for their first meeting, and he could plan for her return within a week.

She would contact him when she was coming just as she did today. He would feel a cooling sensation on his forehead followed by the telepathic transmission of thoughts that would let him know where to meet her. She would be careful to interrupt his thoughts only when he was open to them and to not infringe on his privacy.

Future contacts would be in her spacecraft that she calls a Beamship, so they would have some privacy. Also she intended to take him on flights into free cosmic space, so he could visit the other planets and see the solar system. It was okay for him to bring his camera, for they wanted to encourage him to take many photos and bring them to the attention of the public. She would be more helpful in the future, posing her ship so he could get some very good photos.

Bidding Billy farewell, Semjase then walked toward the spacecraft that was sitting there quietly in the meadow, disappeared inside of the craft and flew away within seconds. Billy took advantage of the opportunity and snapped several more photos as the ship disappeared over the forest. He knew from previous experience that you had to be quick if you wanted to get good pictures of these spacecraft because they changed directions so quickly and disappeared in seconds.

Just as Semjase had said, she began to return almost every week. Each time she would send the telepathic message to Billy, guiding him to a remote spot where they would be unnoticed. Billy would ride his moped to where he was directed and wait for the silver craft to show up. On most occasions she would bring him up into her beamship, especially since the Swiss weather can be so harsh most of the year. Here they could talk and have their meetings in private, and she shared with him the vast amount of knowledge that the Pleiadians felt was important for Earth.

After each meeting, or contact as Billy called them, he would return home and type out what was said. Not trusting Billy's memory, Semjase had arranged for a special computer-like device to replay all that was said at the contact to Billy's mind, so he could type it down just as it was said. The device could read the memory of the meeting that was stored in the subconscious mind of Semjase and send it to the conscious mind of Billy who was sitting at his typewriter. He would then hear the conversation in his head and type it. This was particularly difficult since Billy had lost his left arm in a bus accident in Iskenderun, Turkey on the 3rd of August, 1965, which made typing very difficult. During the transmissions from Semjase, he would sit at the typewriter and be capable of typing 50 to 60 words a minute without stopping. He would normally have someone sitting beside him to change the paper as the continuous stream of knowledge flowed from his mind out onto the typewriter keys. This process would usually last for several hours until the transmission was complete or he was exhausted.

The amount of work became overwhelming to Billy. He was having a contact almost every week, and at the same time he was a father and husband and needed to keep a roof over their heads. His wife, Popi, had two kids, a house, and a husband to take care of, and she wasn't in the mood to hear that Billy was too busy having contacts with a nice-looking woman from another planet and had no time to work. It was several months before she began to take his contacts seriously and started to understand their importance.

At each contact he would usually get the opportunity to bring his camera and shoot 2 or 3 rolls of film. Semjase wanted Billy to get the best UFO shots ever taken as proof to the public that his meetings and information were real. She and the members of the High Council of the Pleiades, who she had to answer to, felt that many people on Earth were ready to make this upward step in their consciousness. The pictures would be proof to some, and to others it would open up old memories of life on other worlds where ships such as these were common. She was well aware that there were many old Lyrian spirits on Earth who had lived many lifetimes on other worlds far more advanced than here.

Billy's pictures began to appear in magazines and newspapers in Switzerland and surrounding countries. They were all beautiful daytime photos that were very clear and distinct. They were so good that many people couldn't believe that they were real. But many of those who did believe came in droves to Billy's home in Hinwel. On Sundays the road to his house was packed with cars from all over, for everyone wanted to talk to the man who was in contact with the star people. Billy had made a promise to Semjase to tell everyone about his contacts and would refuse no one. He underestimated the scope of his promise, for people came by the thousands to ask their questions and look at his wonderful photos. His home life was ruined as people crawled through the windows, went through his drawers, stole his pictures, and made life miserable for himself and Popi. The local townspeople were getting fed up with all of the traffic and commotion. Most of the villagers didn't believe his story and thought he was some kind of con man who was making all of this up. They didn't think this was amusing at all and wanted him out of their town. It wasn't long before Billy was forced to look for a new place for himself and his family to live.

Billy found a nice, old farm in a remote area of the country that Semjase pointed out would have a good chance of surviving the coming disasters around the turn of the century. On a viewing screen in her ship she showed Billy the areas of Switzerland that would be most affected by coming volcanoes, fires, and more importantly, the rising water that was expected from overflowing oceans. These events would be happening around the advent of the twenty-first century. The farm was in a safe place in a little rural area called Schmidruti, about 45 minutes east of Zurich. Here Billy could live peacefully and continue his work safe from the coming natural disasters.

Buying the farm was expensive, especially since Billy had no income other than the pension he received from the Swiss government. He would need some financial help from others in order to buy the farm. As luck would have it, an old friend came forward just at the right time and was able to offer enough money for a down payment on the farm, and things fell into place for him to move his family to their new home.

Over that past year many of those who had come to visit with him had expressed interest in helping him with his work of disseminating his informative *Contact Notes* to the public. So far Billy had amassed over 1,000 pages of *Contact Notes* he had written of his meetings with the off-world visitors from the Pleiades. The information included was on many different subjects, from history to science to consciousness. Semjase had been prompting him for months to get his notes in order and to make them available to the public, and she was most adamant that Billy should speak in public. All of this was proving to be too much for Billy; he just couldn't keep up with the workload, and public speaking was very difficult for him. He had tried on a couple of occasions to speak to small groups in neighboring cities, but he was ridiculed and laughed at and wanted no part of it anymore.

Once the move to the farm at Schmidruti had been accomplished, Billy decided to take Semjase's suggestion that he form a group around him that could help him with his work. They could help him with his *Contact Notes* and other books he was writing, and possibly speaking in public. Billy approached some of his followers who were most anxious to help out with the work, and a group was formed. They called themselves the *Freie-Interessengemeinschaft fur Grenz-und Geisteswissenschaften und Ufologiestudien,* a rather long German phrase which means "Free Community of Interest in Border and Spiritual Science and Ufology." If you don't speak German this is difficult to learn, so to most of the world the group has become known as the F.I.G.U. There were 25 members in the original group, 15 of whom took up residence at the farm where Billy and Popi had just moved. In honor of the special purpose of this new home they would all share, they decided to name the farm the "The Semjase Silver Star Center." The F.I.G.U. members then began to take part in helping out around the "Star Center", or "Center" as they called it, and took on special duties to help Billy with his writing. Some of the F.I.G.U. members helped edit his books, while others answered letters from around the world, and some took day jobs in town to help out with expenses. All in all life started to become easier for Billy, and The Semjase Silver Star Center was becoming well known around the world, and off.

As the contacts continued and his pictures were shown in magazines and newspapers around the world, people everywhere became interested in the Swiss farmer who was in touch with the star people. His contacts continued for almost 3 years and produced hundreds of beautiful pictures, metal samples, biological samples, crystals, and stones from other planets. He was even allowed to take over 30 minutes of movie film of the Beamships in flight which was converted to video tape for the world to see. Here at last was the kind of proof of extraterrestrial contact that people were looking for.

After 115 meetings, the Pleiadians did finally end the contacts on Thursday October 19th, 1978, because they no longer served their interests, but the wave of excitement and intrigue was spreading around the world. Even though the contacts had ended for Billy, they were just starting for the people of Earth.

During the final months of the contacts, an investigative team from America led by Colonel Wendelle Stevens began to publish the results of their findings. In a wonderful and informative book called *UFO-Contact the Pleiades, an Investigative Report,* written by Colonel Stevens, he summarized over 10 months of intensive investigative work that included analysis of landing tracks and photos, testimony of witnesses, detailed study of each contact sight where Billy had taken his photos, and hundreds of hours of conversation covering the information about these beings from the Pleiades. It was an amazing piece of work that captured the excitement and enthusiasm that surrounded our first contact with human life from another world in modern times.

Other members of the investigative team, Lee and Britt Elders, combined their investigative findings with the beautiful, clear pictures taken by Billy and created an informative and stimulating photo journal called *UFO - Contact from the Pleiades.* This very professional book stirred the emotions and provided deep insights into the thinking of these off-world visitors. I purchased the books and began to study them with great interest. The investigative report by Wendelle Stevens was fascinating and captured my attention for weeks, but I was strangely drawn to the photos of the Pleiadian Beamships in the photo journal and couldn't stop staring at it. "This book is important," I said to myself, I just knew it. As I slowly turned the pages, I became more and more certain that this book held some important truths about life from another world. I became obsessed with the book and for days could think of nothing else. The implications were very serious, indeed. Here at last could be proof of the existence of life on other worlds. And if this was true, then think of what we could learn. I had read every word in the book several times, especially the part that said Meier had the opportunity to have physical contacts with these visitors. They had taken him with them in their ships on many occasions for the specific purpose of educating him on a variety of subjects about life, the universe, religion, history, and science. They even allowed him to ask questions put together by himself and a group of friends from the F.I.G.U., who also seemed to be involved in the contacts. The book answered some of my questions but didn't go into very much detail. I was hungry for more and found myself calling directory assistance in Arizona to find the publisher, find the printer, find someone; I had to know more. There was the ring of truth in this book that touched something deep inside of me. I was sure that someone out there was making an effort to get in touch with us.

It took just a few calls to reach the Elders, who were located in a small town in Arizona. They had just returned from several months in Switzerland investigating this case. They were very helpful and answered a lot of my questions, offering some new insights into the experiences of Billy Meier that were not in their book. My phone bill was pretty high for awhile because I kept calling and asking more questions. It turned out that Billy had over 115 meetings with these visitors from the Pleiades and had compiled several books out of thousands of pages of notes taken during his many meetings with these visitors. He was publishing his notes in a set of books called *The Contact Notes,* but the problem was that the books were all written in German and no translating had started yet, so I was cut off from the information.

The investigators told me they had put Billy's photos through many different kinds of analysis and could find no evidence of a hoax of any kind. They had investigated other witnesses who had seen the ships, some of whom had also taken photos of the ships; they even had been to the sights where the photos were taken and reconstructed the photo scene for computer comparison. Small models of the Beamships were made and taken to the original contact sights were Billy took pictures with the same camera for comparison with his own photos. The shots of the models were then analyzed by computer and photographic experts who were able to detect the models in every case. Billy Meier was indeed taking pictures of some unknown type of craft that appeared to be from another world.

Billy had given them metal samples for analysis that he had received from the off-world visitors which was representative of the type of material that their ships were made of. These metal samples had been turned over to a scientist at IBM named Marcel Vogel, who proclaimed he could identify most of the ingredients of the metal, but not the manufacturing process. It was beyond our technology at the moment and clearly not of this Earth because the metal would have to have been made in some sort of vacuum process. It seems the investigators were almost losing their own objectivity, and they were having trouble finding any reason to doubt Billy's claims. He truly seemed to be having contacts with human visitors from another world.

Hardly a day went by during the next couple of years that Billy Meier's experiences were not on my mind. I seemed to have awakened old thoughts and dreams from somewhere deep inside of me that wouldn't go away. I kept my *UFO - Contact from the Pleiades* photo journal out on the coffee table for visitors to see. The book's cover was a beautiful shot of one of the flying Beamships just hovering over a grassy knoll with some logs nearby. The shot was so captivating that anyone seeing it couldn't resist opening the book and asking a few questions. I just had to talk about this with other people. I soon discovered that many people had the same kinds of questions about life that I had, and maybe here within the pages of this book some of the questions could be answered. But one book was not enough; I wanted to talk to Billy, read his notes, and learn more. I had traveled through China, most of the East, 3 trips to the Vatican City, Europe, Egypt, and Japan, putting together pieces of our humanity. My quest had led me down a lot of trails that always came to the same conclusion - we just don't know very much about life and how we fit into the workings of the universe. There was a different theory everywhere you went, all of them based on some truth but usually summarized with a lot of guess work that brought me no closer to the answers I was looking for. We were still confined to this planet with nothing but our own past experiences to guide us. History had left us on our own to create several thousand years of beliefs, religions, and cults, which always seem to lead to war and bloodshed rather than enlightenment. I really had to learn more about this. It was time to go to Switzerland, time to visit the Semjase Silver Star Center and meet Billy.

I finally made arrangements to visit Billy at his home in Switzerland. His letters said it would be okay for me to stay for the summer and learn all I could. His contacts had stopped and the crowds had died down, so it was a really good time to go. I had written to him and explained how I was very interested in the information from his *Contact Notes* that he had published in German, which I couldn't read, and would like to continue my education about his experiences.

I had learned enough to frequently give public speeches and lectures about what little I knew about his experiences. But more importantly, I needed to know more for myself. My need to personally grow and understand myself better was driving me to Switzerland and to the home of Billy Meier.

Since I owned my own business and made my own schedule, I put all of my work on hold, packed my bags, and made arrangements to leave for Switzerland and the little rural area called Schmidruti. This was very exciting, and I felt sure that this was going to be a real time of enlightenment. Actually, I really had no idea of the immense amount of information that was waiting for me. The summer turned out to be an experience that changed my life forever.

The History of Man

During my stay at the Semjase Silver Star Center, my home was a small van parked behind the house with just enough room for myself and a very poor translation of Billy's *Contact Notes* in English. Someone had tried to translate them from German, but whoever it was did not speak English very well. The translation was word for word, as if someone had simply used a dictionary to look up all of the words without regard for grammar or sentence structure. This made the *Contact Notes* very hard to read, so I spent a lot of time trying to figure out what they said.

The little van I was staying in was only a short walk from the main house and afforded me a little privacy, so I had a place to contemplate all that I was learning. I spent several hours each day going over the *Contact Notes* and then spent some time working around the farm and helping out as there was always some work to do, painting the garage or fixing a fence. My nights were normally filled with occupying some F.I.G.U. member's time with thousands of questions or reading and thinking. Usually in the afternoon I would spend some time with Billy, if he was up to it. He had a couch on the front porch where he liked to sit and enjoy the beautiful scenery that surrounded him. There was a small aviary he had built just in front of the house that contained a few birds that would hop from branch to branch, chirping continuously as if they were very busy doing something. It was kind of hypnotic and tranquil to watch them playfully fly around the cage; often I would sit there with him feeling the serenity of nature and soaking up the warm summer of Switzerland.

I was learning a great deal from Billy and the other F.I.G.U. members who lived at the Center. I had been reading my rather poor English version of Billy's *Contact Notes* that he had made during his meetings with Semjase, and I was trying to figure out the chronology of Earth history, but the notes were hard to read, with fragments of history scattered throughout the 1,800 pages. I asked Billy to fill in some blanks for me, and I finally got a better picture of what had happened here on Earth during the past several thousand years.

36

The History of Man

One of man's greatest mysteries is his origin. Where do we come from and why are we here on Earth? The history of our current civilization has been recorded fairly well, so we have a pretty good idea of what has happened the last 6,000 years or so, at least as far as major events such as wars and religious occurrences. But if you wanted to get into a discussion about any possible life existing here before that time, you would be hard-pressed to find any tangible materials to back up your argument.

In order to put together the pieces of our past, we have the writings of the Bible which are widely accepted by many. We also have the Sanskrit scrolls, a group of writings that date back to around 1200 B.C. and contain the religious wisdom of the East. We also have the highly regarded Mayan calendar, a prophetic work that has accurately portrayed the future of man from 2,000 years ago up to a time in the future around the year 2050. And of course there are the Dead Sea Scrolls, a collection of ancient manuscripts discovered in 1947 in a series of caves on the west bank of the Dead Sea in the area of Jordan. These scrolls are Biblical religious texts written in Hebrew and Aramaic around 200 B.C. The Pleiadians regard the Dead Sea Scrolls, the Mayan calendar, and the ancient Sanskrit scrolls as the most accurate representation of our past since they have not been changed or altered over the centuries. They say the Bible has been tampered with on too many occasions by power and religious groups and is no longer accurate.

All of these great historical documents give us small glimpses into our immediate history, but none of them can give us much of a clue about any previous civilizations that may have existed here during the past millions of years. It is generally considered that our civilization is about 6,000 to 8,000 years old, depending on whom you talk to.

The Pleiadians tell us that the Earth is several billion years old and the universe is trillions of years old, certainly enough time for many civilizations to have come and gone. Of course, you will get many disagreements from scientists about how old, big, or long anything is because we simply don't have the technology to understand it all. Most of history is compiled from old records or some form of scientific dating scheme, such as carbon dating. But how could we tell if beings from other worlds have ever set foot here and had an effect on our development? Since the Earth has been able to support human life for at least a billion years, it's quite possible that there could have been many different civilizations that have come and gone.

If the planet had changed orbit, rolled over on its axis, or met with natural disasters of different types, then any traces of these past societies

37

may be under the ocean or buried miles under the ground. It is interesting that every now and then some one comes up with some unexplainable event, like a glass bottle buried in a tomb in Mexico that should be over 10,000 years old or a mechanical device found in the ocean that obviously was made by some form of intelligence but is unrecognizable. How about the report from an American university that summarized that the Earth must have been hit by a major asteroid or meteorite of some type around 10,000 years ago with a force sufficient enough to change the planet's axis, flood all of northern Africa including Egypt, and ruin the atmosphere for years? Those were the conclusions of a team of scientists from studies of debris found on the floor of the Mediterranean Ocean.

The Pleiadians are a very old race with information about many different civilizations going back 22 million years. Since our forefathers were also their forefathers, they have on file every language that has been spoken on Earth for thousands of years, as well as information of the history of man. Now that the knowledge of the Pleiadians is available to us, we can walk through our past and for the first time learn the fascinating truth about the development of man on Earth.

22 Million B.C. - Ancient Lyra

To begin with, in the constellation of Lyra we find the origin of man dating back as far as Pleiadian history extends. Here on these ancient planets are the ancestors of the oldest known form of human life of which they are aware. Twenty-two million years ago ancient Lyrian travelers first came into our system and built a colony. Since these were among the first attempts at space travel for them, it took a long time to reach Earth. When they arrived, they recorded the existence of very primitive human beings here. They found that Earth was a planet where human life had naturally developed over the course of evolution, but it was currently in a very primitive state. The Earth humans were a brown-skinned race who barely possessed any powers of reasoning or intellect and were of no concern to the celestial visitors. Over the course of the next few thousand years many expeditions were made to Earth, resulting in a variety of colonies being formed for short periods of time.

The ancient Lyrians were titans standing 20 to 30 feet tall, from a planet much greater in size than ours. They were white-skinned, with blond hair, and usually had blue eyes, and had a life span of around 2,000 years. They were a warlike race that had not only developed technically, but were quite advanced in the use of spiritual power. They moved their warlike forces around the galaxy and used their great power to take control of many thousands of lesser developed races. Over the years the Lyrian blood line was mixed with other civilizations, creating many different colors and races which spread throughout the galaxy.

Just as their race was at its highest peak of advancement, a huge, destructive comet that became known as the Destroyer Comet found its way into the Lyrian family of planets and 2/3 of their race were killed. Along with the destruction, their technology was wiped out, and they were unable to continue to exercise control over the great empire they had built. The great Lyrian Empire had degenerated back to one planet with no technology to speak of. They were barely able to survive and were faced with the task of rebuilding a civilization which once dominated over thousands of other worlds.

After thousands of years the Lyrians restored their society and again became a dominant force in the Galaxy. Pleiadian history documents that the Lyrians went through a series of civilizations over a period of several millions of years. It was a pattern for them to rise to power, begin to fight among themselves, and then degenerate into a primitive society and start all over again. On some occasions their wars were so brutal that it took millions of years for them to recover from the primitive state left by the destruction.

387,000 B.C. - The First Settlement on Earth
It wasn't until 387,000 B.C. that the Lyrians once again had an effect on Earth. Another war had ravaged Lyra, and many of those on the losing side had fled for safety. They traveled through the cosmos and came to Earth as a place of sanctuary. It was peaceful here as the local humans were primitive and offered no resistance to their high technology. It was decided they would stay and build a colony here.

Back home in Lyra it was discovered that a large group had fled to Earth, and ships were dispatched to come after them. Upon arriving at Earth they were disgusted and appalled to find the conditions that prevailed here. The local Earth humans were being used as slaves and were being mistreated badly. Many were being used in experiments where they were being mated with animals, while others were being disfigured, raped, or maimed. The colony was an example of the darkest side of man. Living in degeneration and filth, it was decided to leave the colony on Earth, take away all of their technology, including their space ships, and leave the 144,207 Lyrian soldiers to their fate on Earth.

This colony died out after several thousand years, and the spirits of the Lyrian soldiers that were left behind became part of the spirit world of Earth. The 144,207 degenerate Lyrian soldiers would now be incarnating here along with the original inhabitants. The effect they would have on Earth would forever steer it away from a normal evolution.

Lyrian history continued to repeat itself for thousands of years until after restoring themselves once again to a high level of technology, they built flight machines with beamdrives and once again moved into the cosmos. Their leaders were great scientists with the understanding of spiritual power, so once again they began to conquer other races. Their leaders soon realized the unlimited powers of the spiritual forces and developed them until they became masters of these great forces, becoming known as an ISHWISH (IHWH) meaning "god" or "king or wisdom." The great power of their spirit allowed them to live for thousands of years as they ruled over countless civilizations.

The Ishwish leaders ruled with cruel power, and eventually the public started a civil uprising. The war lasted for almost four centuries, causing the death of over sixty percent of the population and nearly destroying the three worlds of the Lyra system. It seemed that no one in the Lyra systems would escape this great war that raged 230,000 years ago.

228,000 B.C. - The Flight from Lyra to the Pleiades

An Ishwish named Asael could see the end coming and fled from the wars with 360,000 people in 183 great spaceships capable of transporting over a thousand passengers each, and 250 small space reconnaissance ships that could carry a crew of three. This group of Lyrians wandered through space for many years until they came across a star system with 254 still young, blue suns. There were already a few colonized planets with primitive people living there, but they were no threat to the great Lyrian technology. They landed and built their new society on three different planets around a star they called Tayget. Life was hard and difficult, and it took 300 years for their civilization to grow and adapt to their new environment.

Millions of Lyrians fled the great wars and settled in Orion, Hyades, and the Pleiades.

After the new civilization developed, Asael commanded that they start to explore and conquer other worlds again just as they had done in Lyra. The powerful beamdrive ships sped out into open space and once again reigned tyranny over planets of lesser developed beings and brought them under their control. It was during this time that they came into the system known as the Hesperides. A young, underdeveloped form of human life was there and was quickly conquered and fell into Asael's rule. The Lyrians once again were exercising their power over others and beginning to force their rule throughout the galaxy. It seems that the forces of greed and power were inbred well into the Lyrians as peace seemed to escape them time after time. Millions of years of bloodshed and wars, and still they had not learned to get along peacefully with other races.

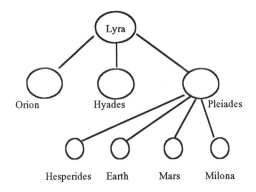

The ancient Lyrians split off to Orion, Hyades, and the Pleiades and started new colonies. The planets of the Pleiades soon flouished and spread out to Earth, Mars, Hesperides, and Milona.

226,000 B.C. - The Time of Pleja

Seventy years of conquering had diminished Asaels lust for power, and his life of bloodthirsty rule came to an end as the father of the Pleiades passed away. Control of the new race of the Pleiades fell to his daughter Pleja, an Ishrish, (the female form of an Ishwish) who, like her father, had the blood of a warrior. Eager to build their great society even farther, she ordered the exploration ships to again seek out new worlds that could fall under her rule. As the ships moved out into space once again to explore, they came across the trail of the Destroyer Comet which so many years ago had been the destructive force that had ended the Lyrian empire. Contained within the tail of the great comet they discovered debris from the planets of ancient Lyra. It was decided to follow the comet for awhile and study its path of violence. This was the destructive force that had changed the history of Lyra and caused death on thousands of worlds, and now it had brought the warriors from the

41

Pleiades into a small sun system and the home of a little planet called Earth.

225,000 B.C. - Earth is Discovered Again

To their surprise they discovered a small group of uncivilized people living there. Some were brown-skinned and could be traced to the origin of life on Earth. Others were of mixed color, but most were white-skinned and had a Lyrian spirit-form. The Pleiadians had stumbled onto a colony founded by their ancient ancestors that had degenerated into a primitive society. Awed by their discovery of human life and common ancestry, it was decided to colonize three different planets in the system and continue the family chain. News of their discovery was sent back to the home planets and apparently sparked an interest in Pleja, for she ordered a great migration to be undertaken. Within a very short time thousands of travelers from the Pleiades came and created societies on Earth, Mars, and Milona, a planet which then existed beyond the orbit of Mars.

It was only a few short years before a small war raged on Earth, and many of the scientists left to return to the Pleiades, leaving the three planets to grow on their own. Plejas was unhappy with this and did not want her new colonies to be destroyed, so she dispatched a fleet to stop the war, and things calmed down again.

196,000 B.C. - War Breaks Out on Earth

The reign of Pleja came to an end, and the people of the Pleiades fell into dark times as they ruined their great society in war. The three planets existed without leadership for over 30,000 years, which was a remarkably long time for Lyrians to get along with each other. It seems that some measure of evolution was finally happening. The scientists of the Pleiades occasionally looked in on Earth and watched as technology developed to a high state, and finally man turned against man once again.

As the wars broke out on Earth, the leaders of the home planets decided once again to involve themselves and sent a fleet to put a stop to it. Earth had degenerated into such an unruly society that it was decided to evacuate the planet and return their people to their home planets. The planet Milona and Mars, which were peaceful at the time, had taken no part in the war that raged on Earth.

The fighting spirit of Lyra did not lay dormant too long though, for it only took forty years before the people of Milona fell into war and destroyed the entire planet in a great explosion. The huge blast pushed Mars out of its orbit, causing complete destruction of all life there and moved the planet into a new orbit. All that remains of ancient Milona is the debris of their planet which is now called the asteroid belt. Once again the Lyrian fighting spirit had caused the destruction of two planets and brought death to millions.

116,000 B.C. - Earth Is on Its Own

Over the next 80,000 years many attempts were made at small colonizations, but none lasted. Earth was left alone with no help from the home planets, for the Pleiadians had too many problems of their own and had no interest in the small colonies that still existed on Earth. As time went by, the little blue planet was thought so little of that on many occasions, groups of renegades were expelled there. It even served as a prison colony for a while.

Earthman has not developed naturally because of genetic engineering by our celestial fathers

58,000 B.C. - The Great Plan

Societies had come and gone in the Pleiades, for the old Lyrians could never seem to get along for more than 10,000 years without going to war. Finally, 60,000 years ago, at a point of high population and technology they decided once again to colonize the Earth. A great exodus occurred as hundreds of great spaceships with thousands of people came and built up a civilization which would last for 10,000 years.

It was a great time for Earth, and the wars in the Pleiades seemed to be left behind. Great cities were built which reflected the advanced thinking and knowledge of a race with a legacy of millions of years. All the continents of Earth were inhabited, and man was living in harmony with himself and the planet. It was almost 10,000 years before the great society began to quarrel and fight among themselves. This time it was the scientists who were the cause of it. They wanted to take control and rule through the hand of material technology instead of spiritual awareness. The technology was so advanced that weapons had been designed that represented a new level of expertise even for the Lyrians. This war was so devastating that it annihilated almost all life forms on Earth and erased every trace of their existence. It brought on a period when savages roamed the Earth and once again lived in primitive villages. The spirits of the original Lyrians who came to Earth thousands of years before, plus all those who had died since were sleeping on the other side.

43

48,000 B.C. - Pelegon, the First God on Earth

For several thousand years the Earth was a dormant place of scattered tribes; meanwhile, a great war was raging on the three home planets in the Pleiades. One of the great Pleiadian leaders of the time, who had captured the hearts of men, was a man named Pelegon. He was one of the more powerful leaders of his time and had earned the title Ishwish because of his tremendous understanding of the spiritual laws. He could see that the future held great devastation for the people that followed him if they stayed there, so he decided to flee the Pleiades and look for a place of safety and refuge. Upon making his decision to leave, he was followed by 70,000 people, including 200 scientists, and fled the wars which were bringing death to so many. It was known to Pelegon that Earth could support life similar to the home planets and was largely uninhabited at the time. Fleeing the tyranny and death that always seemed to follow the Lyrian family, he led his people to a quiet and peaceful Earth to start a new life.

As the Earth grew under the leadership of Pelegon's 200 appointed subleaders, the worst war of all time was still raging on the homeworlds. But under Pelegon's leadership and the guidance of his lieutenants, they populated the many continents of Earth and created a society of love and spiritual growth. Life was flourishing and peaceful as Pelegon was good to his people. He taught them the ways of spirit and how life should be lived by observing the Laws of Creation. This was a society built on spiritual knowledge instead of material greed and power, and it was working.

The true natives of Earth, the brown-skinned race, were in awe of the great power of the Ishwish, Pelegon. They were very underdeveloped in comparison to the settlers from the stars but lived in harmony and peace with them, and Pelegon treated them with respect and love. A master of the knowledge of material life through the development of spirit, Pelegon's seemingly magical abilities caused many stories among the Earthlings which told of his abilities to rule over life and death. One story was passed on that he was once seen floating in air, held up by the power of his mind, and by casting a look at a small tree he caused it to grow. Because of the great power over life and death the Earth people believed he possessed, they called him "God," generating the idea that "God" was a man who held power over life and death. It was Pelegon who became the first god image on Earth and started the concept that we were created in his image.

Finally, in the Pleiades the spiritual leaders were able to overtake the scientists and peace reigned at last. The people learned to trust in the truths of Creation and the knowledge and wisdom of the spiritual laws.

This is a normal process in the development of most races, for in the beginning stages of development man lives entirely by material sense and thinking. And then as he evolves through numerous lifetimes, he slowly learns that he is more than just a physical being and begins to solve the problems of life with more spiritual solutions. At a certain point in the development of a race enough people advance spiritually, and the old material ways of force and power give way to the more spiritual ways of love and light. With this kind of shift in consciousness, societies experience monumental change. This change came to the Pleiadians, and over the next 8,000 years they developed themselves to a very high spiritual level and were at last able to leave behind the long legacy of war and bloodshed of their Lyrian past. They still live by those peaceful standards today.

Nothing was known on Earth of the peace in the Pleiades. Pelegon was still ruler and for the first time in 300,000 years, Earth was living peacefully and happy. The force of his spirit allowed him to live for 4,000 years, during which time he guided the planet to a degree of spiritual development that surpassed anything known in Lyrian history. His vision of life helped this great civilization last for almost 10,000 years before a new Ishwish by the name of Jesas came into power.

Jesas lacked the morals and knowledge of Pelegon and began to rule through power and control over others. He had only ruled for twenty years before the people would no longer stand for their world being ruined and rose up against him, causing war to break out again. After living for thousands of years in peace caused by the love of the great Pelegon, the people wanted no part in a world of war. So by the hundreds of thousands they fled to a nearby star system known as Beta Centauri, leaving behind a war that brought total destruction to Earth.

31,000 B.C. - Atlantis & Mu

There are few myths or fables that capture the imagination of man more than the story of ancient Atlantis. If it really existed, what happened to it, and why is there no trace of its existence? Stories have been passed down for centuries about the huge island continent that existed between what today is called Africa and South America, a place where our forefathers lived in a society even more advanced than ours and traveled the stars. As an example of how Pleiadian technology can change fable to fact, here is the true story of Atlantis and our connection to it.

After the great exodus to the planets of the Barnard Star and the destruction of life on Earth, there was a span of 7,000 years when travelers avoided coming here. The only life to be found were a few scattered tribes of brown-skinned humans who lived in primitive huts. They were the original Earth inhabitants who were still very underdeveloped and were of no interest to the star travelers. Gone was the technology of the great society of Pelegon that had raised the consciousness of man to new heights. The Earth had fallen into a time of darkness and despair.

Light years away lived the descendants of those who had fled the Earth thousands of years ago. Here in the Barnard Star System, a society of human life flourished and lived peacefully. After all, they were the sons and daughters of the great Pelegon, who had taught them how to live in peace and harmony with Creation. This rich heritage provided them with a spiritual advancement that left behind the cries of war and the struggle for power and created a world of peace and spiritual growth.

Among the leaders was a kind and generous Ishwish named Atlant. He was a tall, blond-haired, broad-shouldered man of obvious Lyrian decent. His bright blue eyes and pale white skin painted a picture not unlike his Lyrian ancestors of millions of years ago. He was very popular, and although life there was peaceful and happy, he longed to lead his followers to a new world where they could start a life full of adventure and growth. There were many who decided to follow Atlant, and plans were made to migrate to Earth, a small planet their ancestors had lived on and was hospitable to human life. Here they could create a whole new world.

At first only a few came and found the Earth to be rough and untamed. After piloting their great ships over most of the Earth's surface, they decided to build their first city on a large continent that was located just above the line of the equator which had a warm climate good for living. Having lived peacefully for thousands of years, their technology had developed to a very high state, so it was only a very short time before the beautiful architecture of the star travelers began to fill the horizon. As the city grew and word reached back to the home planets of the success of their new home, thousands more left the Barnard System and came to Earth. Within only a few short years the great society named after its leader Atlant had populated a large area of the planet.

There are 7 basic colors of humanity in
the universe: White, brown, red,
yellow, blue, green, and black.
6 are represented on Earth

Based on our current calendar, the beginnings of Atlantis would be

46

around 31,000 B.C. Some history of this event still rests with the American Indians and some other races who have for years passed down the story of the great Atlantis. The people of Atlantis were kind and generous and lived peacefully with the inhabitants of Earth. Although the Earthlings were far less developed, they were accepted into their cities and found jobs and encouragement, for no hate or prejudice existed in the minds of these spiritually developed travelers from the stars.

Atlant had a wife named Karyatide, who was also ambitious and well-thought-of as a leader. She helped spread the civilization to new parts of the planet, founding cities around an area that today we call the Mediterranean. These smaller satellite cities were called Little Atlantis and lived under the same peaceful rule as the large cities.

Karyatide had a father named Muras. He was a powerful leader from the Lyrian chain of families. After the successful beginnings of Atlantis, he came to Earth with thousands of his followers and built a city on the opposite side of the planet called Mu. Named after its founder, Mu grew to be a gigantic city and slowly spread out and founded other parts of the planet. After many years the many cities that fell under the rule of Muras became known as the kingdom of Lemuria.

Mu was situated in the area we now call the Gobi desert, which is an area between China and Russia. As the great society of Mu advanced, they built two underground cities called Agharta Alpha and Agharta Beta that were located directly below Mu. The cities were connected together by underground tube systems which ran for hundreds of miles, carrying the citizens of Mu from one town to another. Eventually, even more underground tube systems were built and connected many areas of Earth. Although most of these underground tunnels have been destroyed over the years, some of them still exist today.

Thousands of years of peaceful living on Earth produced the largest population ever to live here. Almost the entire planet was populated with cities on every continent which boasted a high quality of living and technology. Earth became known as a peaceful and tranquil place to live and attracted travelers from many different parts of the galaxy. Pleiadian history is not completely accurate here, but it is believed that as many as eight more races from different worlds came to Earth during this time and blended in with the great societies of Atlantis and Mu.

From the star called Sirius came a race of black humans who were very highly developed. They were not of the Lyrian chain but boasted a high spiritual level and found it easy to live in peace with the artistic and creative people of Atlantis. There were also humans from the stars of Orion, Vega, and Hyades, who were also descendants of the ancient Lyrians. It was also during this time that a race came and started a new

47

colony on Earth whose origins are still not known. They were an older race than the Lyrians and kept to themselves and were very peaceful. These were the colonies that founded the Asian communities on Earth, a different family of origin, but now part of the ever-changing mixture of the new Earthman. The Earth was becoming a melting pot of races and colors who lived together in peace and love.

16,000 B.C. - Exiled to Beta Centauri

For 15,000 years the Earth lived in peace, the longest time for any civilization to ever make it here. It was a great time of spiritual growth and development for all who shared the Earth. But as things would go, trouble started when a group of young scientists bent on controlling others tried to cause problems. Thirsty for power, the peace of Earth was threatened for the first time in thousands of years. Fortunately, the people recognized the potential trouble and drove the scientists off of the planet. They fled into space towards a star called Beta Centauri, the closest sun system to Earth located just 4.3 light years away. Here they found human life on a planet and lived in exile.

For two thousand years these same exiled scientists and their followers schemed for revenge while they built up great power and increased their life span. Because of their hatred for the rulers of Earth, they plotted to return and seek revenge and eventually attacked Earth, led by the evil Ishwish, Arus, intending to destroy Atlantis and Mu. Robbing, murdering, but only able to take over small regions of land, they settled in the northern area called Hyperborea, which is today known as Florida. The Earth had not suffered through its axis shift yet, so Hyperborea was still north of the equator.

13,000 B.C. - Adam and Eve

The second in power to Arus was a mighty scientist named Semjasa. He and the other followers were under strict orders not to have sex or social interaction of any kind with the original Earth inhabitants, who were very underdeveloped and even genetically from experiments performed on them by the Lyrians years ago. Keeping to himself, Semjasa defied the orders and worked in secret, performing his genetic mixtures with animals and the subdeveloped Earth humans. He created many different forms of creatures and humans as he searched for a way to improve on man. In one experiment he mated an Earth female, called an *Eva,* with the higher evolved and older Lyrian genetics and created a more intelligent Earthman whom he called an *Adam.* In the Lyrian language Adam simply meant Earth human, and was not his name. The Adam, by the way, was blond, blue-eyed, and stood about 16 feet tall.

48

The experiment worked so well that Semjasa tried it again and created another Adam, a female. Both of his Adams were great advancements in the human form and were more like the Lyrians than the Earth humans. As their intelligence and evolution had been greatly improved, he decided to keep them alive for study and kept their existence secret for many years. When they reached maturity, he mated the two Adams together. This was the beginning of the legend of Adam and Eve.

The two Adams had a child called Seth, who became the first born son of the new human race on Earth. It had been 22 million years since the Lyrians had first used the Earth humans to create all manner of ape-like creatures and ruined the natural evolution of the Earth human, and now Semjasa had created the beginning of the wise and intelligent human race. It was his hope that he been able to set things right and repair some of the damage caused by his ancestors so many years ago. Even though the natural evolution of Earth had been altered so many times, he had succeeded in giving Earthman a new chance to survive and grow. This was the birth of our current civilization as we know it.

The ape was created out of experiments
mating man together with monkeys
and is not a natural developing
creature

Arus and his band of terrorists continually started small wars around the planet, but these little skirmishes hardly had any impact on the great society of Atlantis and were not much of a bother for hundreds of years. Eventually Arus died, and his son Arus II continued to attack remote areas, taking control of what is now India, Pakistan, and Persia. They came in contact with the Sumerians, a peace-loving people who wanted nothing to do with the army created by Arus II and fled to the north for safety. The Sumerians were tall, dark, and the descendants of the Syrians who first settled on Earth at the same time that Atlant started Atlantis. The Sumerians moved into the mountains and became an influence on the people living in India, Pakistan, and Iraq. The region they lived in was called Sumer and was a part of what is called ancient Mesopotamia. Later their ancestors would found cities known as Ur, Uruk, Kish, and Lagash, which have all become major archeological sites in southern Iraq. The great knowledge of the Sumerians was handed down through the centuries and is preserved in pictographic and cuneiform writings that are still being examined today. The Sumerians are, for the most part, responsible for preserving the knowledge of life that was known during the time of Atlantis.

India was then called Arya, and after a few centuries split from Arus II and made alliances with the great cities of Mu and Agharta. These small wars, which had no effect on the great power of Atlantis, lasted another fifteen hundred years. Arus II grew old and was dying, but he succeeded in infiltrating his leaders into Atlantis and Mu, causing enough dissension to begin the talk of war.

9498 B.C. - The End of Atlantis and Mu

The cries of war caused panic, and by the thousands they took to their Beamships and fled to the Pleiades for safety. The war instruments of Atlantis and Mu were of very large size and power. The army of Atlantis contained 4.83 million fighters in large ships, plus 123,000 small individual Beamships and 16,431 remote ships equipped with the most sophisticated heat dissolving beams. They also had 24,230 medium-class ships which were armed with terrifying weapons. But even with all this power, Mu was superior in technology and boasted weapons of greater force.

The scientists of Mu, knowing of the coming events, ordered a fleet out into space to search for a large asteroid in the debris of the destroyed planet of Milano. Finding it, they attached a powerful drive system to it so that it could be hurled at Earth as a weapon of destruction. As the attack of Atlantis started, the leaders of Mu ordered the giant asteroid to be launched, but it was too late to save Mu. The Atlantean fleet dissolved the city of Mu almost instantly. All traces of Mu were melted away, which is evident by the smooth, flat ground in the Gobi desert where it once stood. The underground cities of Agharta were damaged and thousands were killed, but many survived the great holocaust.

Rapidly, the giant asteroid was steered toward Earth with the dedicated pilots attached to it. Propelled by the great technology of the scientists of Mu, the huge asteroid of death was racing at incredible speeds toward Earth when some of leaders and scientists of Atlantis detected the oncoming asteroid. They knew there was no way to stop it, so they fled into space leaving the millions of inhabitants of Atlantis to die.

The asteroid hit the atmosphere and burst up like a supernova, generating heat of over 34,000 degrees. The asteroid exploded less than 110 miles up, and in a thousand small pieces hit the Earth like a shotgun blast. The continent of Atlantis melted beneath the heat of the blast within seconds and the floor of the Atlantic Ocean was broken, causing volcanoes to erupt and bring the sea to a boil. Water from the ocean hurled upward to heights of twenty miles, causing a tidal wave over a mile high to rush over the landmass of Atlantis. It continued on across the area we call the Mediterranean and flooded Northern Africa and the land of Egypt. By our current calendar it was exactly the year 9498 B.C. on June 6th, when the great civilization of Atlantis sunk below the Ocean.

The Planet Earth rolled over on its axis causing the seas to flow over the land, and volcanoes filled the air with smoke and fire. As the planet changed its axis and came to a rest in a slightly different orbit, the geography of Earth was forever changed. If you can picture the Earth as it is now, envision rolling the planet over until the state of Florida is where Greenland is now. That was the position Earth was in before the great war.

Florida used to be called Hyperborea and was the home of Arus and his warriors. The survivors of Hyperborea moved underground after the great holocaust and now live under Mt. Shasta in California. The great continent of Atlantis, which was originally north of the equator, slid under ocean and is now resting in the area of the Atlantic ocean. From what I can ascertain from reading the *Contact Notes,* if you drew a line from Puerto Rico over to Northern Africa, you would be outlining the northern border of where Atlantis was. This huge land mass formerly connected the continents of Africa and South America but now is barely a memory. Remains of Atlantis can be found on the ocean floor off the west coast of the Bahamas in a small group of islands called the Biminis. Here on the floor of the sea oceanographers have discovered the remains of what appears to be an ancient city and have uncovered roads, walls, and other monuments which may tell the story of the last days of Atlantis. Also south of Puerto Rico, deep, down under the water, you can find the tops of pyramids built by the Atlanteans that still rise up through the ocean floor. This is all we have found so far to remind us of the greatest society that ever existed on Earth.

9448 B.C. - Jehovan Controls the Earth

Soon after the war of revenge by Arus II, he was murdered by his third-born son, Jehovan, who seized power over the Aryans and the other two remaining nations of life on Earth. The tremendous destruction caused by the asteroid hitting the Earth had left the atmosphere unbreathable on most parts of the planet, driving the survivors underground. It was fifty years before the air began to clear up and small tribes of people began to once again be seen on Earth. There were three basic groups of people left after the destruction:

51

First Nation: The descendants of the Armus people who lived in the area known as Armenia since 33,000 years ago, who were immigrants from the Pleiades system.

Second Nation: The scattered tribes of Persia, India, and Pakistan, who were known as the Aryans at that time.

Third Nation: A world-wide spread of Gypsies called Hebrews, which in the ancient language of the Pleiades was *Hebrons*.

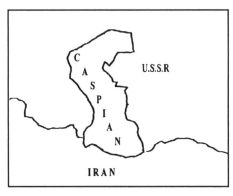

An Ishwish named Jehovan governed the three tribes until 7,000 years ago when he was murdered by his only son Jehav, who, like his father, called himself the creator of man. During this time, a group of 160,000 Great Aryans deserted the rule of Jehav and wandered through the lands to the east, moving into the area between the Caspian Sea in northern Iran and Arahat Mountain in Turkey. This area was full of the descendants of the Sumerians, who led the local people with great discipline because of their highly developed knowledge of spiritual powers. The Aryans attacked and pressed the people under bondage and created a new state. Deprived of all techniques, the Aryans soon began to mingle with the natives, and all previous talents and knowledge soon disappeared and was forgotten forever.

It was only 1320 B.C. when Jehav was murdered by his first son, Arussem, who had two sons named Salam and Ptaah; they were more peaceful in nature and stood up against Arussem, driving him and his followers out of power. Arussem did not have the power to fight back, for his followers were few and his technology was no match for the great armies commanded by his sons, so he secretly returned and hid in an underground city below the Gizeh Pyramid in Egypt. He made plans to take over the world by controlling the thoughts of world leaders and filling their minds with lies, deceit, and delusion. Meanwhile, Ptaah and Salam governed together and created peace until Ptaah was stricken by a disease and died in his 93rd year. This left Salam to rule until be became old and weak, turning the rule over to his son Plejos in 40 B.C.

Plejos was a peaceful ruler and had aligned himself with the High Council of the Pleiadian System. Arrusem, meanwhile, had been governing his band of wicked followers called the Bafath and hiding in Egypt since 1010 B.C. He was taken over by a wicked leader named Henn, who the Hebrons called Jehova. He was known as the cruel one to his followers.

In 80 B.C. Henn was overthrown by a new leader named Kamagol I. He and his followers had to hide from the power of Plejos, so were forced to live below ground under the Great Pyramid in Egypt, their technology was failing and their life spans dwindling. His son, Kamagol II, was even more wicked than he was, and as soon as he was old enough he challenged his father for power. He not only took over control but put his father in a deep, dark dungeon and left him there for years until he died. He was one of the last long-living leaders and would die in 1975, leaving 2,100 of his evil followers behind. By this time the Bafath, deprived of most of their technology, were controlling the minds of 723 Earth people through telepathic means, and these 723 represented their last hope for controlling Earth.

10 A.D. - The Pleiadians Leave the Earth

Two thousand years ago, Plejos, the last Pleiadian System leader on Earth, was informed of the peace agreement between the Pleiades System and the High Council of Andromeda. A new era of spiritual growth and peace had come to the Pleiades, causing Plejos and his followers to want to return to their home system. It was decided to leave someone behind who could carry on the teachings of the Creational knowledge taught by the Pleiadians. They would need an Earthman who was a leader among men and who could carry on the teachings of higher consciousness.

This human was called Jmmanuel. He was not of Lyrian decent, but was a very highly evolved spirit-form capable of the highest order of spiritual understandings. It was arranged for Jmmanuel to be born from a father of high evolution from the Pleiades named Gabriel and an Earth woman of Lyrian decent named Mary. As the Pleiadians had hoped, Jmmanuel easily grasped the teachings of spirit and provided the foundation for what is today called Christianity. He lived for 115 years and brought the truth to all he could through his teachings. Seventy-four years after his death in the year 189, his name was changed to Jesus

Christ, and his teachings were written down to form the religious teachings that prevail today.

The Pleiadians draw our attention to the fact that we have spent more energy killing each other over Jesus than we have spent learning from his teachings

Plejos and his followers had returned to the Pleiades and ended thousands of years of Pleiadian and Lyrian influence. They would not return until 1685 A.D. It had taken thousands of years of bloodshed before spiritual understanding had overtaken the material warriors and brought peace to the troubled Lyrian spirit-forms in the Pleiades.

The Codex

Here on Earth still live the spirits of the first travelers to Earth, the 144,207 Lyrians who came here to escape the wars on their home planets. Two thousand of these old Lyrians were the leaders that were responsible for the abuse and experimentation of the original Earthmen. It was their conduct that set the pattern and leadership for the most decadent and immoral society yet to live on Earth. As their spirits passed away to the other side they took with them a sort of karmic, or spiritual, debt from the material life. Imbedded deep within their spiritual consciousness and their akashic records are the memories of their many violations of the Laws of Creation. Each time they have returned to material life, they live under what is called the *Codex,* a karmic debt that must be repaid.

We are more than just material bodies with a consciousness. We are spiritual beings who go through a series of material lives in order to evolve through experiences learned during the material life. All spiritual beings are consciously connected to the Creational Energy, which is the true eternity of all things. Our spirits would not be able to have consciousness without the life force energy it receives from the Creation, or God Force as some call it. It is this life force energy, a kind of cosmic electrical force, that empowers the spirit so it can exist. It is this common connection to the Creation that binds us all together spiritually.

As each person thinks each thought, it carries like a ripple through Creation and has some effect on all things. The Creation itself is the spiritual energy of the universe; each of us is a spirit-form from that energy. Our connection is through a spiritual consciousness that can be

54

sensed through meditation. All of our actions and thoughts then pass through our consciousness and go out into the universe through this spiritual consciousness. This is how we all contribute to the whole of the evolution of the Creation.

If our actions are of a violent nature, such as in murder, these actions affect the balance of the consciousness of Creation. Our actions and thoughts do not simply dissipate or disappear but are recorded in the ethers of the universe in what are called akashic, or etheric, records and are a part of the spiritual being of Creation.

The actions and murderous deeds of the 2,000 leaders of the ancient Lyrians had an effect on Creation and are recorded in the akashic records of Earth. If you take the life of another through murder, then Creation records this within the spiritual consciousness of the spirit-form and keeps track of it as a debt owed.

Let's say you murder someone through a violent act. Their spirit-form then passes on to the other side while you live out your material life for another ten years, and then your spirit-form passes over to the other side as well. This action is recorded within your own akashic record and the record of the one you killed. It has become part of the events of Creation and cannot be undone. But since we are beings of energy, the debt can be repaid through the Laws of Energy which are ruled by Creation. Here is how it works.

Once you have murdered someone and you both have died, both of your spirits are on the other side and no longer in material form. The debt you owe can only be repaid in the material, so nothing will happen as a consequence of this action on the other side. However, once your spirit-form and the spirit-form of the one you murdered are both back in the material, the debt can be settled. It is not necessary that you know each other. It is only required that you both be in the material world at the same time. If the person who was murdered becomes ill or is suffering spiritually somehow and is in need of strength, he can take from the life force energy of the murderer to help himself. This is not a conscious act, for neither know each other or have any memory of the previous murder. They do not even have to be in the same area of the planet or in close proximity to one another. It is a natural function of energy in Creation that moves life force energy from the murderer to the injured party. The victim will receive a flow of energy which is taken from the life force of the murderer and will start to feel better. The murderer, without knowing why, will suddenly lose some of his life force and perhaps become ill in some form. Since the debt is a spiritual one, it is not necessary that the material consciousness of either party have any idea of what is going on.

For the 2,000 thousand Lyrian leaders who murdered and committed violent crimes of genetic engineering against their fellow man, they have many spiritual debts to pay. Living a material life with a spiritual debt to pay is called living under the Codex. It may be discovered by an individual through meditation, for the recordings of his thoughts are available in his akashic record, a band of energy around the Earth where all thoughts exist.

As we are moving into the New Age and the vibrational level of the Creational energies are increasing, most of the old Lyrian spirits are coming back into material life. For some there are many debts to pay. It is this Codex which will silently move them to be the light workers of our new world, for they are driven to help out their fellow man and make a difference. Most will never know why they are driven or that they live under a Codex. But by virtue of their older and more experienced spiritual self, most will find themselves playing a part in the development of the new world.

The Pleiadians are well aware of these old spirits and know that they can be awakened and can help to be a force for good in our society. They have allowed pictures of their Beamships to be taken which will stir feelings in some; others will be slowly awakened by the teachings of Creation and the understanding of spirit. They believe that if they provide the right teachings, the right words and ideas, the spiritual consciousness of thousands of old warriors can be slowly awakened. And if fed the knowledge of love and light, they can be brought to the front lines again to fight for a world that is sadly lacking in human understanding and spiritual knowledge.

Having lived previous lives on worlds more advanced than ours, their accumulated spiritual wisdom will keep them from being easy prey to the illogical thinking which holds most Earth men in spiritual stagnation. Theirs is the ability to rise above the common man and be the leaders of a new era. They are the visionaries, the creative thinkers, the scientists, the writers, and leaders who can envision a world greater than our own. Most of these old Lyrians have been prominent in history each time they have come into a material life. Since they have many more lifetimes and have accumulated much wisdom and experience, they will usually feel uncomfortable on Earth and try to change it. A sense of being out of place or in the wrong time is not unusual. Many may have visions of other worlds far more advanced than ours and long to leave here.

During my visit to Switzerland, there was an occasion when I was visiting with one of the F.I.G.U. members about the Codex, and I was shown a book which recorded the lives of many of the old Lyrian spirits. Each page provided the names and accomplishments of many different

56

spiritual beings. As I looked through this book, I was surprised to see so many historical names. Truly, the old Lyrians have been working on the Codex for thousands of years. For better or worse, they always seem to make their mark on society in some way.

The book went on to say that there were 5 different colonizations of Lyrians on Earth, some more violent than others. They had been the white seed that had forever changed the evolution of man on Earth. Currently 2/3 of the white race on Earth is of the Lyrian genetic as a result of these 5 colonizations.

As I flipped though the pages of the book, most of the names were unfamiliar to me, but on one page there were the names of 12 different spirits listed. The page looked different from the others, so I had to ask about it. The names were of a special group of Lyrians who were now all in material life on Earth. The Pleiadians had given the names to Billy, and he was to watch out for these 12, for they would be drawn to him for reasons which were not explained to me.

I was told that they believed that I was one of the 12, possibly number 4 based on the information I had given them about my dreams and my family background. Other considerations as to why they thought I was one of them were not explained to me. I inquired as to whether or not any of the other names had shown up, but was told they had not. As of 1987, so far I was the only one. The other 11 names were not familiar to me either.

The Future of Earth

Through the awareness of how our current civilization came about, we can begin to see ourselves in a new light. The white race on Earth is not superior to other races, only older than most. If two-thirds of the white race is of the Lyrian decent, then they have lived more material lifetimes than other races and have more of an obligation to be teachers and role models to those who are younger. As we learn more about our origins and our history, perhaps we can start to come together as one people - the people of Earth.

It is easy to see, by the history of the Lyrians, that man has chosen the path of power and greed to guide his destiny, instead of the more spiritual path of love and understanding. Here on Earth are the spirits of many of these old Lyrian warriors who are still playing a part in our development as a civilization. We can learn a great lesson from this legacy of history. Here we are again, a planet of diverse people whose leaders refuse to get along, but instead play a dangerous game of "King on the Mountain." Just as in the Lyrian past, we are in a dangerous position where we have the technology to destroy our civilization, and it is in the hands of power-crazy men who are obsessed with the lust for control over others. The sickness of prejudice rules their thinking as they finance wars so man can kill one another.

If we are to have peace on Earth, we must rise up against the negative thinking that controls Earth. We must use the power of love and light to diffuse the anger and hostility that causes us to fight. I have always liked the expression, "Suppose they gave a war, and nobody showed up." If the teachers of the New Age can use the power of their light to show others how to live with unconditional love and balance in their lives, we can convince a lot of people to "Not show up." The answer lies in the knowledge that we are spiritual beings and are all connected together in Creation. If we can see each other as spirits and not material beings of color and race, we can discover the spiritual bonding that will lead us to peace instead of war.

Earth is moving into a time of spiritual awareness. As the high energy of the New Age takes its effect, more and more Earth people will begin to discover their spiritual self and develop the powers of higher consciousness. As this event naturally happens, these spiritually aware people will provide the evidence that we are more than just material beings. Others will see that there is more to life than just the material existence, and a consciousness will develop to oppose the cries of war and hatred. For the first time in the development of our current civilization, there will be a more spiritual and peaceful solution to our problems than war. Earth will start to learn that we can all live together in peace if we shed the need for material power and greed. Real happiness in life does not come from the attainment of material possessions but from the inner peace and love that is found on the spiritual path.

At first these spiritual arguments against war will be laughed at and disregarded by the powers that rule. Spiritual people will be regarded as unrealistic and crazy. But very quickly, within a few short years, we will see the tide shift as the people of Earth are drawn more to the spiritual way, which provides a way to live in peace and harmony. Eventually, over the next hundred years the acceleration of higher energy will so dramatically change the consciousness of Earth that a whole new society will emerge that will forever change the way we live together.

If, however, we do not learn from the history lesson given to us by the Pleiadians, we may become just one more chapter in the ongoing list of past civilizations that have destroyed themselves.

The Chronology of Earth History

This chart shows important moments in Earth history based on information from the Pleiadians. Dates are only estimates to show the chronology of events.

22 Million B.C. The first Lyrians come to Earth and colonize.

387,000 B.C. 144,207 Lyrians come to Earth and settle here, forever changing the genetics of Earthman.

228,000 B.C. A Lyrian leader named Asael leads 360,000 Lyrians to a new home in the Pleiades.

226,000 B.C. Asael dies and his daughter Pleja becomes ruler. The system is now called the Plejas.

225,000 B.C. Pleja scout ships discover Earth, and colonies are founded here and on Mars and Milona.

196,000 B.C. War breaks out on Earth and its people are evacuated to the Plejas. 40 years later Milona destroys itself and becomes the asteroid belt. Mars is thrown out of orbit and all life is gone.

116,000 B.C. For the past 80,000 years several small colonies have been tried by the Lyrians. Mostly exiled criminals.

71,344 B.C. The Great Pyramids are built in Egypt, China, and South America by Lyrians.

58,000 B.C. The Great Plan. The Pleiadians build a great society on Earth that lasts for almost 10,000 years.

48,000 B.C. Ishwish Pelegon comes to Earth and builds a wonderful society that lasts for around 10,000 years.

31,000 B.C. Atlantis is founded by a man named Atlant, who comes with his people from the Barnard Star system.

30,500 B.C. The great city of MU is founded by Muras, the father of Atlant's wife Karyatide. His empire is sometimes called Lemuria.

30,000 B.C. The black race comes from Sirius.

16,000 B.C. Arus is exiled from Earth for trying to start wars. He hides out with his followers in the Beta Centauri star system.

14,000 B.C. Arus and his men return to Earth and settle in Hyperborea, which is the current location of Florida.

13,000 B.C. The scientist Semjasa, the second in command to Arus, creates .

	two Adams, who bear a child named Seth. This becomes the legend of Adam and Eve.
11,000 B.C.	Arus II attacks the Summerians, who flee into the mountains.
11,000 B.C.	A group of ET's of unknown origin arrive, led by a leader named Viracocoha, who controlled the city of Tiahuanaco. His base was on an island named Mot. He provided the inhabitants of Easter Island the tools to build the strange statues there which represent him.
9500 B.C.	The Pleiadians cause the old spirit-form from Lahson to come to Earth.
9498 B.C.	Atlantis and Mu destroy each other and ruin the planet. The air is not breathable for 50 years. All survivors are driven underground.
9448 B. C.	Jehovan, the third son of Arus II, takes over the 3 remaining tribes left on Earth and becomes the ruler.
8239 B. C.	The Destroyer Comet passes closely by Earth and causes the Atlantic ocean to part.
8104 B.C.	The Biblical Flood.
6000 B.C.	Venus is pulled out of its orbit around the planet Uranus by the Destroyer Comet and is in orbit around the sun.
5981 B.C.	The Destroyer Comet comes close to Earth, causing great destruction. It also changes the orbit of Venus.
4930 B.C.	The Destroyer Comet once again passes close by Earth, causing tidal waves of destruction.
5000 B.C.	Jehav, the son of Jehovan, takes over rule.
1500 B.C.	The Destroyer Comet passes by Earth, causing the Santorini Volcano to erupt. It also pulls Venus into its current orbit around the sun.
1320 B.C.	Jehav is murdered by his son, Arussem, who has 2 sons named Salem and Ptaah.
1010 B.C.	Arusseam is driven out of power by his sons and hides out under the Great Pyramid with his followers. They call themselves the Bafath.
600 B.C.	Henn takes over from Arusseam and rules the Bafath. Henn is called Jehova by the Hebrews.
568 B.C.	A group of Andromedans come to Earth. They are responsible for the lines of Nazca.
80 B.C.	Henn is overthrown by Kamagol I.
40 B.C.	Salem turns over power to Plejo his son, the last Pleiadian ruler

	on Earth.
10 A. D.	Plejos returns to the Pleiades after procreating the spirit-form of Jmmanuel to carry on the teachings of creation.
32 A. D.	Jmmanuel is crucified on the cross.
115 A. D.	Jmmanuel dies and is buried in Srinagar, India. He leaves 3 sons.
189 A. D.	Jmmanuels name is changed to Jesus Christ and his teachings are re-written to form Christianity.
1000 A.D.	Kamagol I is taken over by his son, Kamagol II, and imprisoned for life until he dies.
1937 A.D.	Kamagol II's second in command is called Aruseak. He decides to leave on his own. He becomes known as Ashtar Sheran and tries to influence the people of Earth.
1937 A.D.	Eduard Albert Meier is born in Bulach, Switzerland.
1975 A.D.	The Pleiadians start physical contact with Eduard Meier.
2004 A.D.	Possible conflict with an alien aggressor.
2255 A.D.	The year the Pleiadians predict the Destroyer Comet will return to Earth.

Life in The Pleiades

Billy likes to talk about what he has learned from the Pleiadians. His contacts were mostly all with Semjase, the Pleiadian woman whom he obviously has great memories of and spoke of fondly. I could even feel a little sadness in him when he spoke about her; it was obvious that he greatly missed her. I remember one night in particular; we were standing outside under the clear, beautiful Swiss sky, and he was pointing out into the stars to show me where the Pleiades were. I was asking him about the planet Erra where the Pleiadians had come from and if he ever had the chance to go there. According to the information I had learned so far, he had not visited the Pleiades or seen their civilization. But I was wrong; he had traveled there in 1984 with Quetzal, the Pleiadian base commander on Earth, and spent 3 days learning about this advanced culture.

Quetzal had frequently come by to see Billy after his normal contacts had stopped with Semjase. They had become good friends, and Quetzal had invited Billy to return to the home planet of Erra with him. Quetzal needed to return there for some reason, and Billy was welcome to go with him.

Visiting The Pleiades

Even though Quetzal had been stationed on Earth for many years, his home was still in the Pleiades. Whenever he had the chance, he would return for a few days to once again be among the level of consciousness that was more comfortable for him. Here he could relax and let the concerns of his command vanish for a while and enjoy the serenity of his home world.

As he and Billy approached Erra, Quetzal explained how their society had developed into a peaceful world of unity and harmony. Billy was well aware that the Pleiadians had not always lived like this but had won their peace through thousands of years of war and struggle, a lesson that he hoped would be understood on Earth.

As the speeding beamship broke into the Pleiadian atmosphere, Billy was surprised to see that the terrain looked so much like Earth. Not only was Erra mostly water, but the mountains and forest reminded him of his own home in Switzerland. There were no large cities with towering buildings as on Earth, but instead the small population of Erra was spread out into smaller communities that spanned the planet. Even within these local communities people lived in more rural settings and kept a distance from each other. It was like they were living with nature, tucked away in little settlements that were almost undetectable from the ground.

As they flew over several small populated areas that looked like cities, Quetzal explained that almost all of the manufacturing and production of products for living was done on other planets in their solar system so as not to upset the ecology on Erra. They had long since developed a balance with nature that was well-protected. Nowhere on Erra was there a smoke stack or pollution of any kind. The atmosphere was perfectly clean and healthy and helped contribute to their long life span of over 700 years, and their good health.

The beamship touched down on a landing area at Quetzal's home. The ship's drive systems were shut down and Billy and Quetzal stepped out into a beautiful, clear, and sunny day. One deep breath of the high oxygen content was all Billy needed to be reminded of how poor the air on Earth had become. Quetzal had informed him that on Earth the oxygen content was dropping to very dangerous proportions which would lead to disease and the damage of nature. Here on Erra Billy's lungs gasped as he felt the surge of pleasure from the clean air. Just the idea that the Pleiadians were being so careful with their world was very pleasing to see.

The main house was white in color and resembled a dome structure not unlike some future-looking homes on Earth. Quetzal showed Billy around and explained some of the technology that was built into the home that monitored the air, communications, food supply, sleep, health, and many other aspects of living. Organic intelligence much like that of the Beamships was also present here and was built into the house and helped created a high standard of living.

Located just a few hundred yards from the main house was another similar looking home that housed another of Quetzal's families. He had two marriages and two families of children. Here on Erra this was very common as you can certainly love more than one person, and in a society that has all but eliminated emotional problems such as jealousy, most Pleiadians entered into more than one marriage. In Quetzal's case his marriages were quite successful and were providing him with many hours of pleasure with his wives and children.

Many Pleiadians have gardens but don't actually work in them. The task of maintaining the gardens and food supply was normally carried out by machines. Quetzal was proud to show Billy that he was working his own garden with a set of hand tools that Billy had provided him with from Earth. It was quite an odd thing for Quetzal to be out working in his own garden without machines. He even had garden gloves, seeds, and shovels from Earth, which had attracted quite a bit of attention from his neighbors, for they had never seen this before. The idea of working with the soil and getting your hands all dirty was quite a novelty and was catching on with Quetzal's friends.

Beyond the garden was another interesting looking building that had special interest to Quetzal. He had taken advantage of his travels to many worlds and started a collection of different kinds of vehicles. There were many cars, bikes, and trucks from Earth as well as many other travel vehicles that were very unusual and strange to Billy. Quetzal had over a hundred strange contraptions in his little museum and took great pride in understanding all of them. He often worked on them and kept them all in good running condition.

The Pleiadians have long understood the power of thought and the spiritual bonding that connects all living beings together through Creation. Because of this they are very protective of the consciousness of thought that is created by all who live there. Over thousands of years of development their thought processes are tuned into one another at very high levels. If visitors to Erra project negative thoughts, they will be asked to leave the planet so as to not disturb the wonderful balance of thought energy that everyone enjoys.

The ability to project your thoughts to another place on the planet is very common and is the socially accepted method of visiting. Telepathy, the ability to communicate by thought, is practiced by most of the population. Devices such as phones are nonexistent. Try for a moment to envision what life would be like if everyone on the planet is contributing part of their thought energy to a common pool that was used to protect the health and well-being of the planet, the animal kingdom, the food, and the health of all inhabitants. There would be no greed, hate, anger, or negative thinking, but only true understanding and love between everyone.

Even though most communication is mental, there is still a tube type of system to travel around the planet. You can travel to almost anywhere on the planet in a very short time. This tube system is mostly above ground and available to everyone. When you are riding on the tube, there is no sensation of movement as the problems of gravity and energy have long been overcome by Pleiadian science. The tube cars are something like our monorail systems on Earth but are far more advanced and intelligent. As with other structures on Erra, the tubes can think and carry on a conversation with you about your destination and answer any questions you may have about the scenery or topography of the planet.

Billy was only able to stay on Erra for 3 days with Quetzal and found it very hard to return to Earth. Life in the Pleiades was such a joy to the spirit that returning to the low consciousness of Earth was very difficult. Quetzal had made it even harder by suggesting to Billy that he could move here with his family if he liked and leave the cares of Earth behind. This was a hard decision, indeed, for life on Erra was very stimulating and creative. All the way home Billy was thinking about it, but knew he would have to stay on Earth to fulfill the mission that he had put so much energy into.

The trip back to Earth took around 7 hours and gave Quetzal a chance to educate Billy on many other facts about his planet and its people. There were many similarities about Earth and Erra that were not accidental. After all, Earth had been originally colonized by the Pleiadian ancestors who had brought with them plants, animals, and foods from their own worlds. Over the past several thousand years Earth had become much like Erra in many ways.

The Pleiades

The Pleiades are a small cluster of stars located in the constellation of Taurus, the bull. During the winter months you can look to the Northern Hemisphere, and if you look closely, you can see six little stars in a small cluster that are sometimes mistakenly called the Little Dipper. There are actually 7 stars in the Pleiades cluster, but usually only 6 are seen by the naked eye. Depending on the time of night that you look at them, this little cluster may look like a small saucepan with the handle on the left side. If this is your position, then you can move your eyes to the star in the top right position. It is named Taygeta and is the area where our visitors from the Pleiades come from. If we were able to fly towards Taygeta and continue on by it for several more light years, there would be a group of 254 blue suns. Here our ancestors live in a Solar System much like our own.

Much has been written about the Pleiades throughout our history. They are sometimes called the "Seven Sisters," or the "Daughters of Zeus." In the Bible they are mentioned frequently as the "Seven Stars." The Kiowa Indians have a folk tale that says seven Indian maidens were being chased by bears. The Great Spirit came to protect the maidens by raising a giant tower to block the bears' path. The bears fought to reach the escaping maidens and left the powerful claw marks that are seen today on the Devils Tower in Wyoming. The young maidens were then placed into the sky and became the 7 stars of the Pleiades by the Great Spirit who protected them.

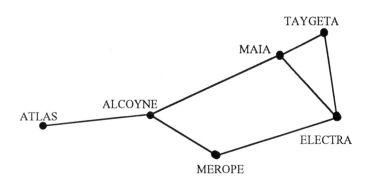

The Pleiades also show up in ancient Egypt for those who study the geometry of the Great Pyramid, Cheops, on the Gizeh Plateau. Many unusual mathematical coincidences present themselves, for instance, the rotation of our solar system around the Pleiades is 25,827.5 years. If you take two base diagonals of Cheops which are 12,913.75 pyramidal inches and multiply them by 2 you get exactly 25, 827.5. Is there a connection?

In 1771, an astronomer named Charles Messir was the first to chart the sparkling Pleiades. From atop a hotel in Paris, he charted 45 stars in the system. The Pleiades later became designated as M45 on the star chart. Several other observations and mappings have been made since and now it is believed that there are more than 2,300 single stars in the Pleiades.

Erra, the home planet of the Pleiadians, is located in the system around Taygeta approximately 500 light years from Earth. It is just 10% smaller than Earth and is rotating in a system with 8 other planets. They now occupy 4 of the planets with cities and manufacturing. Only 400 million humans live on Erra. They have concluded that this is the ideal population for their world for several reasons. Their understanding of how the universe was created and how it is evolving along with the Creational Spirit has led them to regard planets as part of Creation that are also evolving, and they treat them with respect just as they do animals, trees, and all other forms of life in the universe.

Population control has come about in a desire to keep their society spread out and sharing the resources of the planet equally. There is also the consideration that they like to live in connection with the spiritual energy produced by nature. This seems to require keeping the population at a certain level so as to not overpower its energy or draw too much from it. This is a rather refreshing attitude since here on Earth the resources of our planet are considered to just be for the taking, and most people give the planet no consideration at all; and if they do, it's just thought of as some giant mud ball that we live on, and we can do whatever we want with it.

Many years ago when the Pleiadians first traveled to Earth, it was because of the similarities of the two planets. Not only is our atmosphere similar, but nature is much the same on both planets as far as oceans, mountains, etc. Over the years the similarities are even closer since samples of plants, minerals, and animals have been taken to the Pleiades and developed there. It is for this reason that the Pleiadians have found the Earth very comfortable to visit.

Language

The Pleiadian language is not so dissimilar to our own as far as the sound and phrases. For instance, in their language an hour is called an *odur,* a day is called a *musal,* and a month is called an *asar.* It seems that the forefathers of the Pleiadians who visited Earth influenced our civilization many times in our past, and they have left behind the influence of their language, which has worked its way into some of the languages we have on Earth. For instance, citizens of Erra may pass each other on the street and offer a simple greeting to one another by saying, *Saalome,* a word which means "Peace in Wisdom." In Hebrew we find the word *Shalom,* which means "peace," and is normally used as a greeting or farewell. This word was influenced by distant relatives of the Pleiadians over 9,000 years ago.

Erra, the Home Planet

The planet Erra has a green atmosphere which they control, that contributes to their health and stressless way of life. They sleep only four hours a day because they have advanced methods of psychic control that induce a deep sleep quickly. Most of the food is still grown in the ground and is affected by their collective thoughts that control the digestive system, so they don't have to eat as much and the food seems to last them longer. They explained that on many occasions they have brought foods, plants, and animals from Earth and other worlds, which gives them a rich selection and variety to choose from.

They have a very high technical understanding of how food affects their thinking processes. They are primarily vegetarians but sometimes indulge in small amounts of meat when they feel they are becoming a little too dreamy or light-headed. They have discovered that meat gives you grounding in your thinking, so they have engineered a small animal which looks something like a rabbit and that supplies their meat. They normally would not eat another living creature, so this one was chosen because of its low evolution.

On a visit to Erra, we would find it to be about the same size as our own planet Earth, with the passing of day and night, temperature, and climate all very comfortable to us. As Billy experienced, even the air would be healthy for us. The oxygen content of the air is 32.4% with traces of argon and other gases at .3% and nitrides around 67.3%. Surface gravity is equal to 1.0003, just slightly higher than Earth, and the density is 5.521, while the inclination of the axis is 22.99 degrees. The diameter of the planet at the equator is 12,749 kilometers as the planet travels at 11.19 kilometer per second through space. They have a rotation of 365 1/4 days, compared with our 365 day year. A day on Erra is 23 hours and 59.4 seconds, which is almost the same as ours here on Earth. They have 13 months with a compensation every 23 years.

Living in a Parallel World

When the ancestors of the Pleiadians, those ancient Lyrian warriors led by Asael, were traveling through space looking for a home, an error was made and their fleet slipped a part second out of normal time and landed in a Pleiades that is not on the same time pulse as Earth. Because of this, if we were to fly to the Pleiades that we see in the night sky, we would not find any life there but instead a uninhabitable planet with a very young, blue sun. The Pleiadians live part of a second out of the time frame that we are in. When they come to Earth, they have to make a slight adjustment in their instruments to compensate for the difference in time in order for their ships to be seen or else we could not perceive them at all.

The Pleiadians are far older than us in reference to the number of lifetimes they have led, and they now live a more spiritual life. This means they are experiencing and learning more with their spiritual senses than with their material senses. This use of spiritual abilities could be, in part, how they have contributed to their long life span of over 700 years.

They are human just like us with few physical differences. Their skin is whiter than ours as a result of higher evolution. It is a natural function of evolution that the body material becomes less dense with less pigment through multiple lifetimes, and the Pleiadians are several million years older than us as spirit-forms.

When they first settled on the worlds that they now live on, they were

68

7 to 9 meters tall. (21-27 feet) Their body size changed quickly within a few lifetimes because of the planet they live on, and they now are about the same size that we are. Their average age is now between 700-1,000 years, mostly due to the control of spiritual energies gained through numerous lifetimes.

They have no medical problems as we have, for they control health through psychic balance. They feel that here on Earth all of our medical problems are caused by illogical thinking. As we create thoughts, we are forming bolts of energy which have an effect on the cells in our body. These thought energies can be measured in polarities, such as positive or negative charges of electricity. If we continue with illogical thinking, we are creating charges of energy that depolarize the cells and have an effect on the performance of the individual cells which leads to illness.

It has long been known in some societies on Earth that our thoughts play an important part in our health and can contribute to a longer life, especially in the Eastern cultures where meditation is practiced as a means of controlling their thinking. Here in our Western culture we don't try to prevent illness through control of our thoughts, but instead, wait until the illness is obvious, and then we treat it with chemicals and drugs which are designed not to treat the source but to override the symptons. That's why we have so few cures and recoveries from illness.

The Pleiadians say they are not superhuman with the great powers that we may think they possess. They are men and women like us who benefit from the knowledge of many lifetimes. They are not teachers or missionaries and do not come on behalf of any god to give us the long-awaited peace, as Creation does not confer any obligation on them. They understand our right of free will to evolve on our own, and they remind us that peace will only come when the people of Earth take responsibility for their own future and learn to create their own reality. Relying on or believing that someone else or some other power is going to bring peace will not make it happen. They feel an obligation to other life forms to help, but not to interfere.

The Pleiadians are not superhuman with
great powers. They are human beings
just as we are and must constantly
strive for perfection

Born in the Pleiades
Pleiadian men and women marry and have children just like we do.

Probably the major difference in being born in the Pleiades is that their understanding of the reason for a birth is different from ours, due to their spiritual development being so much more advanced. Here on Earth we are at a loss to prove the validity of reincarnation, but in the Pleiades it has become an exact science, allowing them to understand "who" is being born and what the purpose is of the coming life.

You see, many of the more spiritually advanced leaders on Erra have the ability to make a spiritual connection of some kind with the incoming person and "read" who they have been in the past life and what their purpose is for coming into this new life. A mother, for instance, will make a point of trying to find out what name the incoming person wants to call themselves, since they feel a person's name is an expression of not only their spiritual development, but has meaning relating to the path of education that they are on. They think of the incoming spirit-form as a person who has lived other lifetimes and is beginning a new one for a specific reason. Because of this, they are reminded that this incoming spirit-form has led many lives before and is now coming out of a sleep-like state to start another life. The idea of age means nothing when you consider that all of us have been young, middle-aged, and old many times before. To think that you are better, smarter, or somehow more advanced than someone younger than you is incorrect.

When a woman becomes pregnant, she opens a "window of opportunity" so that a spirit-form may come back in to the material life. The decision as to which woman the spirit-form will come into is not entirely up to the spirit-form, although there is a tendency for a spirit-form to stay within the same family if possible, which opens up the possibility that your great-grandfather may become the son of your grandchildren. Creation itself has something to do with the mechanism of parent selection; this process is not completely understood by the Pleiadians. They have advanced to a point of spiritual understanding and cognition that allows them to procreate or cause people to be born at a certain time such as they did with the old spirit-form from Lahson, but they seldom do that. They are also able to contact a spirit-form when it is on the other side, if they want to, but do not recommend it, saying it is uncomfortable for the spirit-form and is not very interesting anyway, for the spirit-form does not know any more than it did when it was in material life and usually does not want to be bothered.

Once a woman becomes pregnant, within three weeks the incoming spirit-form will decide whether or not to inhabit the new body that is being created. Abortion is allowed only during this time; this is the level of understanding and morality on a Pleiadian world. The mother and father both contribute some of their genes in forming the body for the incoming person. Later as the brain is forming, the incoming spirit-form will send impulses to signify how many brain connectors to create, so the "wisdom" the spirit-form is carrying from the many accumulated lifetimes can be handled by the brain once it is formed. Once the brain is developed, the spirit-form then transfers a copy of all of its wisdom into the acids of the brain where it will reside.

During the following months of pregnancy, the mother will attempt to make spiritual contact with the incoming person to become better acquainted, so she will have a better understanding of how to help out this person with their new life. They are able to understand, for instance, the path of learning that the individual is on. They can look into the previous lifetime and see if there are emotional instabilities of any kind that need to be dealt with, or if there were events during that life that left trauma or mental illness that should be addressed. They can tell if the spirit-form is happy and well-balanced or plagued with hostilities and anger and what may have caused it. During the pregnancy, the mother will be able to learn much about the person coming in so that she may have a better understanding of how to assist them in their new life.

Since Pleiadian women are not possessive of the incoming person and do not consider them a creation of their own, it's more like a partnership with another spirit-form. There is a more open attitude taken towards raising the child and sharing its development with others in the community, especially with other members of the family. This would seem very peculiar on Earth since we think of our children as our own creations to mold in our own image. How often have you seen a proud parent boast that his son will become a great football player, doctor, or work in the family business? And isn't it common for us to guide our children to an image that we hold of them? If we stop for an instant and view our children as people on a path of discovery and learning of their own, we might start to find some explanations for behavior that we are not able to understand and personality traits that don't make sense to us. If we recognize that these are people who lived lives before and have brought forward wisdom from previous lives, we can begin to understand why we all have different aptitudes, different levels of intelligence and knowledge.

We are all on our own paths of discovery and learning and need different information at different times in order to continue growing. We do not learn the same lessons in life at the same time, so we must learn to give each other space to seek out answers to questions that are needed for our continued spiritual growth. Life is like a school where we are all in different grades and different classes.

Once the individual is born, they have the capacity to understand their past lives and their chosen lessons in the new life. Since the Pleiadians do not treat children as their own property, they give love and attention to all children and help each other with their education. Newly born people are helped emotionally and mentally by shielding them from the negative influences until they can learn to think and understand themselves well enough to cope.

The first ten years of their lives are spent in education which helps them gain complete understanding of who they are and the path of growth that they are on. In other words, they are helped to understand the meaning and purpose of their life before they have to go out and deal with it. Only positive influences and environments are provided during these years, so they can become completely secure and well-balanced within themselves, and then they are exposed to the more negative forces now that they are better able to deal with them.

Here on Earth there is not yet an understanding of how to communicate well enough with an incoming spirit-form to learn about their previous life, so we can't understand how to help them. We are simply born and thrown into a hostile world and forced to manufacture defensive emotions and behavior patterns to survive. Our lives on Earth are mostly hard and difficult since we have no idea why we are here and what we are supposed to be doing, not to mention living in a civilization which is controlled by men of power who seek control over others instead of a world based on love and wisdom.

After the first ten years of self-discovery, the next seventy years of life in the Pleiades are spent in education; maybe up to twenty professions are learned. Once they leave their education years, they work four hours a day and spend another four hours pursuing the proper balance of creativity and spiritual growth. Since Pleiadians believe the purpose of the material life is to gather information through the physical senses and feed the spirit the wisdom learned from experience, the emphasis is put on personal growth and achievement based on what is good for the individual.

The basic philosophy is understanding the importance of personal spiritual growth by taking 100% responsibility for themselves and not relying on a god, myth, idol, or any other outside influence to solve their problems or take care of their own learning. Instead, the ability to communicate with higher consciousness is taught, so the individual can come in contact with the Creational Spirit which guides all beings in the universe. Only through understanding and cognition of the Laws of Creation can one hope to evolve to higher forms of consciousness.

Economics

The Pleiadians have no economics as we know it, but do have a system of sharing the resources of their world. Each person is encouraged to develop to their full potential and then bring those abilities into society. Material possessions are all provided, based on their contribution to the community. They carry no coins or credit cards; as a matter of fact, they mentioned that we have the only paper money that they have ever seen. They are in contact with many worlds but have not found another planet so totally engrossed in the pursuit of money as we are. They even observed that we use economics as a weapon; we actually make war with economics instead of simply using it as a method of keeping score.

On a Pleiadian planet all things are provided in their society since achievement for the sake of material possessions leads to greed, hate, and anger and detracts from spiritual growth. Since most of the citizens are telepathic, it is not possible for them to deceive or mislead each other and provides for an environment of truth and honesty between all. Because of this, everyone is able to share in the resources of their world in accordance with their contribution without the fear of greed and power. This has made their life more pleasurable and creates an environment where the quality of life is considerably higher.

Government

The Pleiadian civilization spent thousands of years at war until they came across a race of highly-developed beings in the Andromeda Galaxy who were in the last stages of physical life. By the calendar here on Earth this would have been around the year 10 A.D. This race of beings were far more advanced than the Pleiadians, for they had lived many more lifetimes and accumulated almost total knowledge of the material existence and the logic of Creation. A time had come for the Andromedans when they evolved beyond their physical senses and consequently relied solely on their spiritual consciousness for daily interaction. A decision was made to take the advice of these advanced beings and to abide by their suggestions, which led to peace and the end of war.

The Pleiadians now have a High Council composed of the more spiritually advanced, who interpret the wisdom from the Andromeda beings and spread the information to all four of their planets. All citizens in the Pleiades take part in the decisions that are made which make the laws by which they live. This is done through a system of voting similar to ours, only it takes a very high percentage of the voting public to agree before anything is passed. In some cases everyone must

73

agree before a change is made. This is done to encourage a feeling of unity and peace and to take into consideration the views of everyone before making changes.

The Pleiadians are a member of an alliance of civilizations that take advice from the beings from Andromeda. This includes thousands of different societies scattered all over the Andromeda Galaxy and our own Milky Way and numbers about 127 billion. Not all developed races belong to this alliance, but those that do adhere to certain rules governing civilizations such as ours.

In the Pleiades, each planet governs itself in a unitary type system but are subordinate to the High Council, which is located on Erra and is the central government. The Council is comprised of half-spiritual and half-material or semi-spiritual/semi-material creatures, who are human forms of life with enormous knowledge. It is the High Council's function to be in contact with very high pure-spiritual forms for advice, which is impossible for pure-material forms of life because the energy oscillations of the spiritual spheres are too high for the average Pleiadian.

They belong to an alliance, including races from a neighboring universe called the Dal Universe, which tries to regulate peace in certain areas of the universe through the use of giant spacecraft. The patrols that watch over Earth report that there are many space travelers who visit here. Each year around 3,000 ships enter our atmosphere, but only a small percentage are interested in making contact, and then it is usually only telepathic. There are 7 other races besides the Pleiadians that maintain bases here on Earth at present.

Alliance with Earth

We are told that the Pleiadians abide by rules that do not allow them to interfere in our political or power structures here on Earth as long as we are confined to our own solar system. Once we have the technical ability to leave our solar system under our own power and move out into free space, then we will come in contact with other races, including the Pleiadians, who will try to influence us. They want to make it clear that we, the people of Earth, must be very careful to whom we align ourselves, for there are many races out there who are very barbaric and would take us over in a minute or destroy us altogether. They hope that we may choose to align ourselves with them and other peaceful races, but the time is rapidly approaching that we may have to defend ourselves from an attack from space, for Earth is very well known in this area of the Galaxy. The Pleiadians afford us some measure of protection by making their presence known to incoming ships through a network that surrounds our planet, but it is not clear to what extent they would go to defend us from invasion.

Occasionally ships piloted by dangerous
races come into Earth space and
take humans for experiments

Love and Marriage

Pleiadians fall in love, marry, create families, and raise children just as we do. Although nothing is known about the marriage ceremony, we have been told that multiple marriage are common. It is quite normal for Pleiadians to be involved in 2 or 3 marriages at the same time. This system seems to work quite well for them due to an emotional stability in their society that has all but eliminated jealousy and possessiveness. Families will generally live on the same land but in different houses, while the responsibility for raising children is shared by all.

Divorce is not allowed since they feel this is an offense against the Laws of Creation. If the marriage laws are broken, the partners are exiled from the planet, but this rarely happens. They believe in many kinds of love, especially in friendship and marriage which are very closely related, as well as the love of all creatures.

If the rare case happened that a Pleiadian chose to marry someone from another race less spiritually evolved than themselves, then it is provided that the spiritual evolution of the less evolved life form could be accelerated to meet the evolved level of the partner. This is done through a transplant of brain acids which contain the evolutionary wisdom of the higher evolved individual which can be put into the lower evolved life form, causing a rapid increase in their development. Apparently this process works quite well and becomes a permanent part of the evolution of the life form.

Landing on the White House Lawn

There is no plan to land on the White House lawn. They have listened to the thoughts of most world leaders and believe that all Earthly governments are only interested in power and control and have little interest in anything else. An examination of the thoughts of our leaders shows them all to be power-crazy individuals who look at extraterrestrials as a source of power to conquer the cosmos when, in fact, they cannot even create peace on their own world.

A possible meeting was once discussed with certain officials of the

American Government, and the Pleiadians agreed to meet with a small group. As the Pleiadians listened to the thoughts of the officials who were planning the meeting, it was discovered that the officials were planning to kill them at the meeting sight so that they could obtain the Beamship the Pleiadians came in. This sort of thinking has led the Pleiadians to having no trust of our officials and making any sort of commerce with us almost impossible. It is estimated that it may be around 300 years before any kind of social contact may be possible with us due to the enormous gap in our spiritual and moral understandings. It simply isn't in their interest.

Open Contact

The Pleiadians are still here on Earth and occasionally visit Billy and others that they are interested in, but we have not reached a time of public awareness and open contact as a society. It's very exciting to think that this may be a possibility within a few years. For me, and for many of you, the ability to go and visit a civilization on another planet is a very exciting idea. To visit another world and see how they live would be a dream come true. Being exposed to so many new ideas, experiences, and so much knowledge would probably be overwhelming. It would certainly be hard to return to Earth after experiencing the consciousness of a higher-developed society. When this does happen and some of us get to visit the Pleiades and return to tell of our experiences like Billy did, the Earth will forever change and leave behind its adolescence. The paradigms that hold our society together will vanish and be replaced with new concepts and ideas that will leave a great mark in history.

The Beamships

Photo Proofs

Over a two year period Semjase allowed Billy to take hundreds of photos of her spacecraft. She did this purposely as a method of proof to awaken the minds of Earthmen to the idea that we are not alone. Over the years millions of people have looked at Billy's beautiful pictures and felt something stir inside of them. To some people it brings on feelings of familiarity or just the excitement of knowing someone is out there. In any case, there is no question that Semjase's decision to let her ship be photographed has gone a long way in opening up the minds of many people on Earth.

Silvano Sees a Ship

Since Billy had been allowed to take photos of the Pleiadian Beamships, I was curious if any of the other F.I.G.U. members had ever taken any. Billy had over a thousand pictures that he shot over a 2 year period. It seemed likely that some of the others around the Center might have had an opportunity to take some also.

I spent most of my mornings helping out around the farm. It was great exercise and gave me a chance to somewhat earn my keep. The work around the Center was organized by a fellow named Silvano. He was a young man who had brought his wife and baby to the Center to learn about Billy's contacts. He had decided to stay on for awhile to learn what he could and worked the farm in exchange for his room and board. I had spent a lot of time with Silvano over the past few weeks, and of course we had spent many hours discussing the Pleiadian material.

Silvano was a very kind and friendly person. He had a big smile and open face that let you know immediately that you were welcome in his life. His sensitive nature and his inquisitive mind had led him to Billy to discover what he could about the messages from the stars. In this respect we had a lot in common.

I asked him if he had ever taken any pictures of the Pleiadian

77

Beamships and he remarked that he hadn't. He had seen them but didn't have a camera with him at the time. It had happened on a clear, sunny afternoon, just as he had finished some of his chores and was cleaning up in the kitchen. He was washing his hands in the sink and glanced out of the window that offered a view of the large valley that spread out next to the Center. At first he thought the light was playing tricks on his eyes because a flash of silver was dancing in the sunlight about a mile away. Catching his attention, he looked closely out the window as the silver flash began to move slowly across the valley.

Silvano quickly moved from the sink and out the back door to get a better look. The silver object had moved in closer and he could clearly make it out. It was a round, silver Beamship just like the ones in the photos Billy had taken. It suddenly changed directions a couple of times as it quietly flew over the trees. Then with a quick move it came closer, stopped, and hovered in the air. It was gently rocking like a boat in the water, an action that Billy had described several times himself. Then without making a sound, it suddenly just blinked out of sight and disappeared. Silvano was just left standing there with a big smile on his face. He had been at the Center for over a year, and now he had seen real proof of the existence of the Pleiadian Beamships.

A Birthday Party

I had become pretty good friends with a lady named Bruni who was kind enough to spend many of her evenings with me answering all of my questions. She had moved to Switzerland from Germany with her son to also learn from Billy. I told her about some of the experiences that Silvano had, seeing the Pleiadian Beamships, and wondered if Bruni had seen them as well. She remarked that she had seen them on several occasions but remembered her first experience more than the others.

It was on February 3rd, 1984, Billy's birthday. Bruni had just become a member of the F.I.G.U. and had only been at the Center for a couple of weeks. Since she had a son and a job in a neighboring city, she had taken an apartment in the nearby town of Wila in order to be close to the Center and her work. In honor of Billy's birthday she had gone to the Center to have dinner with the rest of the group. They were all sitting around the kitchen table when all of a sudden Billy straightened up in his chair, his soft blue eyes became brighter as if something was happening to him. Bruni couldn't help notice the change and was just staring at him when someone mentioned that this was common when he was receiving a telepathic message from the Pleiadians. Apparently he was about to have a contact.

Popi, Billy's wife, had gotten him his coat; after all, it was wintertime and very cold in Switzerland. As soon as Billy was dressed, he walked to the back door of the kitchen, adjusted his coat and walked out the door. Bruni was naturally very excited by all this and rushed over to the window to see what was going on. By the time she reached the window, Billy was nowhere in sight. He had vanished without leaving a footstep in the snow. Bruni was very excited but was soon calmed by the others who had become accustomed to this sort of thing.

It was only a few minutes later when suddenly Billy reappeared from the living room. He didn't appear cold, his jacket was undone, and there was no snow on his boots. Billy informed everyone that he had been gone for a couple of hours. It seems that Semjase had come to see him on his birthday. Even though he had been in the ship with her for a couple of hours, she had shifted time and returned him about 10 minutes after he left so as not to spoil the family party in the kitchen. Bruni was quite excited to have witnessed this event, which cleared any doubts she may have had about Billy's experiences.

Bruni said that she often sees the Pleiadian Beamships in the sky around the Center. It is not uncommon to see them late at night simply flying by as if to say hello. Since I seemed so interested, she produced a photo album that contained many photos of the of the off-world craft. These had all been taken by Billy on different occasions. The interesting part was that many of these photos have not been seen before by the public.

One interesting photo was of a Beamship that Bruni called the wedding cake ship. It was a new experimental design with some kind of round metal balls all over it. It did look a little like a wedding cake. I had seen one picture of this ship in America, but here were over a dozen photos of this strange craft in trees, over vans, and on the ground in front of the farmhouse. One special picture that caught my eye had been taken right over the van that I was living in behind the main house at the Center.

Another shot that fascinated me had been taken of the ship as it was hovering a few feet off the ground among many trees. The size of the ship was obvious in comparison to the surrounding trees. It also looked very alien compared to the normal saucer-like ships. Bruni explained that the Pleiadians allowed Billy to take pictures of the older saucer-like ships since that image was more comfortable to most of us and would not cause as much fear.

The next day at the Center I saw Billy and asked if I could get copies of some of the photos for myself. He was happy to oblige and suggested that I look through all of the photo albums. There were around 1,100 photos in 5 large albums. They were all numbered, so I could easily identify which ones I wanted. I picked out about a dozen that caught my eye and later that afternoon Popi gave me the copies.

I think that was the day that I started staring at the sky a lot. I had a camera with me and became a little excited about the idea of capturing a photo myself. I realized that it had been several years since the contacts had stopped, but if they still came by for an occasional hello, perhaps I could get it on film. I asked Billy if he knew when they might be coming by, for I would very much like to see one for myself. He just smiled and nodded his head.

The Pleiadian Beamships

On Earth when we see a strange object in our skies, we call it a UFO or flying saucer. UFO stands for Unidentified Flying Object, but we may have to coin a new phrase now that we are in contact with the Pleiadians and know where they come from. Perhaps we could call them IFO's, for Identified Flying Object. The Pleiadians, however, call their small ships Beamships. The name comes from one of the first drive systems they developed, which relied on a light-emitting device to create power, hence the name Beamship. The ships are equipped with 2 drive systems, one for speeds up to the speed of light and another for beyond the light barrier.

A Beamship is a small spacecraft capable of carrying 3 passengers from one place in the galaxy to another. It is a very common way to travel for the citizens of the Pleiades. Many different sizes and shapes are made, depending on the intended use. The saucer shape that is often seen on Earth is used on planets where there is an atmosphere or water. Giant ships of unusual shapes are also used to house and transport large numbers of Pleiadians in open space.

The Pleiadians allowed photographs of the Beamships to be made purposely. They are aware that a great number of people on Earth have lived previous lives where the Beamship technology was used. Because of this, when we see the photos most of us will not be afraid. For many people the sight of the Beamship may actually seem familiar and jar some old memories. At any rate the design of the ship will seem nonthreatening and comfortable to most of us and provide a level of proof that life on other worlds does exist.

Beamships are 7 meters in diameter carrying a crew of 3 and have interplanetary capabilities. They are most commonly used for short trips around planetary systems because of their small interior. If longer trips are required or more passengers need to be transported, then large ships that are more comfortable are used. The Beamships only weigh 1.5 tons and do not have time-travel capabilities like some of their other designs.

Beamships are used like we use cars. They
are usually made for the individual and
are connected to their thinking
through organic intelligence.

The engines use an implosion type instead of explosion, causing matter to be converted back into something useful. The energy of the ship goes out the bottom of the ship and is reclaimed at the top. As it moves around the ship, it seems to distort all that is around it, causing the trees and all the surroundings to bend and distort. The field of energy around the ship causes the bottom to appear blue in color. Some of the distortion is caused by the energy screens that are projected by the ship for protection.

Pictures of the ship are only possible when they allow it, for the screens of the ships can also control the line of vision. In many of the photos the Beamship is over a house or small community while the pictures are being taken, but no one could see the craft.

The antennae guide beam on top of the ship is used to detect different kinds of energy. As an example, on one occasion the Pleiadians asked for some photos that had been taken of the ship which included the antennae on top of the craft. They wanted the negatives and the camera for awhile because they wanted to see how sensitive the film was to picking up the energies. An examination of the film by the Pleiadians revealed the energies from Saturn around the antennae as they suspected. Billy was told that these energies would have an affect on our thoughts, causing many people on Earth to be grumpy or moody for the next few months. This strange energy would also cause the magnetic energy created by the ship's drive systems to be visible to the naked eye for the same period.

The inside of the ship has 3 seats which fold into sleeping couches. Most of the console of the ship is filled with different kinds of screens for obtaining information. There is a greenish-yellow light inside the ship which is generated by the windows, and they appear orange on the outside. These windows are intelligent and control the ability to leave the ship. If the atmosphere outside is hostile, the windows will sense it and not allow the "pit" of the ship to open without the person wearing protective clothing. As the ship leaves the atmosphere, the color of the windows becomes clear.

The shape of the ship is designed for the least resistance in an atmosphere and provides the largest surface area to enable the drive system to be the most effective. The ships are protected by an energy force field that allows the atmosphere to glide away instead of pushing against it. This protection field must be designed in such a way as to give a little so as not to create resistance or else it will slow down the ship, keeping it from reaching the speeds it must attain for travel. The protection field also neutralizes the attractive force of our planet. They are, in a sense, diverting gravity. The ship then acts as a planet itself with its own gravitational force. The clothing that they wear can create the same effect as the protection girdle on the ships. They are worn outside the ship when on hostile planets. There is no feeling of movement inside the ship when it is flying, for it creates its own specific gravity and protects the inhabitants from any outside forces. Even when the ship is making sharp turns at tremendous speeds, there is no awareness of movement.

There are many different types of information screens built into the consoles of the ship. They can be used for information about flight, planets, and life forms. The screens can be telepathically controlled like many of the functions of the ship and can display important information about any kind of life form, such as the time of birth and the expected length of an individual's life span. It can also be used to interpret the thoughts and feelings of an individual.

The trip from Erra, the Pleiadian home planet, takes seven hours to reach Earth; they feel this is a long time to travel in a small ship. The total distance from Erra to Earth is around 500 light years, which is a considerable distance. Here on Earth we are used to measuring things in miles. For instance, it is approximately 400 miles from Los Angeles to San Francisco by car. If we drive that distance, it would take us about 7 hours traveling at a speed of 55 miles per hour. This is the same amount of time it takes a Beamship to travel 500 light years from the Pleiades. We can envision the distance from Los Angeles to San Francisco since it is familiar to most of us, but a light year, how far is that?

Light travels at the speed of 186,000 miles in one second, not an hour. That means that if we multiply the speed of light times 60 we get 11,160,000 miles in a minute. And then multiply by another 60, and we get 669,600,000 miles in an hour. A light year is the distance that light will travel in one year's time, which is 5,865,696,000,000 miles. (That's 5 trillion, 865 billion, 696 million miles). That's so fast that our minds have nothing to relate it to. Here's an example that may help. It is approximately 24,000 miles around the Earth. If we took a flashlight and shined it due east, the light would travel around the Earth 7.75 times in one second. The light from the Sun takes 8.3 minutes to travel

The Beamships

93,000,000 miles to Earth before it hits our eyes. Even if we could travel at the speed of light in a Beamship, theoretically it would still take us 500 years to get to the Pleiades. How, then, are they able to get here in only 7 hours?

The answer lies in the fact that Beamships do not fly at the speed of light, but have the technology to convert themselves into fine-matter particles that can travel faster than the speed of light. This is possible by traveling through what is called hyperspace, thereby making it possible to travel billions of miles in just part of a second. In order to understand this, a brief explanation of time and space is necessary which will make this clearer.

You and I live in a three-dimensional world of planets, suns, and galaxies. It is a material place that we can see and touch. The Pleiadians call it the coarse-matter world since it is material and appears solid.

Time is energy. It cannot be seen, but it is energy that causes the rotation and movement of the three-dimensional world we live in. It is a wave of pulse energy that moves through all matter, causing rotation, movement, and pulsation. Time controls the normal speed of all matter until something comes along and changes it. Time is considered fine-matter since it is not solid and exists only in an energy form. Without time, space would stop moving.

So we live in a space that is affected by the energy of time. The space we live in is comprised of different kinds of matter: carbon, hydrogen, zinc, and the other elements that make up all of the matter in our three-dimensional space. But the universe has other dimensions that do not contain the same matter as the three-dimensional part we live in. Hyperspace is one of those areas. Here, there are different kinds of energy particles that are moving at much higher speeds because time is different, and time does not exist in hyperspace the same as it does in our dimensions.

The Beamships have the technology to move themselves into hyperspace and convert themselves into high-speed particles that exist there. They then can travel much faster, going billions of miles in a part of a second. Once they arrive at their destination, they then reenter normal space and convert themselves back into their original form. The time in hyperspace seems instantaneous, and the passengers will have no awareness of what has happened.

Let's say we have borrowed a Beamship and have decided to travel to the Pleiades. We don't know how to fly it, so we follow a manual of instructions to guide us through the procedure. We leave Earth at 12 noon for the Pleiades and begin to fly out of our solar system. The manual tells us how to set the proper coordinates, so we are going in the right direction. We begin to travel at several million miles per hour and are gaining speed as we go. As we speed up, we begin to feel sick; something is wrong, so we refer to the manual. It says that we are suffering from the effects of the mass speed correlation. What is that, and how do we solve it? The problem is that as we accelerate in speed, our bodies are increasing in mass and we are becoming dysfunctional. If this continues, we will die.

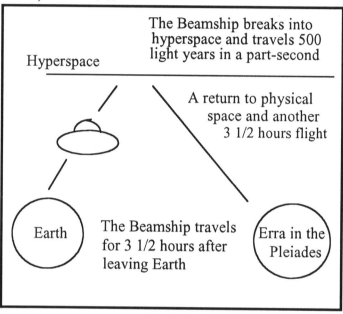

The Beamship breaks into hyperspace and travels 500 light years in a part-second

Hyperspace

A return to physical space and another 3 1/2 hours flight

Earth

The Beamship travels for 3 1/2 hours after leaving Earth

Erra in the Pleiades

If you are in a car traveling down the highway and put your hand out the window, you can feel the resistance of the wind, can't you? Air is very powerful, indeed. If you go fast enough, you can catch enough of it with a wing to fly through the air in an airplane. In other words, air is slowly developing into a mass of resistance. In space there is no air, but there is mass. When you go fast enough, the mass of space will build up just like the wind, and you have resistance. If you continue to go even faster, the mass builds up around your body and crushes you. So the mass speed correlation means that as we increase in speed, there is a build-up of mass that will destroy us and the ship if we continue. So how do we protect ourselves?

The manual says to turn on the protective energy screens that surround the Beamship, and we will be protected from the mass speed correlation. These energy screens surround the Beamship and isolate the ship from the mass of space. This bubble will also protect us from any debris we may run into in space. Energy screens also form artificial gravity, so now we are traveling in a Beamship which is surrounded by a protective field of energy that creates gravity. Inside of the ship we have created a mini-world with our own specific gravitational field, so we are separated from any force of energy outside of the ship. This enables our craft to make any changes in course, and we will have no feeling of it. We are only aware of the gravitational field inside of the ship. We are protected from the mass of space. It feels just like being on the ground with no sensation of movement.

Now that the screens have been turned on, we are feeling better and continue the trip. Soon we notice that we are traveling at almost the speed of light and will soon make the change into hyperspace and reappear in the Pleiades. The manual says we must wait until we are 153,000,000 kilometers (94 million miles) past the last planet's orbit in our solar system before making the move into hyperspace. This is a safety precaution since the changeover into hyperspace creates a rip, or small tear, in time and can sometimes pull objects other than the Beamship in with it. It is also possible to cause a disturbance in the orbit of planets if we are too close. Our instruments tell us that we are approaching the safety distance, so we can get ready to make the move into hyperspace. We have been traveling for 3 1/2 hours. The time is 3:30 on our watches.

Fortunately for us, it says in the manual that the process of moving into hyperspace is automated, so there is nothing for us to do. It even mentions that we won't feel anything during the change. As the ship approaches light speed, we can tell by our instruments that the screens are holding back tremendous energy. If they should fail, we would be crushed instantly from the incredible mass pressing against our protective energy screens. It takes a tremendous amount of energy for the solid matter of the ship and its passengers to be converted into fine-matter that can move in hyperspace. The Pleiadians have developed a technology that uses the tremendous pressure of the mass of space that is pressing in on us as a force to make the conversion.

The first step in moving the Beamship into hyperspace is to turn off the protective screens, which immediately causes an enlargement of the mass. The tremendous energy that is rushing in on the ship is used to facilitate the changing of the matter of the Beamship into fine-matter energy. We are no longer in our material form but have been converted along with the ship into a different form of energy that can exist in another dimension, which is called hyperspace. We have created a distortion of time and dematerialized ourselves.

At the exact moment that we are converted, we must make the move into hyperspace, for if we don't there will be a catastrophe. We have just been converted into particles of fine-matter energy that exists in hyperspace, but we are still in our normal three-dimensional world. In order to make the move into hyperspace, a dilation of time is caused. The theory of relativity goes only to a certain point here. At the exact moment of the dilation of time the breaking open of hyperspace occurs and the ship and crew, in their new form, move into hyperspace (also called *null-time*).

In hyperspace we are moving so fast that we appear paralyzed relative to the normal world. We can cross the 500 light years of distance to the Pleiades in a millionth of a second. The wonderful technology of the Pleiadians understands how to guide us in hyperspace and how to return us to the normal 3-dimensional world at the right location. This is done by reversing the process that put us in hyperspace, causing us to leave this null-time dimension and cause a dilation in time again whereby we are re-formed back into our normal state. Within a millionth of a second we find ourselves outside of the Pleiadian Solar System by a safe distance of 153,000,000 kilometers, or 94 million miles.

A glance at our watch shows it is still 3:30 as our time in hyperspace was so short that we were not aware of any time passing. The whole process takes no more than a millionth part of a second. To our surprise we didn't feel anything. We were out of our bodies for part of a second, though. We were not in material form but were, indeed, in an energy state while in hyperspace; it happened so fast that our material bodies didn't even remember being gone.

It will now take us another 3 1/2 hours to fly into the solar system of Taygeta and land on the planet Erra in the Pleiades. When we get there it will be 7:00 on our watches, for we will have taken seven hours to get there. Thanks to the technology of the Pleiadians, everything went well and we made it safely to our destination.

Things don't always go well, though, as this is very difficult technology to understand and even harder to put into use. While we were in hyperspace, we could have slipped in time and been lost forever. This is caused by the change in speed of our fine-matter energy particles while in hyperspace. If the speed of our fine-matter energy form had accelerated relative to the flow of time in hyperspace, we would have slipped millions of years into the future. If our speed had retarded, we would have fallen back into the past. A single second in the hyperspace equals millions of years in normal space. This means that if our speed had not remained constant for the part of a second that we were in hyperspace, we would have returned to our normal space and would have been millions or even billions of years out of time.

It is possible to remain in hyperspace for longer periods of time to cross greater distances, but the technology to control the speed while in the fine-matter state is critical. Most races experience difficulty with this process, including many of our forefathers who have had to fight these same problems and are now lost in time forever. Many time travelers are stuck here on Earth. The dangers of speed are great, and their effects occur at even a few miles per hour. Even in our airplanes we are increasing mass and dissolving matter, but because of the slow speed, the effects take a long time, possibly hundreds of years. At high speeds it is reduced to decades or even a few years. As the speed increases, the danger of our thought patterns being damaged increases.

The Metal of the Beamships

The metal used in the ship is a soft metal which is a combination of materials from lead contained in the atmospheres of stars. Some of it is found in water, some from different plants as well as different ores from stars in stages of destruction. They then convert the lead substances they have assembled in to this soft metal, treat it with chemicals to make it hard, and then it undergoes another process, which they are not allowed to disclose, in order to make the metal suitable for Beamships. The final product is an alloy which is basically a copper-nickel-silver-alloy and also contains gold for certain Beamships.

We could not produce the alloy on Earth, since not all of the ingredients are available here. For the most part, the chart of elements is the same throughout the universe, so you can find the same metals wherever there are planets that support them. We have most of them on Earth, but not all. Even though we could produce the alloy from our known metals, it would not be the same. We must first develop space travel in order to get to outer space to find some of the components in stars and giant gas planets where metals of greater density exist.

Some of the technology to make the metal of a Beamship will be discovered in the giant gas planets of Jupiter and Saturn

You Can't Steal a Beamship- It Dissolves

A special form of intelligence is bred into the cell structure of the metal that the Pleiadian Beamships are made of. This is done for the protection of the craft in case it is stolen. Once the Beamship is separated from its owner, a special coding in the metal causes it to begin to dissolve and break down. This was demonstrated by furnishing a small piece of metal from the ship to Billy. He took it home and placed it on the kitchen table to see what would happen. Within 24 hours of being removed from the ship, the metal had deteriorated into dust.

Stealing a Beamship would be almost impossible anyway, since the onboard computers are organic and capable of highly intelligent thought. They operate with a very high state of artificial intelligence that not only performs most of the tasks on board the ship, but will protect the pilot when outside the ship. The concept of computer chips and wiring that are used on Earth for our modern-day computers has been improved on by the Pleiadians to a state of organically grown intelligence that can communicate, think, and run the processes of the ship.

Gravity

Gravity is of electromagnetic nature with two unitary but contrary forces. It works to attract as well as to repulse and is connected to the mass itself. The Earth exercises the coherent, and the second factor is itself the generation and use of what we call gravity. Gravity and electromagnetism exist at the same time and appear as attraction and repulsion. One of the contributing factors for the development of gravity is the warmth of the planet and the cold of the cosmos, the solid center of the planet and the atmosphere. These factors are important for the development of the gravity and the force of anti-gravity, which varies at different points on the Earth.

Telemeter Ships

The Pleiadians have small reconnaissance ships called telemeter ships which are used to gather information about us. Most of these ships are unmanned and range from 9 feet in diameter to small basketball-size devices. They are normally controlled by radio-type signals that are broadcast from their underground complex. Some of the telemeter ships also have on-board intelligence and can pilot themselves and make decisions on their own. All of the little reconnaissance ships can be directed and influenced by telepathy.

The 9 foot version has room for one passenger and can be flown manually if need be. The telemeter ships are used mostly to monitor all of our different languages, for this is a particularly interesting study for them. They have recorded all of the languages that have been spoken on our world for thousands of years and continue to monitor our thinking processes to better understand the logic of why we live the way we do. It is very puzzling to them, for instance, how we can live in such a corrupt and negative environment and yet do nothing about it.

Communication on the ships is by a process similar to our radio, but the signal travels in a different manner. The signal is attached to faster-than-light particles called tachyons and is projected through null-time, so it arrives at its destination almost instantly. In this way messages and signals can be sent across vast distances of space and be received very quickly.

"Beam Me Up, Scotty"

We have all watched Star Trek as the captain and crew are beamed down to a planet below from the transporter room. A very similar process is used to bring people up into the Beamship. Special matter converters onboard the ship can break the matter of the body down into fine-matter and then reassemble it inside the ship. In the case of Billy's contacts the Beamship would usually position itself overhead, perhaps as high as 3,000 feet, and then within an instant he would find himself standing inside of the "pit" of the ship. There is no discomfort or feeling of any kind. It is also possible to lift someone up into the ship by using an anti-gravity type of device in which they are very slowly raised up through the air.

The Wedding Cake Ship

In 1981 the Pleiadians were working with a new technology and had designed a special kind of ship that operated on a different scientific principle. It was designed with a special drive system that did not necessitate speeding up to tremendous speeds to make the hyper-space jump possible like in the little Beamship, but instead could make the jumps while almost standing still. Because of its unusual design, it has often been called the wedding cake ship, for its appearance is round and has a ring of small metal balls around the ship, giving it the appearance of a decorated wedding cake.

A race of people who are friendly with the Pleiadians, called Timers, had discovered long ago that within the three-dimensional part of a galaxy there existed corridors or canals where material particles could not exist. These canals were out of normal space and time and could be entered at slow speeds. Once the technology was worked out on how to find the canals and enter them, the ship could move within that galaxy and reenter the material realm at almost any point within the same galaxy, and very little time at all would have passed. The way it looked in the material dimension was that the ship would simply blink out as it entered these null-time canals and seemingly blink back in when it reentered. The canals only exist within a galaxy, limiting the distance of the jumps, for there is a field of energy that forms around a galaxy that is used to facilitate this process, and this doesn't work in free space between galaxies.

This means that unlike a Beamship, which has to move 94 million miles out into space before moving into hyperspace, this new craft can simply dematerialize and move itself into these canals and "jump" to where it wants to go, a much faster process that appears almost magical. This new process was just being learned by the Pleiadians, who understood very little about it but could at least build and operate the drive systems that had been designed for them by the Timers. The technology had been used to build a very large mother ship, but this was the first time it had been tried in a smaller vehicle. The test ship appears in the photos taken by Billy to be smaller than the normal Beamship. From my knowledge of the surroundings where the photos were taken, I would estimate that the ship was only about 12 to 15 feet in diameter. Billy only saw the ship on one occasion but was allowed to take photos and a movie film of this experimental ship in 1981. This was the last time he ever saw the wedding cake ship and the last photos taken of any Pleiadian craft.

The Mothership

The technology for the wedding cake ship was downsized from the design for the largest and newest spacecraft built by the Pleiadians. A product of information provided by the Timers, this large galaxy-class ship measures 17,182 meters, or almost ten miles, in diameter. It was assembled in space and is not designed to be used in a planetary atmosphere. It represents a major breakthrough for the Pleiadians, for it is the first ship of its kind that can bridge the gap between universes.

On Earth we would term this giant spacecraft a *Mothership*. The main part of the ship looks like a large egg standing on end, while and on the bottom there are 3 smaller, round sections that are interconnected by huge braces. The three smaller sections have another brace extending out of the top and hooking into the main part of the ship above them. One of the round objects provides a hatch, or hanger, where visitors can store their smaller craft while they are onboard the huge city.

This is a completely self-contained world capable of providing a home for over 140,000 people who live onboard. Most of these people enjoy living in space and very seldom return to the home planet. Everything is provided for here, including a large area constructed to duplicate the outside conditions found on a planet such as gardens, lakes, and small mountains so the inhabitants can commune with nature. Living

90

quarters, schools, manufacturing facilities, virtually everything that is needed to sustain life is onboard, for the great ship has been designed to be a complete living situation for its crew and is completely self-sustaining.

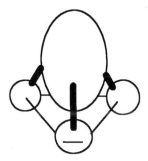

The Pleiadian Mothership is shaped like a large egg. This is the first of its kind in the Pleiadian fleet.

Since the population was so large, they designed huge airways that connected the different parts of the craft in order to move people around the ship. These airways run inside of the huge braces that hook the three smaller sections of the ship to the main body. This allows passengers to easily move from one area of the ship to another. The largest airway extends all the way up the middle of the main part of the craft. This giant open airway allows access to any level of the ship on small floating platforms that are used to move people up and down the airways and make it easy to get around.

The air inside of the great Mothership contains not only a higher content of oxygen than on Earth, but other elements have also been added that reduce the need for sleep and keep you awake longer. It is very similar to the atmosphere on their home planets. Along with the air, another consideration is the food. Just like on the surface world, the crew of this great ship eat a very light diet of vegetables and fruits. They have engineered the food so that by simply munching on small amounts of these specially grown fruits and vegetables, they can reduce the need for sleep to as little as only 4 hours per day while hunger can be calmed for as long as 90 hours, if necessary.

The Command Center for the great Mothership is located at the top of the main body of the ship and is where everything is controlled. Here hundreds of Pleiadians and androids assist in the control of the ship.

The androids are created organically by their scientists to do specific tasks. They do not have a spirit as humans do, but are programmed with tremendous intelligence to do certain functions. Most of the functions of running the ship are done by androids since they are very well-suited for this kind of work. They can stay alive for long periods of time, are disease free, and can be programmed for any kind of work, personality, and character. They are used extensively all throughout the Pleiadian society to handle most of the manual labor and technical work as they can be programmed with very advanced intelligence. The androids do not contain computers as we know them, but their brains would be an extension of the idea of a computer, and are organically made from human material grown by their scientists. For spiritual reasons the Pleiadians do not believe in the idea of cloning, so they have instead advanced the concept of a computer into this level of technology.

You can see right through the ceiling of the Command Center. Even though it is solid, you can see the stars overhead as if you were outside. They have a way of projecting some kind of radiation beam at the ceiling so that you can see through it, causing it to appear invisible. This way everyone working at the Command Center can see exactly where they are and where they are going, not to mention that the view is spectacular.

Visitors from many parts of the universe come together on this great craft, so communication would be a problem without the special language converters that are worn. It can read your mind and pick up your thoughts just before you speak. It then creates the words you need to say in the language you have selected and causes you to speak it. When you normally learn a language, you practice for weeks and build your vocabulary and learn all the grammar. The converter already knows the language, so it only has to know what you want to say, and then it feeds your mind the knowledge of the language you have selected, and you can speak it. It contains the knowledge of thousands of different languages and allows good communication for the many different species that live and visit there.

Time Travel

Being the latest in technology, the great ship can move in time, something that is not possible in most of the smaller Beamships. As explained earlier, the older Beamship breaks into hyperspace to move through the vast distances of space. Hyperspace can be utilized in different ways. When the small Beamship breaks into hyperspace, this is a form of time travel where time and space become paralyzed, or a better way of saying it might be that time and space push against each other, causing a complete standstill of time and space. Just at that point

92

timelessness and spacelessness are passed by at immeasurable speeds in a part of a second, without any shift of time in the real world. In effect, this is time travel in stagnant time where the Beamship appears at its destination at the same time it leaves its starting point. For a brief part of a second, it actually exists at its destination and its starting point at the same instant. This process is nothing more than a technically generated dematerialization and rematerialization process, where no time passes because of shifting or distortion. You could say that this is time travel without any time actually passing.

In a common time travel into the future, time and space are simply paralyzed and no time passes in the material realm, yet to move in the timeless and cause time to pass in the real world, other factors are necessary. When this is done, time is not paralyzed and there is a shift in the timeless. The ship and its passengers will move forward into the future, skipping through time that cannot be reclaimed. If it were possible to monitor this event on your watch, you would see that for every five seconds that pass in normal space, you would move one second forward into the timeless.

This is made possible by regulating the time between dematerialization and rematerialization by the speed effect, for only in the timeless itself can the shift in time be controlled. The timeless can be broken down into a tremendous number of intervals which is beyond the complete understanding of the Pleiadians, but they know enough about it to manipulate it. For instance, a single second in the timeless is equal to millions of years in normal space. This means that if the ship would penetrate into the timeless and slow down or stop, they would move so far back in time that they would never again see their home worlds. Just the process of remaining for a few seconds with lowered speed in the timeless would cause many billions of years to pass on Earth. On the return to normal time, Earth would have evolved billions of years and would have disintegrated into dust, while the occupants of the ship would return to normal space and only be a few seconds older. This may all seem fantastic, but it is the way it works.

Even the brightest Pleiadian scientists do not fully understand all of the complexities of time and space and are still puzzled by many inconceivable details. They have solved some of the problems and secrets of time and space but continue to work towards a better understanding. The knowledge and necessary understanding of the technology for passing through the universe has been discovered, but they, too, are only at the first stages of development in these areas and have much to learn. Their current level of science, though, does allow for the possibility for travelers to step into the timeless and experience eternity.

The future is not a fixed thing, but merely
a projection of events based on
the present

Touching Eternity

During the jumps in hyperspace a certain amount of time actually passes in this fine-matter dimension. This makes it possible for the Pleiadians to actually hold themselves for a period of time in hyperspace, and while they are out of their material bodies, they make a spiritual bonding with eternity and can return to normal space with full cognition of the event. At one time or another almost all of the members of the crew have experienced this, and they have their own truth about the existence of the Creation and the wonders of spirit that are contained within it.

In order to touch eternity, several minutes in the timeless are necessary to make a spiritual connection that will provide a meaningful experience. This will require that time and space be paralyzed while they purposely hold back the rematerialization of the ship for seven minutes while moving in the timeless for only a millionth part of a second. Because of the difference in the speed of time between hyperspace and the three-dimensional world that we live in, the clock in our normal time will advance by 5 times, which is equal to 35 minutes.

One other unusual occurrence that will take place for the crew on the ship is that instead of getting older by 35 minutes, they will actually experience a rejuvenation of 28 minutes. This is because as the ship is in the process of making the leap, it will be held in a state of dematerialization for a period of 7 minutes while not moving in time, so everyone aboard will all have aged 7 minutes. The ability to hold the ship in a dematerialized state for 7 minutes occurs because of very advanced technology which can control the speed effect and keep the ship from slipping in the timeless. Meanwhile in the normal world, the clock is moving 5 times faster, so time will have advanced by 35 minutes when the ship rematerializes. This means, of course, that on Earth 35 minutes will have gone by on their watches, while only 7 minutes will have gone by onboard the ship, so in effect the aging process has been slowed down by 28 minutes and the crew have become younger.

Here on Earth we are still wondering about Creation and what spiritual effect it may have on us. If we were allowed to travel onboard the great craft of the Pleiadians while they were holding themselves outside of time to touch the eternal force of Creation, we would for the first time in our brief lives feel the real truth of Creation and be filled

94

with the understanding of the great eternity that controls all things. Once out of our material bodies and into the timeless, our spirits can sense our connection with Creation. By being able to stay there for several minutes, we would slowly become aware of the love and knowledge that is the spiritual force that runs the universe we live in. Here in Creation is the absolute force and truth of all life, the calm, peaceful, and deeply serene feeling of love and togetherness that we are all part of. Here we can sense our connection to the Creation and know we are spiritual beings that are a part of all that is happening.

For just a few minutes we would only be our spiritual selves without a body, feeling the power and enlightenment of the greatest force of all. There could be no better way to understand who we are and the meaning of our lives than to be in touch with Creation directly as a spirit-form.

A Visit from the Pleiades

One night about midnight, after I had been at the Star Center for about 6 weeks, I was walking down the road toward the house and noticed one of the F.I.G.U. members standing out in front. He motioned to me to come over and watch the sky. It was a beautiful night high in the hills of Switzerland, the sky was clear with a million stars painted against a black canvas. He didn't speak English very well, but he motioned for me to stand and watch the sky where he was pointing. He pointed to his watch for me to wait just a few minutes, which I did. Soon he raised his hand and pointed toward the eastern sky. I shifted my view to where he was pointing and there it was, rising up from the horizon, a streak of white light moving at a very fast rate. It climbed up steadily and then leveled off and began to race across the night sky in front of us. Appearing as a steady stream of white light, the object was moving considerably faster than anything else I had seen in the sky. It was kind of like a shooting star, but rising up instead of falling. Then it took a slight turn and kind of bent right up into the sky and began to blend in with the stars. I was just standing there in amazement when my sky watching partner turned to me and said, "Quetzal." That was the name of one of the Pleiadian pilots who frequently visited Billy. He was apparently leaving the underground base that the Pleiadians still have in Switzerland, and who knows where he was going. I had just seen my first Identifiable Flying Object. Now it was true for me, too.

How the Universe Was Created

The summer was turning out to be an even greater experience for me than I had hoped for. I was able to spend a lot of time with Billy and came to better understand this man who had been in touch with human life from other worlds. We would stay up late at night together watching the stars or just talking around the kitchen table. I was a night owl, too, so it worked out well for both of us. He liked to talk and seemed tireless when it came to discussing man's role in the universe.

Our conversations would usually end up in the kitchen, which was my favorite spot for listening. Billy was very comfortable there as it was the center of activity for the whole farm and had a real homey and friendly feel to it. The kitchen was not very big, certainly not roomy enough for the 15 people living there. One end of the room had a doorway leading outside and a window over the sink with a view overlooking the valley beyond; the other end had a couple of shelves containing a small radio and some pieces of paper that were kept there so that people could take notes whenever they had time to sit down and talk to Billy. I usually had my own notebook with me, but in most cases I found myself going for the note paper on the shelf just like everyone else because you never knew when Billy would be in the mood to talk.

I had just finished painting the garage one afternoon and was in the kitchen cleaning up. Billy was sitting alone at the table having a cup of his favorite coffee. It was times like this that I could get some questions answered, so I asked him about the shape of the universe and what it looked like. He seemed in a mood to talk, so I grabbed some note paper off of the radio and started taking notes.

Pleiadian Science

To most of us the universe is some large, unknown area full of galaxies, star clusters, black holes, and light years of endless space. We have no concept of how big the universe might be, its shape, or how it started. Modern science talks of a "big bang" theory which seems to

96

make sense, only very little is understood about it, and most of us would agree that there is some kind of "God Force" or Creational Energy, that must be responsible for life as we know it. While science is busy trying to unlock the logic of the Material Universe, our spiritual leaders are trying to better understand the role of Creational Energy. Seldom do these two schools of thought agree or understand each other, but eventually they must come to a common understanding, for the material world and the spiritual world are both part of the universe that we live in and one can't exist without the other.

In order to better understand how our universe came about, let's start with the basis of understanding of Pleiadian science. They have not only been able to travel outside of time to explore the very beginnings of our universe, but have traveled beyond its barriers and learned from other races far more advanced than themselves about the infinite evolution of the Creation.

Our universe is inside of a much larger realm of Creational Energy that the Pleiadians call the Absolutum. There are 10 to the 49th power (that's 10 with 49 zeros) number of universes in this large and almost incomprehensible realm of spiritual energy. They have only been able to experience traveling in one other universe so far, but they have some understanding that each universe seems to be slightly different in size and development, yet are similar in shape. It is believed that the Absolutum is within an even greater Creational Force, but nothing is known of that.

The spiritual energy of the Absolutum is called a Creation. A Creation remember does not exist in material form. It is intelligence in a form commonly called spirit. It is a nonmaterial living form of life made up of the spiritual energy of all of the life forms that are within it. This large body of Creational Energy called the Absolutum is a living life form itself and must continually strive to evolve. Evolution is learning. The process of thinking creates energy that forms into logical sequences of thought and creates knowledge. As knowledge becomes more complex it turns into wisdom learned through experience. It is the wisdom learned from experience that creates spiritual growth. **In order for spiritual energy to evolve, it must create material life forms that develop energy through thought engaged in experience.** This means that the Creational Spiritual Energy of the Absolutum knows that it must create material life forms in order to continue its growth through evolution. These material life forms are called universes. Here is how the process works.

Every living form in the universe is a part
of the Creation and contributes
to its evolution.

97

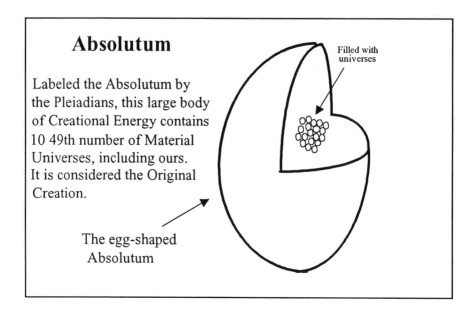

Absolutum

Labeled the Absolutum by the Pleiadians, this large body of Creational Energy contains 10 49th number of Material Universes, including ours. It is considered the Original Creation.

Filled with universes

The egg-shaped Absolutum

First the Creational Energy of the Absolutum has a thought to continue its growth by creating a new Material Universe. This thought is concentrated until it becomes a unique consciousness of its own. If we could see the energy of this small thought, we would discover that it is shaped like an egg. At this point the small thought is floating in the large pool of spiritual energy in the Absolutum between the already existing universes that are there. This small thought has contained within it the *idea* that it would like to create a Material Universe. This little thought takes up no more room in the Absolutum than a flea. The Creational Spiritual Energy of the Absolutum is doing this so that it can continue to evolve as all living things must do. It has taken a small part of itself and started a new Creational Spirit that will develop a Material Universe. For clarity, let's call the Creational Energy of the Absolutum the *Original Creation,* and the new thought that is the beginning of our new universe will be called the *New Creation,* or simply the *Creation.*

The Spiral

After years of thinking, our New Creation is still a small thought that is reasoning and figuring out what it must do to grow. Since thought is energy in motion, a close examination would reveal that it is moving in a spiral formation. The spiral is a multi-dimensional spiral that directs the flow of the energy of our small thought. This spiral pattern was naturally created by the Original Creation when our thought was formed and will control the flow of energy in our New Creation forever. A multi-dimensional spiral pattern would be impossible to draw here in our three-dimensional world, but the drawing below can give you and idea of how it might look.

The Spiral

The spiral pattern that energy follows in the Creation. It dictates the flow of energy that contains the spiritual knowledge of the Creational Universe.

The Sohar

The knowledge contained within our small thought is oscillating along the path of the spiral in a pulsating fashion. It is growing in intelligence very slowly; after billions of years, the small egg-shaped energy spiral has evolved its understanding of how to continue its growth and explodes into a bright light called the Sohar. Along with some help from the Original Creation that started it, the tiny New Creation has expanded to the size it needs to be in order to develop the Material Universe. It has literally pushed its way in among the many other universes in the Absolutum and taken over the area it will need to develop the new Material Universe. There are no stars or material matter at this point, only spiritual fine-matter that has the wisdom and knowledge it has learned through billions of years of reasoning and a little help from the Original Creation that started it.

The bright Sohar now appears between the many Universes in the Absolutum and has just contributed to the evolution of the Original Creation and to the New Creation by virtue of its experience. The Sohar has taken its position, and added itself to the 10 to the 49th power number of universes that currently exist here.

Our New Creation will always be a combination of spiritual energy and material matter, but at this point only the spiritual matter exists for it is still evolving to the point where it understands how to create matter. This is a slow process and takes trillions of years because the New Creation is slowly gathering knowledge which must be learned step by

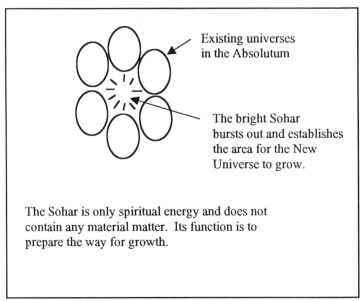

Existing universes
in the Absolutum

The bright Sohar
bursts out and establishes
the area for the New
Universe to grow.

The Sohar is only spiritual energy and does not
contain any material matter. Its function is to
prepare the way for growth.

step. Never can a life form jump ahead in development, but must always learn everything through the slow process of experience. This is a fact that rules all life forms. You might say it is one of the first Laws of Creation.

The Ur

Once the New Creational Spirit has reached this level of development, it receives a helping hand from the Original Creation in the form of a special energy called the Ur. This is the first and primary spiritual force of the Original Creation, and it is responsible for creating timelessness. The Ur is a highly evolved spiritual force that is also capable of creating other spirit-forms. In this case it provides the New Creation with the ability to think in a more rational manner. It also provides feelings, understanding, sense and reason, and the idea of life.

The Forming of the New Material Universe

The New Creation now uses its new thinking and reasoning abilities to create space and time, two factors which begin to form the matrix of the coming Material Universe. First the New Creation begins to create belts of energy which separate space and time into seven different layers or bands of spiritual energy. In appearance this would look something like a tree trunk. The center of the New Creation contains the highest evolution of energy and is labeled the Absolute. The second band is a slightly lower evolution of energy and is not as bright. The third and fourth bands are diminishing in force of energy and will serve different purposes in the continuing development of the new Material Universe. The fifth band is most important, for here is where the material part of the universe will form. Only in the fifth band will there be stars, planets, and material life forms. All of the other bands are different forms of spiritual energy that play a part in the development of the material band and will always be of a spiritual nature, not containing material matter. It is the purpose of the New Creation to develop the material band as part of its continuing evolution. The spiritual energy of the New Creation can think and reason and it has feelings, but in order to evolve, it must develop life forms which are capable of higher levels of consciousness. This is the purpose of the Material Belt.

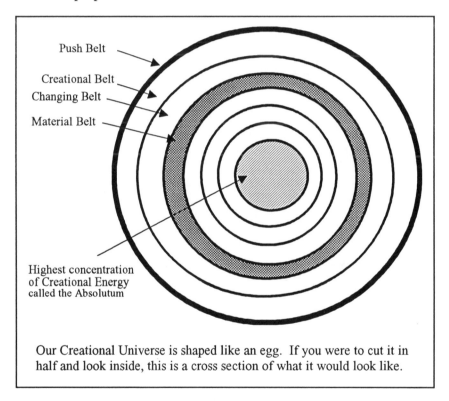

Push Belt

Creational Belt

Changing Belt

Material Belt

Highest concentration of Creational Energy called the Absolutum

Our Creational Universe is shaped like an egg. If you were to cut it in half and look inside, this is a cross section of what it would look like.

Between the fifth and sixth bands there is a layer of energy called the Changing Belt which is involved with converting from one form to another. This sixth band is sometimes used for space flight as time is different here, and great distances of time and space can be passed through in a matter of seconds. The 7th belt which forms the outside layer of the universe serves the task of protection and keeps out the energies from other universes. Since a universe is a material thing comprised of elements based on the evolution of the Creation that formed them, material matter from other universes which exist at different levels of evolution may not be compatible with ours, so the Push Belt protects us as well providing a kind of skin which repulses the other universes.

Creating Matter

As the Creation continues to evolve, the spiritual energy becomes more complex and more intelligent. As it continues, the mass of that energy also increases. This is because thought is energy, and as thought becomes more complex, it increases in force creating density. The building blocks of solid components - the neutron, proton, and the electron - are generated by this. This forms the atoms of the chemical compounds which then in their three aggregate forms create the solid outer wrap, something our scientists understand. This means that original energy is absolute matter, and original matter is absolute energy. The entire universe consists of matter and energy. Coarse-matter = matter, fine-matter = energy.

The Evolution of Matter

The original Sohar of bright light that established the area where the Material Universe would develop contained only the idea to do so. But this idea of light contains intelligence. This idea was only energy in a thought-form. As thoughts continue they form into consciousness, and consciousness forms into will. Will is then concentrated until it becomes dense enough to be called fluffy matter. Fluffy matter is energy in motion which oscillates according to the pattern of the multi-dimensional spiral before it is gas. Here is where the blueprint for all elements starts. As fluffy matter continues to evolve, it forms the first gas, hydrogen. Now we have an element with a positive charge in the nucleus and a single electron around it. Matter is being formed, and matter is energy in motion that contains intelligence, intelligence that contains the ongoing wisdom of the New Creation that started it.

There are 7 levels of matter smaller than the atom for us to discover

It is possible to create machines which convert matter to energy and vice versa. Matter is a sizable idea. All energies can be turned into solid matter. It is only necessary to concentrate energy very strongly and concentrate it very highly. This is done naturally and very slowly over trillions of years by the New Creation, for from it came the idea which started the process. The force of the spirit condenses and concentrates the idea to fine-matter energy, and with more concentration it then becomes coarse-matter. This is the process which will slowly evolve the spiritual energy of the fifth band into a Material Universe full of stars and planets and life forms.

Time Begins

As the energy of the material band begins to evolve and becomes more dense, the element of time provides motion. Time is an energy that moves in waves of pulses causing the rotation, movement, and pulsation of coarse-matter in the material belt. This happens before the energy has become gas and is in a state of concentration referred to as fluffy matter. This only happens in the material band because time as we know it only exists here.

As time speeds through the material band, it moves in a predetermined pattern set by the multi-dimensional spiral. This spiral provides a path which moves energy through multiple dimensions. The Pleiadians have discovered over 22 different dimensions so far and feel that there are many more. Each dimension differs in the kind of elements of matter which can exist there. Some dimensions have material time as we know it, and others move at speeds far beyond ours, while others are infinitely slow.

As time passes through the Material Belt, the fluffy matter will begin to rotate and pulsate according to the speed of the pulses of time. As evolution continues, the fluffy matter will slowly become the gas which will make up the stars that form the systems we live in. Eventually planets form to provide the way for higher life forms.

While this process of evolution is continuing, it is time which makes it all work. By controlling the speed of all of the subatomic particles that make up matter, the three-dimensional world that we live in - the stars, planets, and space - hold together and form the appearance of a solid material world that we perceive. Without time, matter would be forming randomly and would never evolve into solid formations such as the stars and planets.

We perceive the world around us with our eyes, and that tells us that things are solid and that they are moving at a particular speed which we call time. We generally think of time as the transition of one moment to another, and we gauge it by a clock. As all matter moves from one moment to the next, it appears smooth to us because we only see it and experience it with our physical senses. Under a microscope we see that

103

matter at its smallest level is really oscillating fields of energy. What we don't see with our eyes is that all matter is constantly in motion, perpetual motion that will last as long as the universe is in existence. Perpetual motion, then, is the most natural thing in the universe; our senses of sight, touch, smell, hearing, and taste are just not capable of perceiving it.

Moving in Time

The energy of *time* is moving through the three-dimensional world we live in, causing the smooth flow of particles which hold everything together. For instance, the moon is really a mass of particles that stay together because time is controlling it. But what if we disturbed the speed of the particles that comprise the moon, what would happen to it? Would it move out of time?

First remember that at the smallest level the moon is just a mass of spinning particles. Each particle has three stages of oscillation. The first state is a positive charge, the second is a 0 state that has no charge, and the third state is the negative charge. Billions of times per second the particle is oscillating between these states. The particle is in material form during the positive state. As it moves into the 0 state, it is no longer material matter but becomes antimatter, or nonmaterial. In the negative state it is once again matter. The speed by which it oscillates through the three states is controlled by time which is moving in waves of pulsed energy. All of the particles of the moon, then, are oscillating at a constant speed, so they are positive, nonmaterial, and negative at the same time. If all of the particles are doing the same thing at the same time, they can be formed into something which appears as solid. If the particles were all random, they could not form a solid object.

Understanding this, let's say we develop a machine that can create a time energy of our own, and this machine has a speed button on it so that we can cause the wave of pulses of our time energy to move at any speed that we want. Now let's aim it at the moon and turn in on. At first the particles of the moon will move at the same speed as before, so we can still see the moon. Now let's turn the speed dial on our time machine and bombard all of the particles that make up the moon with our time energy and cause them to oscillate a little slower. As we continue to turn the speed dial and slow down the particles of the moon, it will start to fade away. It is starting to move out of time. It is no longer moving at the same rate as the particles in the rest of the three-dimensional world and is falling behind.

As we continue to turn the speed dial and slow down the particles, the moon will become invisible. We won't be able to see it with our eyes

104

because they only perceive things in our normal time. The moon has fallen out of time and is, in effect, time traveling back into the past. By the way, it won't come back unless we find some way to speed the particles up so that they can catch up with us. Once something is thrown out of time through this method, it doesn't come back.

Remember that time started trillions of years ago when the fluffy matter began to have motion. Since then the matter of the universe began to move and rotate. You might say the clock of Creation started, and all particles of the universe have been moving in time since then. The idea is that time has been going for trillions of years. All of the particles of the material world we live in are moving down a multi-dimensional path set by the spiral formed by the Original Creation which started a long time ago. If we look closely at a small section of the spiral, we see our three-dimensional world moving along at the speed set by the energy of time. Each period of time is still there in particle form. The material world creates a highway of charged particles that can be traced all along the path of the spiral. Spiritual energy is not attached to the path, but flows along with it. Since we are spiritual beings, only our bodies are material; our spirits are not attached to the path, but can move up and down the path and move in time.

Imagine, if you will, a strip of film. Hold it up to the light and look through it. If you hold it still, you can see each individual picture. If you move it up or down past your eyes, the pictures begin to run together and your eyes perceives them as smooth, flowing motion. When you watch a movie, the film is moving past your eyes at 24 frames each second. The film strip is similar to the material world that is on the path of the spiral. Your spiritual self is like your eyes moving over it. A movie film is moving at 24 frames per second and time is broken down into billions of frames per second. All of the particles that make up our known three-dimensional world are oscillating at billions of times per second, creating the illusion of smooth, flowing solid objects.

The human spirit-form is not part of
the coarse-matter controlled by time,
but is part of the fine-matter
world that moves along
with it

If we wanted to see the moon in the year 1,000, it is there on the path of the spiral; all we have to do is find a way to go and see it. The human spirit-form is capable of moving itself in time through methods of meditation. In this process the spirit can separate itself from the material consciousness of the human body and move in time down the path of the spiral and view or visit other time frames. Everything that has gone before us in history is fixed on the path of the spiral and cannot be changed. The future is only a projection of things to come based on the present. It can be changed or altered since it is not a fixed thing. It has not happened yet. This realization tells us that everything in the past is there and can be visited by some means, but the events of the future are being made up. In effect, then, all of our history is existing at the same time like a giant file cabinet of information that can be accessed at any time. All we need is the means to open it up and select what we want to see.

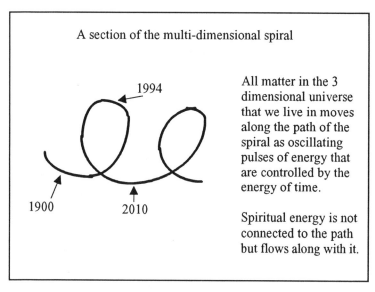

A section of the multi-dimensional spiral

1994

1900   2010

All matter in the 3 dimensional universe that we live in moves along the path of the spiral as oscillating pulses of energy that are controlled by the energy of time.

Spiritual energy is not connected to the path but flows along with it.

We can also build machines which can travel in time, such as the Pleiadian Beamships which move into time by accessing hyperspace. Then through the application of controlling the particles of the ship, they can move in time and reenter the three-dimensional world at a different place on the path of the spiral. This high technology is only possible when a race has the understanding of the spiritual and material realms, since both are needed to fully understand the workings of the universe that make this possible.

The Planets Form

At this point in the development of our universe, trillions of years have gone by. The Creation Universe has reasoned and figured out every step of the way with the help of the Ur energy of the Original Creation. The accumulated wisdom of all that the New Creation has learned is imbedded within it, for as it has learned it all from actual experience. Since our New Creation is within the Original Creation and is connected to it, it has a reference source by which it can learn and try out new ideas. It is no accident that the New Creation is evolving the way it is, for it must follow the pattern created by the Original Creation. Because of this, all Creations are created the same way and must evolve through the same steps of experience. The Original Creation is a blueprint, or guide, of how to do it, and the New Creation takes the blueprint and uses it to create its own Material Universe. Through the process of thinking and reasoning, energy is created, and when the process of thinking and reasoning is correct according to the Original Creation, then that wisdom is added to the accumulated wisdom of the new Creational Universe. This spiritual growth is what evolution is. As the New Creation evolves, so does the Original Creation, so all universes contribute to the growth and evolution of the Absolutum.

As fluffy matter evolves into gas and spirit becomes more intelligent through experience, the galaxies then form. Their movement, rotation, and pulsation is controlled by the pulses of time. Trillions of years elapse during this process as the Material Universe is forming. Then comes the clusters of gas which create the suns and stars, and eventually the planets form around the stars, signaling that the New Creation now understands how to create the mineral kingdom. All along the spiritual energy of the New Creation is learning and growing through the experience.

Once planets are formed, reasoning and thinking continue until the food kingdom comes into existence. All along the way the New Creation is following the blueprint of the Original Creation and using thinking and reasoning to understand the results of its experiences. The development of flora and fauna is just one more step in creating a more complex and higher developed universe.

As the food kingdom is developed, the way is cleared for the creation of animals to eat the food. Fauna, the animal kingdom, is responsible for the evolution of the coarse matter of our bodies. Once the animal kingdom has evolved the coarse body material to a level of evolution that is high enough, it is possible for the spirits of human life to come into material body. Man then begins the material life cycles and evolves the New Creation to perfection through the spiritual energies created by each spirit-form's growth.

Life develops in many different forms, depending on the planet and the sun system it is in. If a world has the necessary elements of water,

107

acids, radiation from the sun, and spiritual evolution, then life forms of varying size and shape will naturally develop. The human form is the most dominant and is found in all parts of the universe where the conditions are correct. The human form also represents a higher level of spiritual development by the New Creation, for it obviously takes more understanding and knowledge to create a human body than it does to create gas, minerals, water, or plants. We are seeing the slow evolution of the New Creation through the learning experience.

The human life form represents the highest order of development. It is capable of providing the New Creation with the highest order of learning experience and thinking that will be added to its evolution. The human form represents the first time the New Creation has been able to create a life form capable of rational thought and reasoning. Each level of development - fluffy matter, gas, minerals, flora, and fauna - has taken a more complex level of understanding and consciousness to create. The human form represents the highest level of understanding and consciousness. Humans can think and experience on their own and provide energy to the New Creation which in turn provides energy to the Original Creation, the spiritual part of the Absolutum. There is a chain of wisdom from the lowest levels to the highest which all contribute to the evolution of all life forms throughout the chain of Creations.

As the universe continues to grow, there is a point where the experiences of the material world can no longer provide new wisdom to the New Creation. There are limits to how high the consciousness of material life forms can expand. In the human form, for instance, there is a point where information gathered by our material senses is not of high enough consciousness to continue the evolution of Creation. The human form then transforms into a higher form of consciousness, which no longer requires the death cycle or the material body.

Our New Creation, which started as nothing more than an idea, has expanded in size and created a material realm from which to gain experience. It has had a mature adult life through the experience of learning from a Material Universe, and now it must rest, for the length of time that a Creation can sustain itself is related to the strength of its spiritual knowledge. Just as it must learn everything in small steps, it can also only learn so much at a time. Learning turns to wisdom through experience.

The New Creation Sleeps

At a certain point in the development of the New Creation, it will cease to expand and begin to contract back into itself. Based on the spiritual evolution of the Creation, it can only sustain its existence so long, and then it begins to contract back into itself to prepare for sleep. The Material Belt and all life forms in it return to a spiritual existence.

One of the problems for our scientists in determining the age of our universe is the speed of light itself. Light is faster in the past than in the future. Astronomers look out into the universe and study light which is billions of years old. New formulas will have to be created that allow for the fact that the older the light, the faster it is moving. The speed of light is also variable depending on gravity and the mass of space it is passing through. As our universe continues to expand, all energies will continue to slow down. Until we have a better understanding of the entire cycle of the universe, it will be difficult to gauge the time until the expansion is over and the contraction begins.

This is a time for the New Creation to contemplate the experiences from which it has gained wisdom. At this point the sleeping Creation is completely spiritual consciousness; there is no material matter. As it rests, it will finish out its thinking and reasoning on the wisdom learned from the experiences the material life forms have provided. Since only the material world can provide the experiences, there will not be any new data, just contemplation of what has happened. Creation has reasoned and learned how to create seven cycles of consciousness, beginning with intelligent light which turns into fluffy matter, then gas, minerals, flora, fauna, and finally the human form. All of these life forms have a level of consciousness that contributed some measure of wisdom to the evolutionary process of the New Creation.

The complete cycle of our New Creation will be 311,040,000,000,000 years, also known by the Pleiadians as a *greattime,* beginning with the First *idea* of Creation and ending as it moves into its sleep period. The first 47,000,000,000,000 years were spent in a purely spiritual form before the Material Belt begin to evolve and the gas started to become stars. The planet Earth is 626 billion years old and the sun is 1 trillion, 730 billion years old, if you date them back to the gas balls they evolved from. Since we are currently in the 47th trillion year of a New Creation which is expected to last over 311 trillion years, it's plain to see that it will be a very long time before the sleep period will begin.

The knowledge the Pleiadians have of the New Creation is due in part to their technology, which allows them to move back in time and study the step-by-step growth for themselves. Combined with the spiritual development they have personally achieved, they have also been able to access realms of higher consciousness and learn from them.

During the sleep time the New Creation rests, contemplates, and prepares itself for a new life. Once this period is over, it will awaken and start the process all over again. Just as before it will start with intelligent light, evolve it into fluffy matter, then gas, mineral, flora, fauna, and then the human form. This time it will start with the accumulated wisdom learned from the first cycle and continue to evolve.

Creation will go through seven complete greattimes of waking and sleeping. Each one will be similar, varying in wisdom and evolution. All greattime cycles, though, will create Material Belts in order to learn from the experiences gained by the evolving life forms. Once it has completed seven greattimes, the process stops and the New Creation will transform into a higher form called an Ur Universe. The completion of seven greattimes is called an Eternity.

1 Greattime	=	311,040,000,000,000 years
7 Greattimes	=	2,177,280,000,000,000 years and is called an Eternity
Cosmic Greattime	=	15,240,960,000,000,000 years

There are three types of universes that the Pleiadians are familiar with so far. Even though it is estimated that there are over 10^{49} th number of different universes in the Absolutum, they have only identified the purpose of three types. First is the Ur, which is the first and primary source of evolution of the Absolutum. An Ur Universe also goes through seven steps of evolution, but it differs in that is does not create Material Belts in order to evolve but instead creates other universes called Creational Universes. The universe that we live in is called a Creational Universe since it creates material life forms in order to evolve. It is the first stage of development in the evolution of universes.

Once a Ur Universe goes through its seven stages of development creating other universes, it transforms into what is called a Central Universe. The function of a Central Universe is not understood very well as they have not been able to enter one, and they rely mostly on the experience of higher life forms for information that it exists.

The understanding of Creation provides us with an answer to the meaning of our lives. Our brief, transitory material lives fulfill the most important task of learning. For it is through learning that we think and create energy with our brains. That energy moves like waves across the universe and has an effect on other life forms, including the planet we live on, the plant kingdom, and all other living creatures. The combined thinking power of more than five billion people on Earth create energy which affects all levels of nature, as well as each other. If ever you doubted the importance of your life, you should know that you are a wonderful and essential part of the Creation you live in, and you share in the responsibility of its evolution. Once you have this understanding and experience your connection to Creation, you will feel the spiritual bonding of all living things.

The purpose of the material life is to provide wisdom learned from experience to your spirit. But it is most important to realize that you are a spiritual being going through a series of material lives to feed your spirit. The food your spirit evolves on is called truth. As you cross the consciousness barrier from material to spirit, you will come in touch with your connection to Creation, and the truth will become part of you. Since you are a spirit-form created from the Eternal Spiritual Energy of the New Creation, you can access the knowledge of Creation through your spiritual consciousness anytime you chose to recognize it. We are all part of the guiding light of the Eternal Creation.

The Evolution of Human Life

The Logic of Creation

Now that we have a better understanding of what Creation is and how we fit into it, the importance of our lives should be clearer. We can see from the steps that the New Creation goes through that there is definite logic to its evolution. Life is not a random series of actions but an orderly, rational, and logical sequence of events that gives meaning to our lives and follows the blueprint designed by the Original Creation and emulated by our New Creation. If we look closely at the evolution of the New Creation and the steps it follows, we can find definite guidelines that parallel our human life.

The New Creation Starts with an Idea

Man is conceived through the idea of his parents.

Creates Material Life in Order to Evolve

We are spiritual beings who come into life through the womb and live a material life.

Earns Evolution through Small Steps of Learning

All wisdom in life is won through experience. Man cannot jump ahead to learn the great mysteries of life; he must learn everything in small steps.

Creation Goes through 7 Stages of Evolution

Just as the Creation goes through 7 greattimes in order to reach perfection and evolve, man also lives through 7 stages of development which follow the logic of Creation.

Creation Has an Awake Period and a Sleep Period

Man is awake during the day, and he sleeps at night. At the end of his material life he will sleep on the other side, and then he will wake to reenter the material world.

Creation Evolves into a Higher Life Form Called an Ur

Man begins as a material life form and eventually evolves into a being of lighter density where the death cycle is no longer necessary. After years of slow evolution he becomes part of a collective consciousness that does not have a material body but exists in pure spiritual form. Collective consciousnesses have 7 spirits.

The 7 Evolutionary Steps of Man

On Earth we are just becoming aware of our spiritual consciousness and its ability to communicate with the eternal knowledge of Creation. The great spiritual minds of the Pleiades have analyzed the development of the human being and discovered how the evolution of the Creation dictates the development of the human spirit-form as well. Just as the Creation must earn its way through 7 greattimes on a path to perfection, so must man. The human life form evolves through understanding learned from experience, following the same design as Creation. There are 7 main levels of evolutionary development with 7 sublevels.

Creation goes through the development of 7 levels of life forms – intelligent light, fluffy matter, gas, mineral, flora, fauna, and human – to complete the cycle of one greattime. It will then repeat that 7 times in order to reach perfection and transform itself into a life form of higher consciousness. As part of Creation, man follows this same guideline and goes through 7 main levels of development, each with 7 sublevels of learning. Man's existence begins as a spirit-form which is connected to the eternal energy of the Creation and ends up a pure spiritual form that returns to the Creational Source, becoming part of the knowledge that directs the growth of the universe.

On the Planet Earth the natural cycles of development occur as they do throughout the universe. First the planet is formed from the primordial gas, which takes billions of years. As evolution continues, eventually the mineral kingdom is formed, followed by the flora, or food, kingdom. The animal kingdom is next since now there is food available.

All along this path of development the spiritual energy of the New Creation is gaining in wisdom that gives it the intelligence to create the next step. As the energy becomes more intelligent, its force, or vibrational level as some call it, increases. It can be seen and measured as an aura around all things.

The animal kingdom plays a very important part for humanity, for it is responsible for increasing the level of spiritual energy on the planet so that human life is possible. Once the animal spirit has developed to its highest potential, the stage is set for the first signs of human life to come into existence. We do not evolve from the animal kingdom, but we owe

113

them a debt of thanks for evolving the coarse-matter from which we create our bodies. The human spirit-form is a unique spirit-form that is created with the ability for rational thinking and understanding; this is what separates us from the animals.

Once the level of evolution is high enough on the planet and the animal kingdom has evolved the coarse-matter sufficiently, the first human spirit-form can come into life. On Earth this happens much the same as it did on other planets, a single-celled creature is made from a combination of plant material and animal feces. This first Earth human life form, a single-cell creature, was really nothing more than slime. Evolution came into play, and as the new human form continued to grow through numerous material lives, it was eventually able to procreate as we do now.

The Pleiadians have studied the process of evolution of the human spirit for thousands of years. They learned that as man goes through his many material lives, he will develop through 7 main steps of evolution that closely follow the same pattern set up by the Original Creation and emulated by the New Creation. Since the New Creation itself revolves around cycles of 7, they have learned to relate the growth of man to these same steps. If we could attend a Pleiadian school, we would learn these 7 steps of evolutionary development of human life, along with explanations of the 7 sublevels.

Step	Evolution Step	Type of life
1	Beginning Life	Material life
2	Life with Reasoning	Material Life
3	Life with Intelligence	Material Life
4	Life with Spiritual Cognition	Material Life
5	Life with Creational Cognition	Material Life
6	Life in Spiritual form	Material/Spiritual
7	Life with Creation	Spiritual

STEP ONE: BEGINNING LIFE

1. Beginning Development of the Intellect

These are the first material lives on Earth. The human form is nothing more than a spirit-form trying to develop its intellect. There is no accumulated knowledge from previous lives, only the intellect of the spirit which has not lived in a body before and can barely take care of itself since it has no understanding of the material world at this time. All humans look the same at this point since our facial expressions, bodies, color, etc., are expressions of experiences, wisdom, emotions, and ego that we have not yet developed. Our lives are short as our spirits have very low energy to sustain the material existence. We also die young due to poor health.

2. *Beginning Development of Spiritual Growth*

Through numerous lifetimes we begin to think and provide wisdom to the spirit. The process of evolution has begun. Simple-minded, we can barely feed ourselves and sustain life.

3. *Beginning Development of Reason*

We can now think and reason a little better. We have lived many brief lives and are starting to build intelligence from the experiences of previous lives. We are 20 to 30 million years old at this point. The counting of age begins with the start of the first material lifetime and includes the sleep period on the other side we call death.

4. *Beginning Use of Thinking*

We can live longer now, for we are able to feed ourselves, start a fire, and build shelter. Our accumulated wisdom is providing us with some assistance since our spirit is now beginning to understand the physical existence better, and it can provide the occasional hunch or idea learned from previous lives to help out.

5. *Beginning Development of Reasonable Actions*

We are still very primitive and living in caves. We don't get along with each other and in our material consciousness have absolutely no idea who we are or why we are here. We are trying to develop some more rational thinking patterns, but it's going slow. We can't even understand each other.

6. *Beginning Development of Thinking and Action*

Rational thinking and understanding are becoming useful in our day-to-day lives. We are starting to understand each other and are starting to work together. Man's appearance is unique, for his body and face are reflecting the experiences and wisdom of his life.

7.   *Beginning Awareness of Reason*
Reasoning and rational thinking are now in control of our lives. We can communicate through language, symbols, and signs. We are starting to form communities and learning to get along.

STEP TWO: LIFE WITH REASONING AND RATIONAL THINKING

1.   *Beginning Development of Reason*
Our ability to reason and solve problems is making a difference. We are still not aware that we are also a spirit-form. We are only beginning to question and look for answers. Life is purely a material existence to us.

2.   *Awareness of Reasoning and Its Use*
We are now aware of reasoning and understand its use. We are searching for answers to our existence. Emotions are coming into play as fear, anger, and hostility begin to govern our lives. We all look much different from each other now since we are noticeably on different paths of discovery and experience. The problems in life are being solved through our reasoning ability and we now regard ourselves as rational, thinking beings.

3.   *Development of Awareness of Higher Influences*
We are aware that there are powers in the world more advanced than our own and are searching for them. We question the power of the stars, sun, and moon and nature around us. We are unsure of our existence and are looking for meaning to our lives. The moon and the stars puzzle us as we search for answers to their existence.

4.   *Awareness of Higher Influences*
We start to develop belief systems such as worshipping idols, gods, and the sun without actually having any knowledge of what we are doing. We are still without knowledge of the spiritual

116

side of life.

5. **Belief in Higher Forces.   Superstition, Fear of Evil, Veneration of Good**
    Here we see the development of religions, superstition, and gods. Our lack of real knowledge of Creation and fear make us vulnerable to powers we don't understand. Most of the current mass of humanity on Earth is at this stage.

6. **First Awareness of the Meaning of our Lives and the Real Spiritual Life.   Development of the First Spiritual Cognition's and Their Use. Spiritual Healing, Telepathy**
    Now comes man's first awareness of the spiritual world. He is looking for answers but has no real understanding. It is the beginning of awareness of spirit and its uses. This will be the first attempt at using the powers of spirit without real knowledge. This is the current position of the average Earthman, who at this level of development can only gain 9.4 months of spiritual growth within a lifetime. At this point we are around 80 to 100 million years old as spiritual beings. Most of the older spirit-forms on Earth would be at this level of understanding. This would be typical of New Age people and border scientists who feel the intellectual curiosity to learn more about life and spirit.

7. **Development of Knowledge and Wisdom**
    The mind is developing and our accumulated wisdom learned from millions of years of lifetimes is creating intellect. Man is becoming aware that there is more to life than his brief material existence.

STEP THREE: LIFE WITH INTELLIGENCE

1. **Development of the Intellect.   High Technology, Advancements in Spiritual Forces.   First Development of Living Forms**
    It is the age of the mind. We can be considered intelligent life forms now. We have broken through the age of ignorance and have advanced well in the sciences. Our awareness of our spirits and our connection to Creation is stronger, for we are learning

117

more about the powers of our spirit. We have learned to create new foods, to crossbreed animals, and are searching for the understanding of how life works.

2.   *Awareness and Exercise of Knowledge, Truth, and Wisdom. Slow Dissolution of Acceptance of Belief*
We are leaving behind the thinking of the past. We no longer accept old myths, idols, and false gods. Real intellect and reasoning are providing us with enlightenment.

3.   *First Usage of Knowledge and Wisdom*
High technology is becoming part of our world. Genetic engineering has led to the creation of the first life forms. The secrets of the universe are beginning to unfold to us as man is learning about his place in the scheme of things. This is the present position of the educated Earth human being, scientist, etc.

4.   *Awareness and utilization of natures laws, development of high technology that leads to the creation of living forms*
Man is leaving behind his old belief structures and is gaining in wisdom about the universe around him. Here we see development in the sciences as man learns to really understand the forces of nature. There is high technology in the field of genetics as we learn to clone our cells and experiment with different life forms.

5.   *The Use of Spiritual Forces in Life*
The development of spirit is now playing a bigger part in the role of man. We have learned more about the ability of spirit to help us in life and are beginning to solve less of our problems by material means.

6.   *Understanding Life Through Wisdom, Truth, and Logic*
Man is on the verge of real understanding of Creation and the Material Universe around him. Contact with higher life forms begins. The spiritual world is now more understood and the true meaning of life is unfolding. Our existence as part of Creation is becoming clearer, and peace among men is starting as the need for material things slips away.

118

7.   *Awareness of the Real Meaning of Life*
Just a few border and spiritual scientists would be at this level. Man has real knowledge now of the Laws of Creation and how to use them in society. Belief systems and religions are fading away as man develops true understanding of his role in Creation. It is understood that gods are actually human life forms with greater knowledge than most, and we now know that gods are also subject to Creation. At this level of development the human can advance spiritually as much as 89.7 years within a lifetime.

STEP FOUR: LIFE WITH SPIRITUAL UNDERSTANDING

1.   *Clear Understanding of Spirit*
We can now live more in harmony with nature and Creation as we have real knowledge about life and spirit. Our thinking is clear, but we have little experience dealing with life using spiritual power.

2.   *The Truth of Spiritual Knowledge and Wisdom*
We begin to experiment with spiritual knowledge and learn about it uses in telepathy, telekinesis, time travel, and control over nature.

3.   *Use of the Spiritual Knowledge and Wisdom*
We now have real knowledge of the spiritual forces as we begin to use telepathy and the other spiritual powers in our day-to-day life. Many of our problems are solved with spiritual consciousness rather than material senses. Our spiritual self is now understood, and we work with the energies of all life forms.

4.   *Cognition of Creation and its Laws*
Through the development of spirit we come to have personal knowledge of our connection to Creation and have a better understanding of the meaning of life and our role within it. The material world is becoming less important to us as we are learning more with our spiritual senses.

5.   *Living from the Creational Laws. The End of the Concept of Belief*
There is a major breakthrough in our development as now we are

119

living from the Creational Laws and have moved into a time of higher consciousness. We are perceiving life with the higher abilities of spirit instead of the simple material senses of sight, touch, smell, hearing, and taste. Our accumulated wisdom from previous lives is being very helpful. Our previous lives and the experiences learned from them are clear to us.

6.   *Controlled Utilization of Spiritual Forces*
The power of our spirit is causing us to live longer. Health problems are vanishing as we control our bodies through spiritual balance. We are beginning to develop a society of integrity wherein we can sense each other's emotions and thinking. The Pleiadians are living at this level.

7.   *First Ability to Create Living Creatures*
We have developed very high technology and can roam the universe. The knowledge of the material life is ours, and we create our own life forms to work for us. Our genetic scientists can preserve extinct species by recreating them in the laboratory.

STEP FIVE: LIFE WITH CREATIONAL COGNITION

1.   *Creating Other Life Forms*
We can greatly extend the life span to thousands of years through a combination of technology and spiritual power. Our lives are becoming more spiritual than material since the force of our spirit and our high evolution allow us access to higher forms of consciousness in Creation. The material senses are not playing a big part in gathering the information to form our life experiences, for more of this is being done by spirit. We are giving advice to other civilizations and helping them with their first steps.

2.   *Construction of Synthetic Livable Creatures*
Our technical knowledge of the material form allows us to create high forms of life that can be mistaken for human. We are becoming more of a spiritual being and spend more time in connection with Creation. Our awareness of the material world is becoming less important to us. Our concerns are for the creation of life and its development.

3. *Spiritual Development for Control of Organic Forms of Life*
We are beginning to develop the force of our spirit to the point where we can control the birth of other creatures. We are developing the ability to control the forces of nature: levitation of matter, the control of gravity, and electricity. We are starting to look and think more alike, for we have all learned many of the same things.

4. *Interest in Mastering Life and all Its Forms*
We are becoming less concerned with our material senses as we search for the remaining knowledge of life and spirit. We are becoming masters of all knowledge of the human form.

5. *Recognition Awareness of Earlier Lives*
We can control time and space with our spirit and can move through our previous lifetimes. We are becoming masters of the knowledge of human life and its development.

6. *King of Wisdom - ISHWISH (IHWH). The Level of a God*
We are now masters of the human knowledge. We are still in material form but have little need for our material senses. We communicate and experience the world mostly with our spirit. This is the level of a god, a material being that has mastered the knowledge of man, a King of Wisdom. In ancient times gods ruled the Earth and controlled the minds of men. It was believed that they had power over life and death, which is not true, for only Creation has that power. There are no longer any gods ruling over Earth, but many people have not relinquished this ancient concept and taken control of their own lives.

7. *The Transition to Spirit Begins*
This is the transition time for the material being. Having evolved through all of the stages of development of man, we are ready to transform into higher consciousness and leave the material plain. We now look very much the same, for we have all assimilated the same knowledge and have arrived at the same level of understanding. We are mostly spiritual and it shows in our bodies and faces. We are at peace with Creation and live with the complete understanding of love and life.

121

STEP SIX: LIFE IN SPIRITUAL FORM

1. *Cognition of Spiritual Peace, Universal Love, and Creation*
The last stage of material life. The experiences that are needed to continue our evolution can no longer be provided by the material senses. We are becoming a pure spiritual form. We are living in harmony with Creation and feel the constant love of eternity.

2. *Beginning of Life as a Spiritual Form*
The material body is becoming dysfunctional and serves little purpose anymore. We are interacting almost totally with our spirit. We no longer require sleep or food since we are becoming a pure spiritual form. Our bodies are becoming lighter in weight as the material is fading away.

3. *Development of Other Life Forms*
The material body is becoming less dense. It is possible to see right through us because our bodies are becoming more like light. The death cycle has stopped and we live continuously in this form. Our existence is almost purely spiritual now, and our time is spent in helping with the development of those younger than ourselves. We are taking part in the education and spiritual guidance of those in the material world. We are several billions of years old now.

4. *The End of the Material Life*
The transition into light body is complete and we are living our first spiritual existence. Our material body is completely gone and we now exist in a purely spiritual form. We use the accumulated wisdom we have learned to help those younger than ourselves. Our spirit now exists with the constant consciousness of love and understanding for all things. We still have awareness of self and our personality. We are around 70 billion years old as a spirit-form. Billions of more years will be spent as a spiritual being striving for perfection before we transform over into Creation.

5. *Collective Consciousness*
Millions of years pass as our spiritual self comes together with 6 other spirits, and we become a collective consciousness comprised

122

of 7 spirit-forms. We still have awareness of self and are actively taking part in the development of human life. This is the same level as Arahat Athersata, the timeless teacher of great masters such as Jmmanuel.

6.   *Final Spiritual Existence*
This is the last existence of the spiritual self. We are in the last years as a collective consciousness of seven. Our personal identity fades away as we reach the highest level of consciousness called the Petale Level. Here all collective consciousness come together as one to prepare for the transition to pass over into Creation.

7.   *Pass Over into the Creation*
Our evolution as an independent human life form is complete. As part of the highest level of consciousness, the Petale Level, we will pass over and become part of the Creation itself. Here we join up with all of those who have gone before us and become part of the great eternal knowledge of Creation which provides guidance and love to all things. We have earned this right through billions of years of experience which has provided us with the complete, accumulated knowledge of all things. We have experienced and completely understood the evolution of a universe.

STEP SEVEN: LIFE WITH CREATION

1.   *Twilight Sleep through Eternity*
Our spirit-forms are part of Creation that will sleep for a period of 7 greattimes, or an eternity. During this time all life and the whole universe ceases to exist. There is no space or time, only the nothingness of sleep. It is not a time for creative thought, but a restful time of cogitation.

2.   *A New Greattime for Creation*
Creation awakens and starts to create a new universe just as before. We are now part of a completely new cycle. Our awareness of self is gone, for we are one with eternity now and are contributing to the spiritual knowledge that guides all.

3. **Creation Starts a New Universe**
    Creation will once again begin its evolutionary cycle by creating living life forms which can contribute to its evolution through wisdom gained from experience. A New Universe will be formed to repeat the cycle of evolution. The energy of the Creation has evolved to a higher level.

4. **Creation of New Spirit-forms**
    Creation is constantly improving and creating new spirit-forms. Spirit-forms are small parts of creation that will evolve by becoming material life forms. Creation will continue to evolve and improve itself through the cycle of life forms. Creation is constantly starting new spirit-forms throughout the complete cycle of Material Universe. Even here on Earth new spirit-forms are coming into life. Since they have no accumulated knowledge or intelligence, we will often think of them as idiots or insane. In many cases they are just new spirits who have come into a material world far too advanced for them.

5. **Moving into Spiritual Form**
    It is part of the function of Creation to continually strive for spiritual greatness by gaining in knowledge. Since the spirit is always awake and never sleeps during a greattime, it is observing and learning at all times. The human form continues to think and provides food for the spirit. Creation is continuing to strive for perfection in itself in order to become an Ur Universe.

6. **The Completion of 7 cycles**
    Creation can not degenerate. It is always moving forward in its evolution. The same applies to the human spirit-form, for it cannot degenerate, either. It is possible to be stagnant or to waste lifetimes without learning anything, but never does the spirit become ill or degenerate. Seven cycles of evolution through the creation of Material Universes will be completed as the energy level of Creation continues to increase.

7. **The Final Improvement in the 7th Period**
    As any Creation reaches the last cycle of its 7 periods and has mastered the highest improvement possible, it will transform into an Ur Universe that is capable of creating other Creational

Universes such as ours. The energy level of the Ur Universe is so great that it can provide cosmic life force energy to several Creational Universes at one time. Its existence is pure spiritual energy. The cycle of evolution of spiritual energy continues.

The Laws of Creation

Since the logic of Creation is absolute and does not change, we can say it becomes a law. Creation always follows the path of the Absolutum. It always has an awake period and a sleep period, and it evolves from a simple idea to a higher form of consciousness through the experiences learned through the 7 stages of development. Creation dictates the laws of physics, math, and the other sciences; we merely discover the knowledge that is already there.

If we can learn to understand Creation and the process of evolution it is going through, then we have discovered for ourselves how to create laws for our society by which we can live. Everywhere in Nature the Laws of Creation are obvious, if only we open our eyes to see.

In man's early development he may praise the sun or worship the moon in hopes that his simple life will be better. That is the level of his understanding at the time, and he will make simple laws for his society. As we progress and grow in experience, which leads to intelligence and higher consciousness, we will make different laws that reflect our understanding of Creation that are more in line with the complexity and level of knowledge of our society. We are continually evolving and changing as a society and must be open to creating new laws and paradigms that will keep pushing us forward instead of holding us back.

We must become aware that all living things are part of the same Creation. There is an interconnection that binds us all together, something like a network of consciousness that I refer to as spiritual bonding. As we think, our thoughts run across the network and affect all other life forms that are connected to it. Thought is energy, and energy contains thought. They are the same thing existing in different form.

Spiritual growth is the forming of logical thinking that is harmonious with the Laws of Creation. When you have perceived something correctly with great clarity of thought, and understood it to the point that it has become part of your life dictating your actions, the wisdom learned from the experience contributes to your spiritual growth. In order to control your spiritual growth, you must learn to take 100% responsibility for your own actions, thoughts, and deeds. You cannot dump your responsibilities onto any other life forms, gods, idols, or cults and expect to grow. No other life form, including gods, can grow for you. When

125

you have learned to face your problems with your own energies given to you through Creation and know that you are part of Creation, you can draw on the spiritual force that is within you and achieve all that you can imagine.

It is unfortunate that we are born into a material world unaware of the great spiritual knowledge we are connected to. When the Earth human learns of the great power and knowledge that is within the spiritual subconscious, he will begin to help others in the world with the right kind of teaching and guidance so that they can live life to its fullest and most rewarding potential. The path to spiritual growth is through the recognition of our role within Creation.

The Equality of Man

It has been said that all men are created equal, and we are. We all start as spirit-forms of equal knowledge. Or I should say, lack of knowledge, for in our beginning state of pure energy we know very little. It is Creation that gets us started on our path of growth.

Once we come into our first lifetime, the learning process starts. We begin to accumulate wisdom from our experiences and create a path of learning that will continue for billions of years as we go through the stages of development of human life. All along this path we are learning different things at different times. It is the accumulated wisdom that contributes to our intellect and our aptitudes, causing us all to be unique individuals on our own paths of learning.

We all need different knowledge at different times because we are on separate paths of learning. As we go through life, we slowly learn all of the lessons of life, but not at the same time. Eventually all of the lessons are learned by everyone, so never can we say that one person is better than another, but just at different levels of learning. It is the wise man who recognizes that he is only older, not better, and uses his older self to help the younger through love and understanding. The man who uses his older self to take advantage of a younger spirit-form, or get ahead at anothers expense, is living in spiritual stagnation and still has some hard lessons to learn.

Peace will come to Earth when everyone realizes that we are all spiritual beings of Creation on our own paths of development, and we make space for other spirit-forms so that they can be who they need to be and learn what they need for themselves, without any judgment or harassment from us. It is the truly enlightened one who recognizes the spirit in his fellow man and sees him not as a material being, but as a spirit-form on his own path of discovery and learning.

Spiritual Growth

In front of Billy's house is a patio for guests who visit the Center. There is a guest book to sign and 5 large photo albums you can look through and see the most beautiful and clear pictures ever taken of Pleiadian or any other spacecraft. The signatures in the guest book are from countries all over the world and attest to the great interest people everywhere have about our connection to the family of man throughout the universe.

I had my laptop computer with me and was busy typing out some details on what I had learned the past few days when a man came walking up the road to the house. He turned out to be from Kansas, where I was born, and had heard about Billy and his experiences like many others, and came for a visit. We had even attended the same college and both had majored in Psychology. He had gone on to become a professional psychologist and started a practice while I had never used my education and ventured off into private business.

I had him sign the guest book and offered him some time alone with the 5 photo books while I tried to find someone around the farm for him to talk to. During the day it was pretty quiet around the Center as most of the F.I.G.U. members worked in town at regular jobs. Billy was in the kitchen, but as usual, he wouldn't come out to talk. It had been years since he had greeted visitors or answered letters; he had become a real recluse as far as the world was concerned.

Freddy and Silvano were out working in the fields, and Popi, Billy's wife, was in town on errands, so our visitor had to settle for me. He could only stay for a couple of hours, so I had to do the best I could to answer his questions. Since he was a psychologist by profession, he was concerned with the development of man and how we think and learn. His questions were among the very things I had been studying lately, so it gave me a chance to explain it as best I could. I had just been typing information into my computer to get things clear in my own head, and now I had a chance to try to explain things to a learned man who had studied the science of humanity.

127

We spent most of the afternoon talking and having a great time examining the Pleiadian concepts with principles currently used on Earth by his profession. It was a great time of discovery for both of us and actually helped me to learn through explanation. I had explained the concept of Creation and how the universe had developed, but most of his interest was about the actual process of spiritual growth; it seemed so different than what was currently being taught in our school system. Since we had both gone to the same college, I was well aware of what he was talking about. The process of spiritual growth as explained by the Pleiadians was quite different than what he and I had learned in school.

The Process of Spiritual Growth

One of the ways that a New Creation contributes to its evolution is through the mechanism of spirit-forms, human beings who create material lives to learn from. During that learning process, wisdom is obtained through experience and adds to the spiritual growth of the individual and the evolution of Creation. Wisdom is knowledge that creates energy. The more we learn, the higher level of energy we provide to ourselves and the Creation. The process of spiritual growth at the material level is accomplished through the gathering of information with the material senses, which is processed by different levels of consciousness and eventually is stored in the spirit as part of the accumulated wisdom of the everlasting spirit.

This process of spiritual growth is a natural one that goes on whether we are aware of it or not. The advantage of understanding the process is that we can be in control of the rate of our growth, the quality of information we expose ourselves to, and develop methods by which we can live a happier life and be in control of our minds. We can also learn to understand the purpose our lives and better understand the path of evolution that we are on. You have only to look around you at the millions of people who are unhappy, depressed, angry, or out of control, and you can see the immediate need for a better understanding of how our spirit works with our material self.

Before we examine the actual process of how we add wisdom to our spirit and create evolution, let's have a look at the levels of consciousness that will be performing the internal work. Once we know how our spiritual self works with our material being, we will see that it is very similar to how Creation works with a spirit-form. Creation evolves by creating a Material Universe through which it can learn. The universe goes through cycles of waking and sleeping while it is learning from experience. The human spirit-form works the same way and follows the pattern set by Creation. It creates a material body, which goes through cycles of being awake and being asleep while it learns from experience.

How the Mind Works

Did you know that modern science cannot detect the origin of thought? We can trace down what part of the material brain the thought is in once it causes a synaptic junction to charge. But the origin of thought, that place in our mind where the idea comes from, cannot be seen or touched since it is not material. The mind is energy, both material and spiritual, and sends information to the material brain to be processed to the cells.

Let's take a look at the general layout of how the spiritual mind and the material mind work together. For the sake of our discussion I have drawn a diagram which will help explain how the mind works.

On the right side the spiritual self is represented, and the left shows the material self. There is no relationship to any part of the physical brain, for this chart only represents the mind, the area of consciousness where ideas are formed.

Let's start on the left side of the diagram, the material side. Before we come into life we are only a spirit-form, but once we are born, we create a material body with a brain and develop a material consciousness. In order for our body to be able to perceive information, we develop the five senses that we are all familiar with, hearing, touch, smell, sight, and taste. You will notice on the diagram that these are all attached to the material conscious mind. This is how we gather information which starts the learning process. You are exercising your sight right now by reading this book. The conscious mind, then, is our connection to the outside world. It is how we make decisions; all of our thinking processes, everything that we consider, contemplate, and speculate on is done here. This is where all of our actual thinking is done.

Next is the subconscious, or unconscious as it is sometimes called. This represents the area of consciousness where we store all of the thoughts that occur in the conscious mind. All of our feelings, perceptions, all that we see, experience, hear, or anything else that penetrates the subconscious is stored here. This is the computer control center of the mind. It is responsible for guidance, control, and all of the internal communication between the different areas of the mind.

Between the conscious mind and the subconscious there exists a sensor, or filter, that all information passes through. Everything that passes from the material conscious to the subconscious passes through this control center. All superficial thoughts, including anything that was seen or heard superficially, will be blocked and not passed onto the subconscious to be stored or considered. Our senses see and hear millions of pieces of information that are around us all the time and are of no particular interest to us; this unusable superficial information is what is blocked out. For instance, if you are sitting at a busy public restaurant with many people hurrying about, eating, reading, waiting on tables, cooking, and engaging in thousands of pieces of information that your eyes and ears may perceive, all this is simply superficial information that you have no need or interest in, so it is blocked out and not stored.

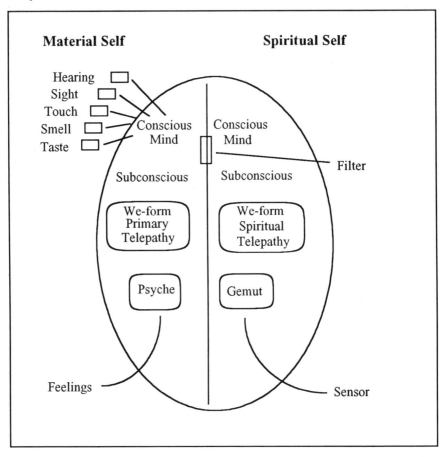

We have an internal sensor called a *we-form* by the Pleiadians. It is the source of what is called primary telepathy that operates through the ears, a kind of hearing that allows one individual to send thoughts and sounds to another. It is short range and cannot be used off of the planet. It is most effective in close quarters to sense what someone else is feeling or thinking. When the phone rings and you think you know who it is, you are using the we-form of primary telepathy. We don't know the real word the Pleiadians use to describe this sensor. That fact that it can sense information from many different sources something like a network, or an inner telephone, brought to mind the term *we-form*. This kind of telepathy can be blocked by the receivers so others can't pick up your thoughts.

The psyche is a storehouse of feelings which make up our disposition or morale. Your emotional feelings and attitudes about the world around you are in here. Here is where you will find feelings of sympathy, melancholy, cynicism, joy, spite, euphoria, optimism, pessimism, depression, anxiety, and fear. From here you may find the feelings of isolation from the world or changing the world for the better. The feelings in the psyche help form the view that others have of us.

Since the material consciousness, subconsciousness, and psyche are created by the spirit-form, the same levels of consciousness exist on the spiritual side as well. The exception is the psyche, for its counterpart on the spiritual side is called the *gemut*. This is a German word which means sensor. The gemut has no feelings like the psyche, but it is able to think and is the connection we have to outside consciousness, for it is our connection to Creation and to levels of higher thinking. Some think of this as the silver thread to the life force or God.

The spiritual consciousness works much the same and acts as a receiver and sender of information to the spiritual subconscious. It works like an observer and gets a copy of all that the material senses pick up.

The spiritual subconscious is a wonderful accumulation of all of the wisdom learned from the many material lives lived so far. It has the ability to draw upon this resource of information and send hunches to the material side when we are trying to make decisions. This hunch is usually the first little thought that creeps into your mind when you trying to make a decision.

Once man becomes aware that he is more
than just physical, he is opened up to
his real spiritual existence

There is also a we-form on the spiritual side which is used for telepathy, but it works slightly differently. Since information through the spiritual we-form is using spiritual force to send and receive, it can transcend the normal distance problem and communicate with others anywhere in the universe. It has almost no barriers of time or distance and is very difficult to block. If one were to receive information from a human on a distant star, this is where it would come from. The message could be sent from many light years away, and it would be so fast that you would think the sender was right next to you. Thought is actually much faster than light and is almost immeasurable in speed. Since it is spiritual in nature, I believe the great speed is because thoughts are networked through the energy of Creation itself, which is everywhere. This is would account for the fact that thoughts can be transmitted almost instantly anywhere in the universe.

Now that we have some idea of different areas of consciousness and memory and what they do, let's follow a simple thought from its inception and see how the mind works with it. For the sake of this example, let's take something that is familiar to all of us, food. Let's go back to our busy restaurant and pick up the menu and follow our thoughts as we try to make a selection.

Our eyes have just fallen on the luncheon special which is beef stew. In a split second we read the letters that say, "Luncheon Special - Beef Stew - $3.98." That probably took our eyes a second to read. During the space of that one second, our material conscious consulted with our subconscious millions of times about what it was reading. As the visual image of "Luncheon Special - Beef Stew - $3.98'" came into view, our conscious mind created a visual image of the letters and sent it off to the subconscious. It was quickly considered by the filter to determine whether the thought was superficial or not, and then passed on to the subconscious. The incoming thought, remember, is energy, and as such it is oscillating at a particular vibration. Each time we think, connecting impulses are immediately created which determine the vibration of the energy and the charge that carries it.

As soon as the subconscious received the image, it quickly checks in its memory to see what kind of data we have on "Luncheon Special - Beef - Stew $3.98." If the vibrations of our subconscious memories connected to this image are in conformity with the vibrations of the conscious mind, then a response is sent back to the conscious mind, via the filter once again, that we have similar compatible vibrations, and the conscious mind quickly produces a feeling of *SYMPATHY*. If the new vibrations sent from the conscious mind cannot make a connection in the subconscious which is agreeable, but is of a degenerated or repelling nature, then the corresponding impulses will be sent from the subconscious back to the conscious via the filter that will cause the thoughts of *NON-SYMPATHY* or *ANTIPATHY*. The thoughts of sympathy or antipathy will rise to greater or lesser extent, according to the power of the vibrations in question.

It should be understood that the conscious mind is not capable of creating a thought on its own. It cannot form it, develop it further, or execute it if corresponding impulses from the subconscious do not stimulate the activity. Although all of the information gathering is done by the conscious mind, it does not know what to do with the new information if no corresponding impulses from the subconscious realm are received. Because of this, the conscious mind and the subconscious *flash* back and forth very quickly in order to develop the thought.

The first reaction may be of familiarity since you have eaten this before and liked it, so that memory is in your subconscious and will send sympathetic impulses back to the conscious. As soon as the subconscious sends back the first impulse, a thought begins to build in the conscious mind. It will continue to flash back and forth at incredible speeds as new information comes in and the thought builds.

The conscious mind begins to build a thought and continues to add new information from the eyes, ears, nose, hands, and mouth. Perhaps your nose picks up the smell of the stew; that is added to the information and your subconscious will send impulses about the smell, letting you know if it likes it or not. Your eyes may see an order of stew on the next table, and that visual image is added, did it look good or not? Perhaps the person you're with mentions they got sick on the stew last week, and that figures into the thought you are building. Within just a second or two a million pieces of data can be *flashed* back and forth to build the thought.

Just as you are starting to form a thought about whether or not you should order the stew, you find out that the cook who made the stew is someone you really dislike. Now you have an immediate negative reaction and send very negative vibrational impulses to the subconscious which will, in turn, respond quite negatively also. The thought of this person quickly triggers deep-seated emotions of hostility and anger in your psyche, and adds that to the flashes of bad memory in your subconscious, and then sends all of that back to your conscious mind. Within a split second your entire mood changes, and you have no interest in the stew or the restaurant and you want to leave.

One's negative thoughts can be very disruptive to a situation. Now you are leaving a restaurant where you have been enjoying the food for weeks just because it is cooked by someone you don't like. As you bolt for the door, your anger causes you to bump into the waiter and knock over his tray, and without excusing yourself you race out the door.
Your mind has just been through billions of flashes, mood swings, emotions, and thoughts. Within the space of a few seconds your whole atmosphere changed, all because of a negative thought that you created.

Your conscious mind and your subconscious process new data and create thoughts like this continually all during your waking state. The memory of these events are stored in your subconscious and serve to influence the emotions and feelings in your psyche. As you sleep at night, your conscious mind is what sleeps while your subconscious is still active, sorting out the events of the day and coming to terms with them.

If you had remained upset the rest of the day and had gone to bed in that state of mind, you would have gotten very little sleep because your subconscious would have kept dealing with your out-of-balance state until exhaustion finally set in, causing sleep. Even then you would not have slept well, for your subconscious would have been trying to solve things, and it would have been sending impulses back to your conscious mind, causing it to think and keeping you from a deep sleep.

Our spiritual side never sleeps and is paying attention to what we are doing at all times. Each time a thought flashes back and forth between our conscious and subconscious, the spiritual side is listening to see if we are learning anything. So far the events of the day have not been added to our spiritual subconscious, where the accumulated wisdom is stored. Spiritual growth is adding wisdom learned from experience to our spiritual subconscious that will be carried forward through lifetimes. In order to do this, it is necessary that we learn from our experiences and make that new knowledge part of us. Once we have full cognition of knowledge and integrate it into our life causing change, then our spirit will add it to our spiritual growth if our new wisdom is correct according to Creation. Let's see how that works in this instance.

You had a sleepless night of worry over how you acted the previous day and decided to go back to the restaurant to apologize to the waiter. As you are expressing how sorry you are for your actions and trying to explain how it won't happen again, the cook walks in the front door. Seizing the opportunity to cleanse yourself even further, you have a long talk with the cook, during which you find out you have been mad at him because of misinformation. There really hasn't been any reason to dislike him, it had all been a misunderstanding, so after some discussion you finish the conversation as friends. Walking away you feel a great relief as the negative energy dissipates, and you have learned something about anger and how to deal with it. You even admitted you were wrong and faced up to the fact that your anger was uncalled for, and in the process you discovered a new friend. You feel pretty good about yourself and even sit down and have the "Luncheon Special -Beef Stew - $3.98."

This new experience is also recorded in your material subconscious; you have made some progress in the emotion department as well, causing the psychic illness of anger to subside just a little. As the following days come and go and other situations arise that normally would have caused you to fly off in anger, you now deal with them with a new attitude. You have learned how to control your anger and have made a difference in your life that will stay with you. The wisdom from this new experience will be recorded in your spiritual subconscious. This is wisdom from experience that is added to your accumulated knowledge and will move forward from lifetime to lifetime. The lesson may have to be repeated several times to really heal your psyche, but now you're on the right track.

Psychic illness is a buildup of emotions which are so negative that we can't live our life normally. Jealousy is about the worst condition to fall into, for it is very hard to recover from it. The many events that lead up to a person becoming completely jealous make it very difficult to recover from.

Psychic illness is caused by the illogical thinking of the conscious mind which slowly creates the emotions through a buildup of negative thinking. When we are born, our psyche is clean and healthy. No one is born full of anger, depression, anxiety, or jealousy; these are all man-made emotions that are created from not being able to handle life's experiences in a healthy manner.

If a person can learn to think in a neutral manner, instead of negative or positive, then he will not create the harmful emotions which rule our psychic feelings. Neutral thinking is the ability to clearly see things as they are without attaching negative or positive judgments to the thought. If we had just seen the Beef Stew as nothing more than just food in a bowl and had not attached any other emotions or feelings to it, we could have had a peaceful lunch with no problems. It was the process of attaching a negative thought to it that caused the difficulty. It is not healthy to attach overly positive thoughts to things either, for they can cause just as much damage in over-inflated egos or attitudes. In the New Age we will all learn more about how to see the world around us in a neutral way and live without psychic illness.

It is very difficult in our current world to grow up without creating many negative emotions because of all the trauma we go through as children. Many adults would agree that most of their emotional problems stem, in part, from a difficult childhood that created emotions which still play a part in their behavior. We are born into a society that does not understand us spiritually. There is no understanding of how we left the last life and what problems we may have starting this one. No one is concerned that we are spirits on a path of learning and need something special. Our society teaches that children are possessions to be disciplined and corrected. Over 50% of the young children in America today are victims of some kind of child abuse, most of it physical. Currently over 1/3 of all children are born into single-parent families and will be denied the natural order of learning that comes from two parents. We are creating an entire generation of young adults who will not benefit from the necessary role-modeling from that missing mom or dad. We can only guess what effect that may have on our society.

For those children who are lucky enough to have understanding parents that make an effort to try to understand the unique qualities of each child, they will grow up with far less problems. When we are young and impressionable, our psyches are forming, and our subconscious is just building its vast memory bank that we will draw off of throughout our lives. If we can go through our childhoods being loved and understood and are taught how to think correctly, life will be one great festival of joy and happiness.

If however, we wind up as adults who cannot control our thinking, life would be a burden of emotional pain. We would then find ourselves riding a roller coaster of negative and positive thoughts, causing our moods to constantly change. Having no control over our thinking, we would have a different opinion on things every day, making decisions almost impossible. Even though most of the world is caught up in this mode of illogical thinking, there is hope as it can be reversed.

Psychic illness can be corrected through the slow process of reestablishing logical thinking. The conscious mind can then start to build new thoughts which will, in turn, create new experiences from more neutral thinking. These new experiences will reeducate our emotions and our psyche will slowly repair itself.

Reeducating a psyche is slow work and can be very demanding. It takes the help of another person who is a more logical and clear thinker, for the stricken person is not capable of helping himself in the beginning. You can't repair a thinking problem with the same illogical thoughts that created it.

The food our spirit lives on is truth according to Creation

Healing a person of psychic illness means healing through the powers of the spirit. An individual must activate his own spirit to heal themselves. This means the power of their spirit must be motivated and become useful. The process of healing requires long explanations of pure logic which will motivate a person to think correctly and use their own spirit. In effect, a person wishing to heal themselves of psychic illness must be prepared to do a lot of thinking, because the person helping them cannot take over the mental work of another person. It is only possible to give them a start in the right direction, but the ailing person must heal themselves. It is their mind that must learn to think correctly so that it will form new understandings and feelings.

It is not possible to simply erase old memories and feelings so that everything will go away. The old memories and experiences must be replaced with new ones. The ailing person must first learn to understand exactly what the problem is, and then be led into new thinking through the aid of visual images so that they may have new experiences to replace the old ones.

In the case of psychiatry, words of logic and self-discovery are relied on too much. The subconscious reacts better to images and visions, not words. Only the conscious mind can use words, and they can be misunderstood or misinterpreted by the ailing person. It is words from which we create visions and images. If we are sick, we will hear words and create images and visions that are negative or illogical, so progress is slow. Many people take the guidance of a psychiatrist for months and years and make little or no progress since the treatment seldom goes past the stage of words on a couch.

On the other hand, if you take an ailing individual out of his environment, away from all of the normal surroundings that he is used to, and give him a new environment with unfamiliar surroundings, he will have to immediately create all new responses to deal with this new situation. Then if he is guided correctly with neutral thinking as he creates these new thoughts, experiences, and feelings, he will become a new person in a very short time. Old memories and emotions will be replaced quickly.

If a person is spiritually weak and suffering and you are strong in spirit and healthy in mind, you can try letting them use your strength while they get theirs back. This can be done by the laying on of hands around the body in the region of the stricken person's aura. The aura is the field of energy around every body that reflects the condition of the spiritual energy. As you think, your thoughts create energy that shows in the aura around your body. If they are sick, it will show in their aura.

If you are strong, you can let your aura mix with theirs. Hold your hands around them in their auric field for several minutes, perhaps hours, and they will benefit from it. The power of your healthy spirit can help theirs get started. Sometimes just the feeling of your healthy energy is enough to make them feel better about themselves and pull them out of depression or despair. You must be cautious to not absorb negative energies from them. This can happen if you are doing this because of ego or vanity rather than love and genuine concern for another. If you try to help someone in order to show off or prove that you are very spiritual,

137

you will do them no good and only hurt yourself. If, on the other hand, you are giving from your heart and expect nothing in return and think with a clear and logical mind, you can be of great help to another. When you are acting with your ego, you are spiritually weak and cannot protect yourself adequately; however, a spiritually balanced person is strong and will suffer no ill-effects.

Our Connection to Creation

On our spiritual side, we also have the ability to be in connection with Creation through the *gemut*. When our spirit-form was created, our connection to the Creation was made through this special sensor. While our spirit is listening to our thoughts and accepting wisdom into the subconscious, it always has the ability to use the gemut to check out our ideas with Creation. It is like an open line that is always there for us, and it can only be felt through the spirit. Our spiritual self will not accept any wisdom to be added to our accumulated consciousness unless it first checks with Creation through the gemut to be sure it is in line with the truth. It is Creation that lays down the laws of evolution and creates the framework for man to live by. If man could learn to think with his conscious mind, using these laws of conduct provided by Creation, not only would his life be easier, but his evolution as a spirit-form would progress much faster.

In religions and different belief structures there is always the faith factor, for it is not possible to prove that God really exists. It is something that we take on faith because our parents or the priest at our church told us so. If you want to prove to yourself that Creation exists and that it is the ultimate source of love and understanding which can provide all knowledge that is necessary for life, then you have only to make your connection to the Great Eternity through the gemut. Here you can feel and experience for yourself the ultimate feeling of the life force that guides all things, and it is available to you at any time you choose without going through any ceremonies, spiritual leaders, guides, or forms of worship. You are always connected to it, for you are a part of it.

The Akashic Records

Earlier I mentioned that thoughts are energy. As your mind builds the thought through the millions of flashes between the conscious, the subconscious, and the psyche, it becomes a charge of energy. The vibrations of this energy are dependent on the level of evolution of the spirit that makes it and the emotions and feelings that helped create it. We are normally used to thinking that our thoughts are safely tucked away inside of our heads where no one else will know about them. This is true to a certain extent, for those around us will have no idea of them. However, our thoughts do not dissipate or disappear inside of our head someplace. Once the thought is created and becomes energy, it has the ability to leave our mind and move out into space. As it does this, it rises up off the planet and becomes part of a band of etheric energy that circles the planet called the *akashic records*. This energy band is called records since it contains thoughts from all who have lived on Earth throughout history and stores it in a very logical way based on level of evolution.

The akashic records are the knowledge of the past. Here the thoughts of everyone are arranged in layers of memory. Each layer or level of memory is a different level of evolution. Remember that thoughts are energy, and the energy is separated by the level of its oscillating vibrations. There is an akashic record around a planet just for those thoughts; there is also an akashic record around a solar system, and one around a galaxy. There may be others that I'm not familiar with. These are the only ones the Pleiadians have mentioned.

The knowledge of the past is protected, so getting into it is not easy. You must earn that right by virtue of your understanding of how the spirit works. It is only accessible through the subconscious of the spirit which activates the we-form on the spiritual side. Once you have learned how to activate your subconscious through meditation, you will also discover that you will need to learn the "key" to get in.

A key is a special symbol understood by the spirit that can unlock a particular memory level in the records. This key can only be discovered through meditation since it is part of the symbol language of spirit. Once you have learned a key that can open a particular record, you can then gain access to those thoughts. Opening a record allows you access to the thoughts of that person which are stored there. This is how you can learn about another person's thinking. The information you will have access to cannot be of higher evolution than your own. So even if you were to try and access information created by some great thinker like DaVinci, you would only be able to access his thoughts that were not of any greater evolution than your own. This is because your mind creates energy that oscillates at a certain frequency determined by your evolution. The higher the evolution, the higher the frequency. Frequencies created by your mind cannot unlock records that require a higher frequency. This is Creation's way of protecting knowledge until you are ready for it. Even if you somehow could get information of a much higher evolution sent to you, there would be a problem of reception. Depending on how high it was, you either couldn't receive it, or it would make you crazy, angry, or emotionally push you beyond your limits. You could even get physically hurt from being overloaded by frequencies that are too high for your mind to handle. It's kind of like a radio that is only capable of handling incoming frequencies up to a certain level. Anything above that level is either missed all together or distorted.

Information from the akashic cannot be spoken,
but can only be transmitted through
writing or drawing

Once you are able to access thoughts from DaVinci, your spirit acts as a receiver and thinks like DaVinci while it is connected. Since this is a spiritual connection, not a material one, the information cannot be spoken but can be written down as in auto-writing or auto-painting. It is not uncommon for some people to have a connection to the akashic and be able to receive information and not even know where it is coming from. If you speak to these people, they will tell you that they use meditation and a key or symbol of some kind to start the transmission.

The akashic can be accessed through meditation. It is not the spirit world, but the records of past knowledge. The spirit-forms who created the thoughts that are there are now living new lives as different personalities. When you are in the akashic records, you are not in connection with DaVinci, just his thoughts that were recorded when he was alive. The spirit that lived a lifetime as DaVinci has now moved on and created another life as a new personality and is no longer DaVinci. It is only his thoughts that are left behind.

Heaven - the Other Side

The akashic should not be confused with the other side, the sleeping place of spirits. This is an entirely different area that can only be accessed by spirit and requires a different technique. The Pleiadians do not interfere with the other side, and feel it is better to leave sleeping spirits alone. For one thing, these spirits don't know any more than they did when they were here, and usually don't want to be bothered anyway.

Psychics that claim to be in touch with dead or sleeping spirits are usually in touch with the akashic records of that spirit and don't know it. The minds of Earthmen were scanned by the Pleiadians and they discovered that only sixteen people on Earth have the evolution and the understanding to actually get in touch with the other side at will. Many people receive images, feelings, or thoughts from spirits but cannot initiate it themselves; they are only receiving. To the Pleiadians and their level of morality, they feel it best to leave the other side alone.

140

Telepathy

The Pleiadians use a form of telepathy to send information to thousands of people on Earth all the time. They have been very open about the fact that they're trying help with our education by sending us ideas and visions that we can use. They are hopeful that by doing this the ideas will stimulate people to use their Higher Selves and educate others who will make a difference in our world. This information is normally sent to us so that we can receive it during our sleep through our we-form on the material side. This means that we may pick up ideas and thoughts while we dream and believe they are our own.

The Pleiadians feel it is morally wrong for them to invade our thoughts and impinge on our free will. If they do not allow us to know the origin of the thoughts, then we will think they are our own ideas. Hundreds of small telemeter crafts of various sizes listen to our thinking and broadcast thoughts for us to pick up. In 1975 they admitted that currently over 17,000 people were receiving their transmissions. They have not told us who these people are or how they select them.

Other travelers from other worlds could also be sending us information as well. In many cases the receiving party may have become aware of the source of these transmissions, for the senders may wish to identify themselves. We should also be cautious, though, as many people create these connections in their fantasies and are in touch with nothing but their egos. In any case, we should always be careful about information and never worship or give special recognition to any source of data. Always treat information for just what it is without glorifying it. It can be very exciting to be in touch with other life forms, but be aware that not all of them are friendly and have your best interests at heart. Imagine the psychic pain you could put yourself through if you allowed yourself to be used by another life form for their use against your own people. An invasion from outer space may not come in ships, but in the minds of our people.

Not only do we receive information from the Pleiadians and other races, but from each other. Remember the we-form on the material side is a form of hearing that can also detect the thoughts of those around us. We pick up feelings and impressions when we are around people. For instance, if you were around someone who was thinking negative or harmful thoughts about you, your we-form would pick it up. Depending on your sensitivity, you would probably feel this and react in fear, caution, apprehension, or anger. You would want to get away from this person as soon as possible. We are receiving feelings and impressions from people around us all the time. Our subconscious is busy defending itself from outside thoughts all the time without our awareness. There are over 5 billion people on Earth who are thinking all sorts of thoughts that create energy we have to deal with. This energy also effects the animals and nature. We are told by the Pleiadians that in some cases earthquakes and storms can be started just by the extra negative energy from the mass consciousness of Earth people which disturbs nature.

The we-form on our spiritual side also can be used to make connections with other life forms. It is dormant in most people since they don't even know it is there. It has the ability to move thoughts in symbol form over vast distances in space. If a Pleiadian wanted to send you a thought from their home planet of Erra, then this is how they would do it. The thought would come to you on the spiritual side, since telepathy on the material side is only for short distances on the planet. The problem that you would have is that the information comes in symbol form, and you wouldn't understand it. It take years of practice in meditation to learn and understand the many different symbols that are necessary to translate incoming transmissions.

Here on Earth we also need to know that beings of higher intelligence can also send information in thought-form into our subconscious without us knowing about it. Since the subconscious is where your memory is, you would think the new thought is your own. For instance, it would be possible to implant a thought in your mind that you have been taken aboard a ship and interacted with extraterrestrials about a special mission they want you to perform. It is not necessary for this experience to have ever happened. The entire experience could be put into your memory and you would believe it really happened. You would argue with anyone that it is real, for you have no way of doubting it yourself. To you it is an actual memory as clear as any other thought. This happens in many cases where ET's want someone on Earth to do something for them. Our minds can be controlled by higher intelligences and we can do nothing about it since we are so underdeveloped as thinkers. It is very hard to block information which comes in through the we-form on the material side, especially if you don't even know that it is happening. If you knew it was happening and wanted to block it, you could, but you would have to be a very powerful clear thinker with good meditation experience, but these are not the people who are chosen.

A Real Time Vision is one that is experienced
in actual time, and cannot be discerned
from reality

Channeling

Occasionally someone tells us that they are in touch with beings from the spirit world or other planets and that these beings are going to speak to us through them. This process is called channeling. It is typical for the person performing the channeling to speak to us in a different voice, as if it were the personality of the incoming being.

The Pleiadians do not ever communicate in this manner because they know it is too inaccurate. They have been quite clear that in no case do they allow the person receiving information to know where it comes from. Since there are so many different ways that we can receive information from outside sources, it is easy to see how anyone could be confused about the origin. We receive information through the material we-form, the spiritual we-form, the gemut, psychic connection to one another, and transmissions from other intelligences such as the Pleiadians that enter our subconscious as we sleep or daydream. Then if we add the fact that our conscious mind makes up its own thoughts from the psyche and the subconscious, it is easy to see how the origin of information can be very hard to pin down. I think that people who channel are receiving information; they are just not aware of where it is really coming from.

If you want to learn to channel, you start with learning meditation and how to enter into a concentration. At some point the individual will suddenly make a connection somewhere and start speaking with a different personality or voice. Anyone who tries this should be careful, so when you start to learn meditation, you must be careful to avoid letting the ego come into play because it will manufacture anything you want, fulfilling your dreams or wishes, and it is done using the emotions and feelings from your psyche.

One of the natural pitfalls to learning meditation is the tendency to create images from your own subconscious rather than creating clear dream images in the awakened state from the spirit. If meditation is done correctly, the first achievement will be the occurrence of vague and, at first, incoherent forms of dream images in the waking state without concentrating upon such images or wishing to see something. These images are distinguishable from the usual dream images by their extreme clarity and distinctness. They also do not exhibit any power of suggestion and will gradually begin to link up with logical forms. The sure sign you are doing meditation wrong is when a different personality begins to appear. In most every case the person channeling is only accessing areas of his own subconscious which may contain information from many sources.

Channeling can be termed euphoric meditation. In other words you are practicing meditation incorrectly and are producing the effect of the second personality from your ego. This can be very dangerous, especially if the individual continues this and lets his ego get out of hand. It can lead to schizophrenia, a condition of psychic illness that is very difficult to recover from, causing the individual to no longer be able to distinguish reality clearly.

If you want to access information from other sources, learn to meditate correctly and use the we-form. No alter-ego voice or personality is required to receive telepathy or visions through the spirit. It is only necessary to learn to enter a meditative concentration deep enough to use your own spiritual force. I have heard many channelers and found no information that could not be expressed using a simple meditative technique. I believe when the information comes in through the foreign voice, it is only being manufactured by the individual himself.

People who show good psychic abilities are often in touch with other people or life forms, for they are sensitive to certain frequencies where reception of thought energy is possible. Good psychics take advantage of meditative abilities but never use a channeled voice to communicate. They are in a wakened state of concentration and use their spiritual force to make connections.

Reincarnation

As we come close to the end of our material lives, there is an inner awareness that knows when death will come. Buried within our subconscious is the knowledge of our life span. Our spirit has the knowledge of how long our material life should be and when we will pass away. This is due in part to the amount of life force the spirit has to sustain the material life, and in part to its ability to transcend time and know what lies ahead.

Fear of death is a result of not knowing what will happen to us after we die. Most religions and belief systems tell us we are going to heaven or hell where we will be judged, disciplined, burned, or who knows what, depending on how we have obeyed their laws. Fear of going to hell and burning forever, or not being able to get into heaven if you sin in the eyes of your priest, is a very strong motivator and gives religions control over millions of people. Fortunately they are wrong, for these mythical places are only the inventions of those who would control you here in the material world.

Onboard a Pleiadian craft there are instruments which allow a person's spiritual self to be shown on a view screen, which contains knowledge about the time of birth, purpose in life, karmic debts, past-life trauma, and the expected time of death, among other things. This information can be read and studied for a better understanding of your life.

The device also has the ability to read the feelings and thoughts of your conscious and subconscious mind. As an example of how foolish the fear of death is, an older man who was close to death was chosen and his spiritual self was projected on the screen. First his conscious mind was read, and the thoughts of his fear of death were very strongly displayed. He was dying of heart disease and was in a lot of pain. He had lived most of his life as a soldier and had been responsible for the deaths of thousands of people. Now he was close to his own death and was behaving like a coward, for fear had overcome him. His life had been one of purely material gains, power, greed, and control over others. He had never taken the time to get in touch with his spirit, touched Creation, or felt the love of those around him.

Changing the screen so it now showed his subconscious revealed that the fear was gone. His conscious mind was almost paralyzed in fear, but his subconscious was fairly peaceful. This is because the subconscious understands what the afterlife is and knows that death is no great horror, but only a change into the other side for a time of rest and reunion with the Creation. The Pleiadians do not see death as an ending, but only a transition in the endless path of spiritual growth that is a natural part of our evolution.

We have the ability to have an effect on our next life in some ways. We can make conscious decisions about our choice of gender, for instance. If you have lived a life as a woman and wish to return as a man, this is possible through generating the will to do so in your spiritual self. Subconsciously we make the decision on gender based on lessons that we are trying to learn or experiences we are trying to have. If during our material life we have become confused about our gender through emotional trauma or other experiences that make us unstable about our sexuality, we may leave the material world in a confused state. If this happens, we will continue to be confused on the other side, for the programming or decision making needs to be made in the material life. When we return to the material world, the state of confusion will lead us to be born as a homosexual. This confusion of spirit will also play a hand in the development of the body and certain areas of the brain which affect sexual attraction. Since this is a form of illogical thinking and confusion on the part of the spirit, it can be dealt with during the material life through a slow process of logical thinking and experiences allowing the individual to discover his sexuality and reprogram himself. For a person experiencing sexual confusion, it is important to program your spirit as to your sexual preference while still alive, as this will control how you will return in the next life and end the confusion.

Once the death process begins, our material senses begin to deteriorate and stop functioning. Medical death occurs when the heartbeat can no longer be detected, and we are pronounced dead. Even though we appear dead and our material body is no longer functioning, the spirit may stay in the body for up to 72 hours before it leaves. In most cases the spirit will separate and leave quickly. There are many cases on record where witnesses have seen a wisp of energy or felt something pass by them as the spirit leaves the body. Scientifically it is even possible to weigh the body after death and measure the weight loss after the spirit has departed. It is believed by some that the spirit energy somehow inhabits small organelles in our bodies called *nisel bodies*. Nisel bodies are not material, but are energy bodies that store the life force energy. When a person dies, the nisel bodies disappear also. If you were to examine a dead cell within a living body, you would find that the nisel bodies in the dead cell would be gone.

The spirit, however, does not die and is very busy taking over the conscious awareness of the self as the material senses are shutting down. While this happens, the spiritual conscious begins to see the light of Creation and a feeling of love and comfort are immediately felt. Thoughts of the material pain and discomfort fade immediately because the material brain is no longer functioning. All thoughts, emotions, fears, anxieties, hate, and other man-made feelings that have been manufactured throughout the material lifetime fade away as the material self is ending.

Having advanced thousands of years beyond us in spiritual understanding, the Pleiadians have studied the passing over of spirits in great detail. They want us to know that our spirit does not leave the planet and go to a heaven or to a hell. It stays right here on Earth where it started. Our spirit-forms came out of Creation and are evolving with the planet, and they stay with it. Our akashic records are only on this planet and are connected to us. It is not possible at our level of evolution for us to be born on another world or dimension. We simply do not have the ability.

Our spirits rest in the band of energy around the planet the Pleiadians call the other side, which is right here with us, only in energy form. Once we pass over, our spirits are still conscious and are aware of the material world for awhile. If we have lived a long time and have died a peaceful death when our time has come, we will slip into rest easily and naturally.

We are spiritual beings living a series of material lives in order to evolve

If we have died unexpectedly from an apparent accident, murder, or traumatic event, we could be uncomfortable for awhile and may not even reach the other side. In these cases the spirit may not recognize that it is dead, or may not want to die, and will slip into another material being instead of passing over into the other side. This will cause the invaded person to become confused in spirit and may immediately start showing signs of unusual behavior. Even pronounced personality traits may shift as the incoming spirit doesn't know where it is and is trying to send messages to the material self.

Professional psychologists are discovering that there are many cases of this happening. Methods of hypnosis have been developed which are effective in making the incoming spirit aware that it is in another body, and that it is time for it to let go and pass on over to the other side. Doctors dealing with this problem actually counsel the confused spirit, letting it know that death has come and that they are in another material body by mistake. In most cases, once the incoming spirit understands what has happened, it will immediately let go and pass over, relieving the individual of the confusion of spirit and returning them to normal thinking. There are thousands of cases of this phenomena on record, providing a wealth of new knowledge about the spiritual world.

Once on the other side, the spirit will rest for a period of time that is dependent on two factors. If you have lived a long life and have added a great deal of wisdom to your spirit, you will come back very slowly. If you have lived a short life and have learned very little, you will come back quicker. This is Creation's way of balancing out the evolution of the human spirit-forms on a planet.

The time on the other side follows the pattern set by Creation as it evolves through cycles of waking and sleeping. The sleep period on the other side is a time of rest and contemplation. No new experiences are gained; that is only in the material realm. The wisdom learned from the material lifetime is considered, or cogitated, and the process of evolution for the spirit continues.

Once the rest period starts, the spirit is no more aware of the material world than we are of the spiritual world. Communication is possible if you know how, and in some cases thoughts do transfer, but for the most part the spirit has no interest in the material realm. When we are alive and sleep at night, our material senses are off and we are not aware of the material world. We are busy finishing out the thoughts of the day or

147

traveling through time and space in our dreams. Awareness of the material returns when we wake up in the morning and begin to use our conscious minds again. Our time in the other side is very much like this.

The other side has different levels of consciousness. When we first enter, we are at a level where we finish out the thoughts and feelings of the lifetime. The majority of the time is spent here, and then we will move through two more levels of consciousness before we are ready to return to a material life.

The average time on the other side is 152 years on Earth. This is an average time, taking into consideration all of the spirits here. This time can vary, of course, as stated before, depending on the length of the material life and its attainment. In the time of the New Age the turn-around time speeds up due to the increase in the vibrations of energy affecting the planet. It is possible that some spirits may return as quickly as 15 years.

Once our spirit has passed through the three levels of consciousness on the other side, it signals the Creation that it is ready to return to the material realm. This signal is somehow connected to the spiritual life force, which is now rested, and the clarity of thought that has resulted from finishing out its thinking from the previous life.

The Creation has a hand in actually moving the spirit into a material body once it is ready. It is the physical mother in the material realm which provides the window of opportunity for it to happen. There is a tendency for a spirit to try and stay within its own family if possible. So if the timing is right, and a female member of the family is pregnant, and the spirit is ready, Creation moves its hand and the spirit moves into the womb.

Considering the average turn-around time is 152 years, this means that your children may have also been your great, great, great, grandmother about six or seven generations back. Here in the New Age where spirits will be coming back sooner, there is a chance of your children being your departed parents or grandparents.

If all spirits lived a long and full life, the family chain would almost follow a normal order of things. Unfortunately because of wars and other reasons, spirits live a shorter life; the normal chain of births gets interrupted frequently on Earth, and people are born into the family out of their normal birth sequence. In my case for instance, I was informed that the Pleiadians felt that I was late in my birth and missed my normal place, and I should have been a child of my grandmother. This means that my mother normally would have been my sister if events had gone right. This interruption of the normal cycle can cause problems in one's growth as a material person.

The spirit will move into the material body within twenty-one days of conception. On a Pleiadian world they have the ability to know when the spirit has made its decision and will no longer permit abortion after that. Once the spirit has made its decision to come in and contact has been made to find out who the spirit is, this is the beginning of the new life. If there is an abortion once the spirit is in the womb, it will return very quickly into another, possibly within hours or days. When we reach this level of knowledge here on Earth, we will see a change in morality and a different view on abortion.

The first choice of Creation is that the spirit comes into a window of opportunity that is as close as possible to the same level of evolution as the spirit. For this and other reasons of stability, the family chain is the first consideration. If the spirit is moved out of its family, as millions are on Earth, it causes a more difficult time during the material life. The positive side is that this can provide for many new things to learn.

Once the spirit is in the mother, it is a very exciting time for both her and the person coming in.   To begin with, the mother should try to be aware during the first twenty-one days when the spirit actually makes the decision to come into her body. Developing your spiritual force through meditation will help you make the contact and discover that a person is coming back into life. It is not being created from scratch, but has probably lived as many lives as you have and is now creating a new life. Be aware that it may be a family member from a long time past. You could study your family tree and see who passed away over a hundred years ago. If you can find pictures of your older relatives, you could meditate on their images and you may make some connections. Image how wonderful it would be to discover who the spirit was in previous lives and how they had lived. If you knew what kind of life they lived and how they died, you could create a special bond with them before they were born. Communication could begin with the new person letting you know what to name them. Names reflect the level of evolution and the path of learning we are on. Names have meaning in spiritual language and will present themselves to the mother if she is open to it.

By realizing that babies are people creating new lives for themselves, we should no longer think of them as possessions that we made, but as people coming into a new life. Life is a cooperative effort by the mother, the father, and the incoming person. The father provides his DNA along with the mother's to begin the formation of the material body. It begins with the spine as the body begins to form. During the 8th to the 15th week the brain is forming and creating all of the connectors it will need

149

for thinking. It is at this time that the spirit of the incoming person starts to take a hand in the formation of this new body. It is the spirit that provides the mapping or information to the DNA on how many brain connectors to create. The spiritual self knows how much accumulated knowledge it will bring into the new body and how many brain connectors it will need to handle the intelligence and aptitudes that will flow in. If you have learned lessons in a particular area in previous lives, the wisdom from those experiences are carried forward into your new life, so you can benefit from them. This is the determining factor in why we all have different intelligence and aptitudes. Millions of years ago we all did start off equal. Equally ignorant, that is, but as our evolution continues, we all learn different things at different times, so our accumulated wisdom is diversified. So you see, none of us are any better than anyone else, just younger or older. It's like going through school and being in different grades. We all go through the same classes and eventually graduate, we just get there at different times. We judge each other or try to sound like we are better than another to make ourselves feel or appear important. In actuality we are only younger or older than each other on our own paths of evolution.

The accumulated knowledge of our previous lives is stored within our spiritual subconscious and is always available to us if we use it. We also benefit from it another way. Once the brain is formed and the connectors are all functional, the spirit makes a copy of its wisdom and puts it into the acids of our brain for the material body to use. We are also connected to Creation through our spiritual gemut sensor. We have our spiritual subconscious to help guide us. We have our spiritual we-form to connect us to the akashic records of our past thoughts, and we have wisdom from our previous lives in the acids of our brain. All of these connections are there to help us in our new material life.

The material for the most part is a product of the DNA of our mother and father, the family genetics. The spirit, though, is reflected across the face. If you could see pictures of your previous lives, you would notice that across the eyes you would look similar.

This fascinated me when I heard it, and thought how unfortunate that photography has only been around for a short time; otherwise, we could all have pictures of our relatives from hundreds of years ago, and we could see this phenomenon for ourselves. Because of my interest in this, one of the ladies at the Center showed me a picture of a Russian woman who lived about 160 years ago and asked me to look at it carefully. I studied the picture for a moment and then glanced back at the lady. It was her. Even though the hair was a different color and the face was a little different, you could see the same eyes, nose, and ears across the face. She had been guided by the Pleiadians to understand this and had found this picture of herself in a previous life.

The moment of birth is very important on a Pleiadian world. Just as the soft spot on our skull bursts forth and is touched by the air, it is affected by the energies of the universe. Because of this, Pleiadian mothers do their best to let the new person be born when they are ready. The feeling is that the person coming in is on a path of discovery and learning, and they will pick the moment they want to be born in order to line up with the energies that will help them. It's quite possible this is all taken into consideration by Creation when the move is made into the womb.

Now that we are born and have returned to the material world, we have a new material consciousness with which to experience life. Our subconscious is empty except for the memories of growth in the womb and birth, and our psyche is healthy and clean, with no emotions or feelings of hate, anger, prejudice, or anxiety. We have been at one with Creation for some time and have just left a wonderful, restful period. All we have to do now is learn how to think logically and correctly, so we can live to our fullest potential through a long and happy life filled with love.

Learning Meditation

I was raised in the Episcopal Church in the Midwestern town of Wichita, Kansas and was considered a Christian just like everyone else there. It wasn't until I began to travel the world many years after leaving home that I became aware of the many different belief structures and concepts of life that exist on Earth.

The concept of meditation was one new idea that I learned to embrace. It has taken on a growing importance in my life. I had meditated before, but what I was learning from Billy was all new to me and took some real brainwork for me to understand. The concepts of meditaton/concentration prove useful in developing personal control, and most importantly are a means to access to the spiritual power in all of us. I had never been exposed to meditation when I was younger. I was only taught prayer at the church. A whole new world opened up to me when I discovered what can be learned and accomplished through meditation.

At the Center Billy has built a mediation room which all of the members of the F.I.G.U. use. They have a regular schedule which they keep on the kitchen wall so that they can keep track of the time spent in the meditation room each week. Since all of the members are learning and studying spiritual growth themselves, the meditation room was a very busy place.

What is Meditation

Meditation is mostly associated with Eastern philosophy, since it is practiced so widely there. But it should be made clear that meditation is a form of concentration which leads to control of the mind and can be practiced by anyone. It is not necessary to adhere to any mystical philosophy, belief system, or religion to use meditation for your own benefit. Even though its popularity lies in the East, it is rapidly gaining in use in Western society as increasingly more people discover the benefits of being able to communicate with the many different levels of consciousness through meditation. It is a method by which we can gain

152

control over our thought processes, develop spiritually, or come in communication with higher life forms such as the Pleiadians.

When we come into a new life, our material consciousness is formed along with our body. Our senses of sight, touch, smell, feel, and hearing are developed for information gathering, and we begin to form new thoughts. At this point our new material subconscious only has the memories of birth, and our psyche is almost devoid of any feelings, emotions, and attitudes. Material emotions and memories are created and collected during the life and do not exist when we arrive. All that comes with us are the memories and feelings of the spirit. Our thought processes are very simple, for we have no material memories or psychic feelings to create them. It is here that we have the opportunity to learn to think properly so that our life can be lived and experienced to its greatest joy.

Most of the worries of the world are
caused by illogical thinking

At the time the spirit enters the body and the new life begins, we are healthy in body and spirit. The spirit cannot be illogical or sick; this is strictly a function of the material self. As the body is being formed, its potential can be degenerated during the pregnancy by drugs, alcohol, mental illness, and illogical thinking on the part of the mother. The new material life will already be damaged and can not live to the fullest ability of the accumulated knowledge gained by the spirit. This can limit intelligence and aptitude and cause birth defects which will impair the ability to think correctly.

If the mother would use meditation during the pregnancy, she could not only communicate with the incoming person, but could control her own thinking and provide for a healthier birth. By controlling our thinking, we control both our physical and mental health and thus provide a good beginning for the new life.

By learning meditation, you develop what is called the meditation *concentration.* This is nothing more than developing the ability to concentrate on a particular object and see it clearly, untainted by feelings, attitudes, memories, and negative and positive thinking, while not allowing any other thoughts to enter your mind. Once this is accomplished, you are in control of your thinking and on the road to developing powerful spiritual abilities as well. There are many ways that meditation can be helpful in your life.

The Conscious Thinking

Most of our entire life is spent in conscious thinking. It is the process of forming a thought from our memories and feelings that allows us to communicate with ourselves and each other. If we could not think, we could not learn or grow and would be no different than the animals with which we share the Earth. Thought allows us to understand our experiences and gain in wisdom, which leads to spiritual growth. Without thought we could not function as living beings.

Even though thought is so important to us, there is very little training on how to perform it. In school we are told what to think, but not how to do it. There is no education on how to think or how to control the thinking processes. Through meditation we will learn to not only understand what thought is, but how to control it for our benefit.

*First there is the conscious mind; its energy
affects the electrical body which charges
the chemicals that feed the cells*

Negative and Positive Thinking

As we create the energy of thought, we give these energies a negative, positive, or neutral charge due to our own way of thinking and feeling and according to our own behavior patterns. Meditation can serve as a means for achieving harmony between the positive and negative and create a state of balance or neutral thinking. You will also learn to know yourself better and exercise more control over yourself.

The Spiritual Powers

Through meditation/concentration you can learn to bring forth the spiritual powers of telepathy, telekinesis, and time travel. These abilities are inherent in the spirit and can be made accessible to the material self through meditation if you are willing to put in the time and effort.

Telepathy is the ability for humans to send and receive thoughts using the we-form sense that is in all of us. The material self and the spiritual self both have dissimilar we-forms which operate differently. Both can be accessed through meditation and can be developed to be useful attributes in our life.

You can also learn telekinesis, a method of moving objects without touching them physically, through the use, again, of pure spiritual powers. For most people this ability may take years of practice to develop the necessary concentration. If practiced every day, the average

154

person may find some success in about seven years.

Meditation can enable you to transfer yourself mentally/visually into the past or future and gain information on various events. These events may be in the past or may be projections of a future that has not yet happened.

The ability to develop and use any of your natural spiritual powers lies in the development of meditation as the tool or mechanism by which you gain access to these abilities. All communications of the mind and spirit are made possible through meditation. You will find it necessary to put in a great deal of time and energy into this practice of meditation/concentration, in the material realm as well as in the spiritual realm, if you expect to achieve any kind of results.

The Concentration

Meditation allows you to see something clearly, observe it clearly and recognize it clearly, without entertaining a thought. First we produce the desire or will to create a meditative concentration, to grasp something or to put something into practice. Then the desire or will must be completely disregarded and put aside so the concentration can be obtained. This means that in order to obtain a pure, meditative concentration - a reflection in the purest form, a clarity of vision of whatever it happens to be - the will must not be carried into the meditation. When you are ready to meditate you do not say, "Now I will concentrate, or now I will meditate, or now I will do this or that." These are the thoughts that form your will to perform meditation and must be set aside, or you will not be able to concentrate in any form.

By developing meditation, we learn to direct our senses toward something quite definite, and then concentrate on it. During this concentration, no other thoughts may be entertained because the concentration may consist only of absolute clarity of vision or clarity of reflection. This means we must observe the object of our concentration while being completely void of any outside thoughts.

Meditation, then, is going to allow us to control our day-to-day thinking and give us access to the powers of our higher spiritual self. Consequently, meditation means this: Learning balance, learning clarity of vision and clarity of reflection, acquiring the ability to transmit spiritual consciousness into the spheres of the past and the future, and acquisition of spiritual capabilities such as telepathy, telekinesis, etc. Next let's discuss the need for meditation and then how to perform meditation, and what it can do for us.

155

The Need for Meditation

When we first come into life, our thoughts are very simple. Our conscious mind is functioning well, and all of our senses are working and are trying to interpret the new world we are in. We can see around us but don't know what we are looking at. We can hear sounds, but have no idea what they are. Touching things is a new discovery, and even the food we eat doesn't seem familiar.

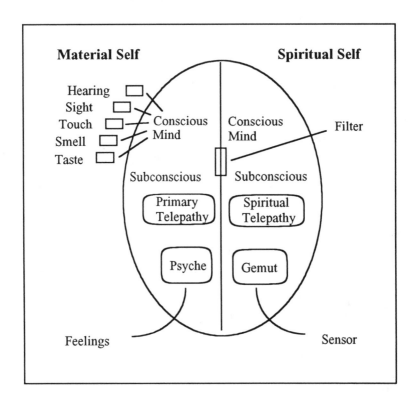

The reason everything is so new and unfamiliar is that the material subconscious has very little information in it. We have very few memories yet, and we have no data in our subconscious to flash us those *Sympathy* or *Antipathy* feelings that we use to form thoughts with.

Remember our conscious mind creates thoughts by flashing to the subconscious to check for any available data that we have on the object on which we are forming the thought. Since the subconscious is where we keep our memories and has nothing to flash back yet, our thoughts are very simple indeed.

The subconscious deals in vision, not words, and portrays its message in dreams

As we continue to experience the world around us, we begin to build up memories from experience in our subconscious. These are new memories about our mother, our crib, the food we are fed, and the many new sounds we hear. Very slowly we begin to create feelings of happiness as we are fed and taken care of. And, of course, there is the love we feel for our parents. These feelings start to form the emotions that build up in our psyche that will also become part of our new thoughts.

The process of thinking is instinctive, so we don't have to figure it out. The flashing between our conscious and our subconscious is built-in and is ready to operate; it only needs data to start building more complex thoughts.

As we get older and continue to experience the world around us, our thoughts will increase in complexity. We came into the world happy and full of love, but as we get older and come in contact with a more hostile and unfriendly world, we start to form new emotions to protect ourselves. If we let this process go unchecked, eventually we fill our psyche with feelings of anxiety, fear, hostility, anger, and depression in order to respond to this new environment. These psychic feelings then become part of our thoughts and how we express ourselves. No one comes into the world angry or prejudiced and yelling at those around them. These are acquired responses as a result of life's experiences.

Through meditation we can learn to control incoming data so that when our psyche is forming, we can handle the fear, anger, and hostility that is directed towards us so that negative emotions do not form. As we are confronted with negative elements in society, we can learn to pause during the flashing process that forms our thoughts and use our spiritual self to keep in balance. When we are young, most of us are overwhelmed with childhood experiences that leave very deep emotional bruises which affect our thinking as we get older. As we reach maturity, we recognize that we are not in control of our thoughts and go searching for ways to rid ourselves of depression, anger, anxiety, and other negative feelings that rule our lives. We turn to self-help courses of different types which make an effort to help us overcome our inner feelings and live a more balanced life. It would have been better if we had been taught how to think using meditation when we were young; then, we would not have formed these negative feelings in the first place. Meditation provides us with the inner strength to deal with any situation and remain in a calm and balanced state.

Since meditation gives us access to communication between the many areas of the mind, it should be taught to everyone when they are young. After all, thinking controls our life, so why not learn to do it better? If we have already reached adulthood, we can still learn to meditate and repair the damage that has been done. Once we learn to control our thinking and bring our spiritual self into action, our lives become easier and more productive.

How to Perform a Simple Meditation

Before getting any more detailed about what is possible through meditation, let's go through the steps of a simple meditation/concentration so that we better understand the process and see what is possible.

There are many methods of inducing meditation, ranging from focusing on a candle light or concentrating on a crystal. You may use any method that suits you, but I prefer to develop the meditative/concentration using breathing, since our respiration connects us directly to our life energy and gives us a sense of well-being.

For best results this should be done in a sitting position, preferably in the lotus position with legs crossed. This type of sitting position should not be looked as the only method, especially in the Western world, as the lotus position can be very difficult because of lack of practice. You must use a position that is comfortable so that your attention is not drawn to any body discomfort which will distract you during the meditation. For myself, I use a soft cushion to sit on since my legs don't fold very well.

You do not want to be influenced by outside energies or sound, so try to find a location that is both comfortable and quiet. If you have room in your home, you may want to build a special meditation area where you are comfortable and not bothered by the outside world. Here you can cleanse your surroundings of negative energies and create an environment where you feel comfortable and relaxed.

It is also important that you free yourself of all worldly objects like watches, rings, necklaces, earrings, or any other jewelry you may normally wear that affects your personality or thoughts. It is also suggested that no clothing whatsoever be worn but that, of course, is up to you. The objective here is to put you in the most balanced state possible, so you can bring out the spiritual being that is connected to Creation and leave the material being and all of its feelings, emotions, and personality behind during the concentration.

The Relaxation

Once we are in a comfortable position, we are ready to relax

158

ourselves. The thinking of the day stores its energy in all of the cells of our body. Some are more affected than others. We can release this build-up of tension by taking 3 deep breaths and releasing them slowly. Deep breathing is very good at releasing energy and bringing the body back to a more relaxed state.

The Breathing Exercise

The breathing exercise is used to familiarize us with the concept of concentration, so we can learn to control our thinking. The objective here is to observe the natural flow of our respiration while not influencing it in any way. Do not hold your breath or intentionally subject it to any artificial rhythm. The object here is to follow the breathing procedure calmly and carefully during the exercise.

Close your eyes and focus your attention on the sides of your nostrils and begin to observe your breath as it moves in and out of your nasal passage. Try to keep in a state of observation and do not become involved in the rhythm of your breath. If you catch yourself affecting the flow of your breath, causing it to speed up or slow down, just relax and become the observer, not the controller. You will probably make an effort to control your breath and may cause it to go even more out of control. Simply relax and let your breath find its own pace, and remember, you have been breathing for years without any help from your conscious mind. Simply become the observer and make no attempt to regulate the flow of your breath. Observation means that you are not influencing the breath in any way with any of your material senses or thoughts; you are only observing it.

Observe your breath as it flows up the side of your nostril and disappears at the top of your nose. DO NOT FOLLOW IT. This would take your attention away from your observation spot.

The inhaling and exhaling usually becomes noticeable as a cool stream of air that keeps moving. Even if your observation is strictly concentrated on the fixed point of the sides of the nose (nostrils), a peripheral awareness of the course of the breath through the body is produced, arising from the light pressure of the air we breathe. No further consideration should be given to it.

As your concentration continues, you will begin to notice exactly where the breath enters the nostril, where it starts to flow up the side of the nostril, and where it disappears. These three spots mark the beginning, middle, and end of the breath and become clearer and clearer as the concentration continues.

Aware of Your Body

If you become very uncomfortable during this exercise, you will not be able to continue and may have to start over. However, if you only become aware of your body, you should simply treat this awareness as an observation which has disturbed the tranquil harmony of the concentration. Simply visualize that the respiration EXISTS, completely independent of the intention of the meditation exercise and discard the awareness of your body.

Unwanted Thoughts

As you continue to observe your breath, it is only natural that unwanted thoughts come into your mind. Since we are not trained in controlling our thinking, our mind is used to racing from one thought to another anytime it wants to. By developing concentration, the ability to focus on only one object at a time, we are serving notice to our material consciousness that we are taking charge of our thinking. This will be something new for most and will require some time to become successful.

As unwanted thoughts jump into your mind, you must order them to disappear and return to your observation mode. It is a good idea before starting this exercise to tell your conscious self that you intend to concentrate now and to not bother you with any thoughts. Tell yourself to hold all thoughts until you are through with your meditation, and then you will instruct it when you are ready to continue normal thinking.

If you could concentrate for 1 minute without another thought coming into your mind, you will have dramatically changed your life

Our mind is used to manufacturing ideas and images for us all of the time, conforming to the internal wish list provided by our ego and other emotions. If we do not take control of our thinking, our mind will continue to make up all sorts of images while we are trying to concentrate. Learning to concentrate will help us begin to take control of our thinking processes, but we must be careful to be honest with ourselves and not allow our ego to manufacture unwanted thoughts and images.

Continued Observation

Continue your observation until a deep feeling of well-being and relaxation is obtained. Allow yourself some time to benefit from this enjoyable state of mind. Relish the moment and become familiar with the location in your mind that has produced this moment as you will want to return here often.

The most important objective during this exercise is to learn to concentrate on any one object for a period of time and keep out unwanted thoughts. Just this simple exercise can begin to restore power to your thinking. By developing the power to concentrate on a single object in meditation, you are learning how to control your thinking and can apply this to normal life by being more productive and less influenced by the outside environment.

Continue this exercise daily until you can concentrate on a single object without any unwanted thoughts for one minute. This may not seem like much, but most people will find it harder than they may expect.

Summary of Exercise

This is a very simple exercise that you can practice any time of day wherever you are. It's very good in a tense or stressful situation to help calm yourself down. I would suggest that you practice the exercise every day before you have lunch. This will serve to compose you from the hectic thoughts of your workday and make your lunch more enjoyable. It also allows you to work the concepts of relaxation, concentration, and thought control into your every day life.

The Uses of Meditation

Through continued use of meditation we can learn to control our conscious mind by pausing during the flashing process of thought formation and allowing our spiritual self to give us advice. We can also learn to program our subconscious to perform work for us while we sleep in order to lose weight or stop smoking, for example.

Emotions that are causing us problems in life can be reprogrammed by creating new experiences that come to happier conclusions. All levels of our mind can be controlled and addressed through meditation. It is this simple exercise that puts us on the road to controlling the communication of all levels of our mind.

Turning off the force of your material
thoughts allows the force of your
spirit to come forward

Meditation is also the first step towards controlling our material mind and letting the power of our spirit come forward. The ability to call forth our spiritual self and make use of our spiritual powers rests in the ability to turn off our material mind and allow our spiritual self to come through. Our spiritual self is always there, listening to all that we do, and never sleeps. Most of us never consider that we can call forward our spirit to offer an opinion, to give advice, or to teach us something about ourselves and our previous existences. And seldom does anyone ever consider using their spiritual self to contact other life forms. However, all of these things are possible through the continued development of meditation.

Pausing

As the Pleiadians listen to our thoughts and analyze how we think, it has become apparent to them that we need to learn some simple techniques of controlling our thinking that can be used in everyday life. One of these simple techniques is called the *pause*.

Most of the problems in the world are not caused by disease or wars, but by our thoughts. How often have we spoken too quickly and said something that we regret, only to ruin a deal or a friendship. When we feel depressed or angry, it is our thoughts that control us. If we could learn to pause as our thoughts are being formed or as our emotions are taking control of us, we could be in control of how we feel. Training ourselves to pause before we speak, and just for that one quick moment consider what we are about to say, can save a lot of misery in the world.

The pause can be exercised as our minds are flashing between the conscious and the subconscious and adding feelings from the psyche. As thoughts are formed very quickly, we must train ourselves to interact in this process by pausing, either as the thought is being formed, or before we speak.

As an example, let's say that your boss has just called you into his office about your work. You're in a great mood as you enter his office, and suddenly he begins to call you a boneheaded, good-for-nothing employee that had better shape up or look for another job. Your immediate reaction is to defend yourself, and you feel your body tighten up as you start to react. At this point you have many choices to make. You could allow his outburst to get you mad and yell back. This would probably get you fired and put you in a foul mood as well. A more controlled response would be to simply let him yell at you until he calms down, say nothing, and keep your job. You may also consider how to say something to calm him down and change his mind about you. There are many options. Just as you are about to speak, pause, and consider what you are about to do. Pause and let your spiritual self come forward and make a suggestion. Pause and calm your body with a deep breath before doing anything. If you allow yourself to pause, your spiritual self will send you ideas or hunches that are always of a more gentle and calm nature. Since the spirit cannot be sick, it does not contain any negative thoughts or feelings. It can be relied on to guide you and give you advice from a more balanced position. How many times have you been trying to think of what to say, and the first thing that popped into your mind was the right thing? That is your spiritual self trying to help out. Learn to acknowledge this first little hunch, and consider it more carefully before pushing on and ignoring it.

The pause can very helpful in controlling your conscious mind and your state of balance. If you find yourself deeply depressed, you can pause, explain to yourself that you are allowing an emotion from your psyche to influence your state of mind, and replace the emotion with another image which makes you feel better. By doing this, you have changed how you feel just by pausing and taking part in the thought process.

It is our thinking, more than anything else, that keeps the Pleiadians from wanting to have open contact with us. Our thoughts are too often plagued with misery, negativity, or feelings that are very uncomfortable for them to be around. It will not be possible for Earth to have open commerce with the planets of the Pleiades until we learn to think in a more controlled way.

The Meditative Immersion Using Colors

While the breathing exercise is good and helps you relax and build concentration, you will want to develop beyond this into a deep meditation, where more things are possible. To achieve this you can use a method other than turning your observation toward your breath in your nostrils. This method of immersion is now toward the eyes in such a way as to concentrate on colors which will appear as the immersion into meditation progresses. There are many methods using colors as a guideline to the depth of immersion into meditation. The members of the F.I.G.U. in Switzerland use the following colors as do many other people.

You begin the meditation/concentration with a matter-of-fact attitude. This means that your knowledge of the existence of the colors is present, but you do not think about them directly. It is enough to know that they exist without having to manufacture them first, so they can very simply be observed. As the meditative immersion continues, the colors will systematically come to your eyes as the depth of the immersion continues.

163

The purpose of the colors is to help you understand the depth of your meditative immersion and the possibilities that you are capable of at any level of immersion.

Before starting this meditation, concentrate your thoughts on what you want to accomplish in your meditation. Your first goal is to create the meditative immersion. Your second goal might be to move in time and see the past or future. The secondary goal must be decided before starting the mediation. Once you have your goals in mind, follow these steps:

- Get into a comfortable position, either sitting or lying down, and loosen up the entire body.
- Close your eyes and deeply breathe in and out three times.
- With your eyes closed, direct your attention to the back of your eyelids and observe the light. Continue the concentration until the color blue presents itself.

(The standard colors of meditative immersion used by most people are: Blue, Green, Yellow, and Red.)

Blue: Represents the color of the presence, the life force, and your existence. This will be the first color to present itself and lets you know the immersion has begun. Once the color blue begins to appear, allow it to occur three times; this will let you know it is time to concentrate on your secondary goal determination, the view into the past or future.

Green: As the immersion continues and becomes deeper into the spirit, the color green will appear. This represents to you that you are changing from conscious thinking to the subconscious. It can also mean that you are beginning to move in time, either from the present to the past, or the future. Allow the green also to occur three times, followed by a deep, inward concentration.

Yellow: Represents the color of the concluded change from the conscious to the unconscious, as well as the concluded change from the present to the past or future. Depending on the individual, it may take several months or years to reach this level, for it requires very good concentration skills. Allow the presence of yellow to occur three times with a deep concentration to follow.

Red: Represents the color of penetration into the unconscious, or penetration into the past or future. It is also the signal that the meditative immersion has been attained and now the spiritual subconscious starts to work on its own in reference to the secondary goal determination, which in this case would be time travel into the future.

Once the immersion is complete and a good concentration is obtained, the color red will slowly vanish and become a veil of mist and will cause the occurrence of vague and, at first, incoherent forms of dream images in the waking state that have not been created by yourself. They must appear without being called or created by you.

These waking-state, dreamlike images can be distinguished from the normal daydream by their extreme clarity and distinct qualities. They remain extremely constant and do not fade away or disappear like sleeping images do, but remain very vivid. If you are performing the meditation correctly, the images will not display any power of suggestion or try to influence you as a sleeping dream might. They will at first seem hard to understand, but will gradually become logical and understandable, and hopefully begin to make sense. These images always display events in their natural order, instead of jumping around like normal dreams.

In most cases these images are hard to understand and will take many hours of time to understand them. This is done after your return from the meditation immersion. The spirit will send impulses from the subconscious to help bring the image to a conclusion. Our normal world makes this very difficult, for there are billions of people thinking on the planet which makes it almost impossible to meditate to any great depth or investigate your new images. If you are serious and wish to continue your meditation beyond this level, it will be necessary to construct a pyramid capable of shielding your mind from the thoughts of the world and all outside influences. If you wish to build a personal pyramid, make it about 6 feet high and use the same relative specifications as the Great Pyramid in Egypt.

Another extremely important factor when producing waking-state dreams is that you must be totally honest with yourself at this stage and not create these images from your ego. Any thoughts that you may have

165

that create these images will be from your own material self and are usually caused directly by your own emotional problems, such as wanting to be popular or revered by others as a great medium etc. Do not proceed any farther unless you can be honest with yourself. You are in no danger if you allow the images to come from your spiritual self.

Return From the Meditative Immersion

Returning from the meditative immersion is very simple and requires nothing more than a simple thought to initiate the return to the material consciousness. You do not need to be concerned about not being able to return from the immersion; there is never any danger of that.

To return, you simply reverse the process of colors that have been used. If you have used the colors of BLUE, GREEN, YELLOW, RED as the meditative immersion colors, they will also be used as the colors to return with. Always use the same colors in reverse mode so that your mind understands what you are doing.

Simply envision the color RED first; it is only necessary to cause the color to occur once at each level. Then replace the color with YELLOW, then with GREEN, and then with BLUE. As you envision the colors, it serves as a signal to your mind that you are returning, and you will gradually come out of your immersion and return to the normal, thinking, conscious state.

Once the color BLUE appears, your material consciousness is automatically restored and you will begin to think in a normal fashion. All of your senses – hearing, seeing, touching, smell, and taste – will immediately become aware of your environment as you return to the present physical life. It's not uncommon to take a few minutes to become fully oriented, and it is normal to feel a little sleepy, like you are floating on air.

Summary of the Meditation Immersion

The meditation immersion is a very powerful tool that allows the individual full access to control over his thinking as well as the powers of the spiritual realm. The method described here is a simple guideline for the individual to follow and experiment with on his own.

It can take years to obtain the ability to use the spiritual powers of telepathy, telekinesis, or time travel. The time will vary from person to person, but you can expect to invest many hours in order to see good results. The degree of results depends on the ability to concentrate and develop a clarity of vision that allows you to see objects as they really are. Combining the meditation practice with modern techniques using sound waves can dramatically improve your results.

Further explanations of certain meditative techniques should be mentioned here to help with your progress and quality of results. Read these ideas carefully and monitor your progress with honesty in order to develop good habits of meditation.

The Power of Observation

The ability to observe objects and see them as they really are is very important in meditation. Objects may be people, thoughts, ideas, visions, or whatever the object of the meditation is. In our normal thinking, we sense objects with our material senses and transfer that image to our subconscious where we receive impulses related to it. After flashing on our memories, attitudes, feelings, and emotions, we may no longer be sensing the object as it really is, but as we perceive it to be.

A typical example may be viewing a beautiful sunset at the beach. When the sunset is first observed by our vision, it will flash through our consciousness, and we will immediately feel the impact of all of the stored-up memories and feelings that we have about sunsets. Within an instant thousands of memories about the sun, water, sky, and other wonderful moments come together and we get a nice, warm feeling about the sunset. After all, who doesn't enjoy watching a beautiful sunset over the ocean?

Because we have so many stored-up memories and feelings about sunsets, we overlook seeing the details that are really there. Instead the object, the sunset, is taken as a whole, and we rely on our stored-up memories to form the observation. This is common throughout life as we call upon our memories and feelings to observe things around us.

In meditation we want to set aside all preconceived memories, feelings, and emotions and observe things from the very beginning as they really are. We want to purely observe the object as a receiver without influencing the object through our own form of will, and without exerting any influence or evaluation on the object. If we are going to meditate on a sunset, we want to set aside all of our memories, feelings, and preconceived notions of what a sunset is and discover it all over again by purely observing it in the meditation.

This would be accomplished by entering the meditation/concentration and not allowing any unwanted thoughts or preconceived ideas of what a sunset is to enter our minds. We would concentrate on the image of the sunset and observe it, just as we observed our breath in the breathing exercise. We fix our observation on the sunset and become the observer. As our concentration continues, we will begin to receive impulses from the sunset. Very slowly the sunset will present itself to us. First we will become aware of the color of the sun; then, it's shape. Very slowly our observation of the sunset will continue to fill in the smallest and most minute details of all that we are concentrating on. We will become aware of all of the colors around the sun, the water below, and the sky around it. As our concentration continues our spirit will add the feelings of Creation, and the sunset will take on a completely new meaning to us. Acting as a receiver, we will have allowed the sunset to present itself, or "speak" to us, causing a sensation of spiritual bonding and love that we never thought possible. Complete relaxation and feeling a harmony with nature and Creation will flow into our meditation. By letting go of our normal thinking processes, we have allowed the power of our spirit to come through.

Clarity of Vision and Reflection

Once our abilities of concentration and pure observation lead us into meaningful meditation, we will begin to receive visions and images from different times. When we return from the immersion and begin to reflect on what we have seen and encountered, it is important that we do not allow our material memories and emotions to distort or taint what we have seen.

Just as clear observation is important to build a truthful concentration, we must also be able to reflect on what we have seen, clearly. It is important to remain in a balanced and neutral state of mind while we reflect on what we have seen so that we can learn from it.

Time Goes by Quickly

When you are meditating, time can pass by very quickly. It is not uncommon to discover that 15 or even 30 minutes in meditation can seem like just a couple of minutes. Because of this it is a good idea to have someone watch the time, so you can be brought out of the meditation at a definite time. This is because once you are in a deep meditation/concentration, you lose control of time and have no idea how long you have been there. Your spirit is connected to the timeless and is not used to a watch or timepiece. It is only your material senses that have a sense of time. If you are meditating alone, you might want to set a clock radio or music player of some type to start playing after 30 minutes. This should be very quiet so as to not shock you. Don't worry if you are meditating in bed before falling asleep because the mediation will find its end after you fall asleep.

Neutral Thinking

In your normal daily thinking process you should learn to think neutrally. I call this being in balance. The idea of neutral thinking is that we should develop a discipline of thinking that prevents us from having negative or positive thoughts in any form. This is accomplished in part by the pause which intervenes during the flashing as our thoughts are made. As we become more in control of our thinking, it is much easier to keep out unwanted negative and positive thoughts that throw us out of balance. Of course, in normal life we all have thoughts that are varying degrees of negative and positive. It's just part of our normal learning process. Developing the concept of neutral thinking gives us control over our thinking and allows us to be more neutral, or balanced, when we need to be. This process also gives us more control over our negative and positive thoughts, so they do not have as much control over us.

It is also desirable to keep negative and positive thoughts out of our concentration and only allow purely neutral thoughts to be applied. It is our negative thinking that makes open, public contact with the Pleiadians impossible. We have over 5 billion people on Earth who are thinking with no control. They are creating energies uncomfortable to the Pleiadians and harmful to ourselves and nature. If we could teach the whole world to think in a more balanced way and to keep out the more exaggerated negative and positive thoughts, most of our differences would vanish overnight.

The Boomerang

One of the problems in dealing with our own thoughts is that it is sometimes hard to discover what constitutes a negative or positive thought. We are not used to analyzing our thinking and saying, "Oops, there goes a negative thought," or "Now I'm thinking positively." Most of us are not even aware of our thinking and haven't given much thought to what kinds of thoughts we are creating. We are comfortable that our thoughts are not heard by anyone else, so we don't have to be to concerned about what we think. Besides, who is to decide if a thought is negative or positive?

If we wanted to analyze our thoughts in order to clean up our thinking and learn something about ourselves, there is a logical way we can monitor our thoughts and see if they are positive or negative and know what kind of effect they are having on the universe. It's called the *boomerang*. When a thought is created inside of your head, it does not stay there. Even though we are not consciously aware of it, our thoughts leave our physical body and go out into the universe. Thoughts are much faster than the speed of light and can penetrate deep into the cosmos instantly. Your thinking blends in with billions of other thoughts and takes its part in the scheme of things. Most importantly, just like a boomerang, our thoughts reach a certain distance and then turn around and come back to us. The boomerang effect is the process of sending back the thought you sent out, but in a slightly changed form.

There are two parts to a thought. There is the thought itself and then there is the energy that hurls the thought out into the universe. When your thought speeds out into the universe it will eventually come to the end of its travels, and like a boomerang it will turn around and head back to where it came from. Another interesting part of this process is that the thought will become polarized by the energy of the universe and return in a slightly different form. The thought itself will not change and will return in the same form as when it left, but the energy that hurled it out into the cosmos will return in the opposite polarity to when it left. If we pay attention to this process, we will be able to learn for ourselves the effect our thoughts are really having. You see, we may think we are thinking very positively, but perhaps we are not. Ego can get in the way and distort our thinking. By using the process of the boomerang as a means of analyzing our thinking, we can really learn what is going on in our minds. This, of course, requires a certain honestly with ourselves, as we might not always like the result. Let's see how this works.

Even though it is of importance to us, the actual thought itself is of little relevance to the universe. It is the charge of the hurling energy that has an effect throughout the universe. If you are thinking about your relationship and how much you care about this person, the thought is very important to you and you would probably consider it a positive thought. Let's say the thought is about how anxiously you are looking forward to seeing your lover on Saturday night. You're dwelling on this idea and envisioning going to dinner and spending time with each other. To you this is a very positive and happy thought.

As you think these thoughts, they speed out into the cosmos. Your vision of having dinner together, the thought you created, is intact. As you create this thought in your mind, a small form of energy that will hurl this idea out into the universe is also formed. This hurling energy has an electrical charge created by you. It may be negative or positive depending on the true meaning of your thinking.

As the thought reaches the end of its travels out into the cosmos, it slows down and begins to depolarize. The thought of having dinner stays the same, but the hurling energy depolarizes and switches poles. If the hurling energy had been negative, it would now be positive and vice versa. The thought and it's hurling energy now are speeding back towards you. The thought is still the same, but the hurling energy is now in its opposite form.

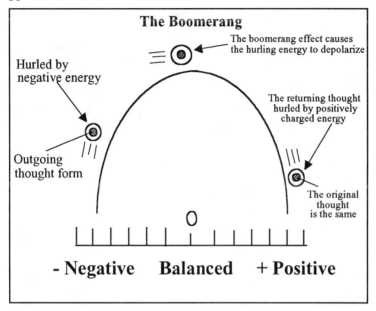

The distance the thought has traveled is dependent on the power of your thought and the force of your spirit. It may return to you quickly within a few minutes, or sometimes it may take up to 3 days to return. Consider also that you may continue thinking this thought for some time and send it out millions of times, each one returning at different times. The power of the *returning* hurling energy is equal to the power of the *sending* hurling energy. If you have sent out a thought that was hurled by very large amounts of negative energy, you will receive one back with very large amounts of positive energy.

As the thought returns, your mind acts as a radio receiver and picks it up. It has returned and entered your mind for consideration. This is an automatic process that happens continually in your mind. This forces you to once again think the same thought but it has returned encompassed within a hurling energy of different force. What left your mind as a positive and happy thought will return with a negative charge causing you to think the same thought of having dinner with your lover, but you will feel the effects of the negative hurling energy that came with it. Your mind will immediately consider the upcoming event of having dinner with a slightly different viewpoint this time and send the thought out again. This happens millions of times, causing us to consider something from many different views. Our spiritual selves watch this process and are not affected by it, but our material minds can become confused, angry, depressed, happy, sad, or can even cause sickness in the body as a result.

If we send out thoughts intentionally and watch for their return, we can learn how we are really thinking and work out the answers to our problems. For instance, we may have ulterior motives for having dinner with someone and not be consciously aware of it. The boomerang effect will draw our attention to the true meaning of our thinking and make us face up to the idea of what we are really up to. Even though others don't hear our thoughts, we must face up to them ourselves. You cannot lie to yourself or fool your spirit. In the end you must learn to be honest with yourself. If you do not, you will make yourself sick.

The boomerang process will help us learn more about ourselves. We are working toward a time of development where the strength of the positive and the negative are equal. This is balance. Once you can form a thought from a completely balanced viewpoint, it will return the same way. A balanced thought is one that does not contain a negative or positive hurling charge; it is neutral and returns the same as when it left. The feeling of a returning thought that is in balance can be felt by your spirit just as a negative or positive one can. You will be able to feel it and learn to recognize the neutral polarity. There is a feeling of contentment that comes over you when you know you are thinking logically. It is a form of spiritual bonding that lets you know you are in alignment with the universe.

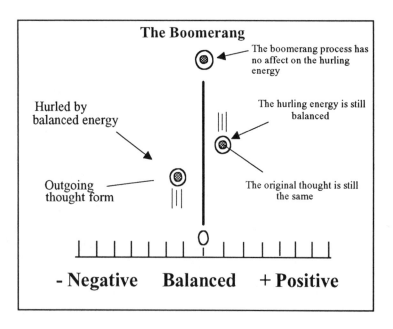

The Boomerang

The boomerang process has no affect on the hurling energy

Hurled by balanced energy

The hurling energy is still balanced

Outgoing thought form

The original thought is still the same

- Negative   Balanced   + Positive

We must have positive and negative thoughts in order to learn and grow. It is a natural process of growth. If we only created positive thoughts, we could not develop. The boomerang is a way of monitoring ourselves and learning to face the truth about our thinking. Here we discover that our material thoughts are filled with many devious spikes put there by inflated egos and emotional problems. Just the stress of living in our everyday world pushes us to defend ourselves with rather creative thinking. Our spirits cannot become sick or create illogical thoughts and are not affected by ego and emotions. Learning to think in a more balanced way through the use of our spirits is the path to higher consciousness. Using the boomerang and being honest and open with ourselves is a sign of clear thinking, intelligence, and growth.

The Echo Effect

While the boomerang effect is most useful for an individual to learn about himself, another interesting phenomenon occurs when a group of people all send out the same thought together. In a boomerang the hurling energy is depolarized by the universe and returned to the sender, forcing another consideration to the thought. If a group of people all send out the same thought at the same time, it forms a large block of energy at the location of the thought it was projected toward and echoes back to the group without being depolarized. Here is a better example.

Suppose you get together with 1,000 other people at a rally to support world peace. The speaker is doing a wonderful job of creating a vision of harmony and love for the world, and everyone is feeling a beautiful uplifting of spirit. He then asks everyone to concentrate and send out a thought of unconditional love directed at a young child who is lying stricken with illness at a nearby hospital. A large picture of the child is brought out on stage and positioned so that everyone can see it. Within a few minutes the energy from all of those thoughts converges on the photo. The combined thoughts of unconditional love begin to have an immediate effect on the nearby child. His stricken body starts to benefit from the great power of love and gives him strength to battle his illness.

The incredible concentration of similar energy that has been focused on one spot forms a block of balanced and loving energy. Within an instant there is an echo effect as the block reflects the energy from the people and sends it right back to them. The hurling energy has not gone out into the universe and been depolarized, so it will be returned to the senders just as it was sent. Since 1,000 people were able to send out beautiful thoughts of balanced energy, they will feel the echo effect of the same energy come over them. This will magnify the beauty of the moment as the feeling of unconditional love is increased from the echo.

This is a common effect with large crowds that are led into thinking the same thing at the same time. If people are caught up in a large crowd that is thinking happy and beautiful thoughts, then those happy thoughts will increase and magnify even greater. Likewise, this also has same effect on large crowds that are taught to hate or are being led in anger.

For instance, lets consider millions of people in a small country that are being led by a religious leader who hates America. If he can get them all to think the same thought of hatred and anger towards America at the same time, two things will happen. One, the thought of hate will be formed in America and have an uncomfortable effect on the people here. Two, the thought of hate will echo back to the millions who are projecting it an cause and even greater intensity of hate to occur. This is how radical leaders whip their followers into shape and exercise control over them. Do not think for a moment that many of these leaders are not aware of this technique and use it to their advantage over an ignorant populace.

The ability of a large group to create great amounts of energy through focusing their mental energy on the same thought will be the key to the control of the world shifting to those of higher consciousness in the future. While negative power leaders are adept at controlling crowds and creating hate and anger which destabilizes the world, more positive spiritual leaders who also understand this technique can use it to create tremendous energies of unconditional love and balanced thinking to provide comfort to those who need it.

Our Health Is Controlled by Our Thinking

The Pleiadians tell us all of our illnesses are caused by our thinking. This is very true since the energy formed by our thinking finds its way into every cell in our body. As the mind forms a thought, the polarity of the energy, whether negative, positive, or neutral flows through our bodies and rests in our cells. The constant build-up of negative energy brought on by our thinking leads to the degeneration of the cell and eventually to disease. Sickness at this level is nothing more than energy in cells that is not polarized as it should be. To keep ourselves healthy, it is important to learn to think in a neutral or balanced state as much as possible to keep our cells healthy.

Since our thoughts can play such an important role in our health, it can also lead to affecting our life span. Many Eastern philosophers believe it is good to slow down the beats of the heart to increase life. Most important is to think with balanced, neutral thinking and keep your mind active by challenging it with creative thought.

174

*All sickness found on Earth is
caused by illogical thinking*

Use Mediation to Control Problems Such As Smoking, Eating, etc.

We can use the techniques of mediation to overcome simple problems such as smoking or overeating. These troublesome habits become reinforced due to laziness, illogical thinking, pleasure, pain, fear, and any other number of emotions we attach to things and then we can't stop. Once we are in control of our thinking, we can intercede in these runaway reflexes and stop them.

Give yourself a goal in mediation to stop smoking and let your spirit come forward and direct your subconscious to quit. We have trouble changing our thinking because we are weak at controlling things. Your spirit is not weak and can overcome simple problems quite easily.

Spiritual Bonding

Throughout the book I have made several references to spiritual bonding. This phrase means that you become connected or bonded at a spiritual level with some other life form. This refers not only to your connection to Creation but to all life forms, including other humans, animals, plants, and to all of the universe. You see, spiritual bonding is the process of projecting out your own spiritual energy and making contact with spiritual energy from any other source.

Meditation teaches us some of the basic principles of controlling our thinking and allows us to develop control over our thoughts and our level of consciousness. We have already talked about some of the basic principles of pausing, flashing, and concentration that contribute to balanced thinking. We also now understand the value of controlling our negative and positive thoughts in order to find that balanced level. Meditation can then be a valuable utility in developing the state of mind that is best for spiritual bonding, and makes it easier to return to that state whenever necessary.

You see, we are all spiritually bonded to one another all of the time. Whether we are aware of it or not, our thinking creates energy that is projected in the aura around our bodies. As we come in close contact with others, our auric field touches theirs and affects them. Normally our auras only extend a few inches out from our bodies. When the power of our thoughts becomes more concentrated, our auric fields can extend out for several feet and have a much larger effect.

If our thoughts are negative or hostile, we harm those around us; if they are loving and understanding, we can warm their hearts and fill them

175

with happiness. If 1,000 people get together and become hostile all at once, they create a huge field of energy that starts affecting others, and pretty soon you have an angry mob on your hands. If the 1,000 grows to millions who learn to hate, all of society is affected.

Did you ever stop to think about what the planet and nature must do to defend themselves from the huge field of energy that is built up by billions of illogical, prejudiced, and hateful people? At this level of energy the planet and nature are stirred up and we have the human contribution to earthquakes, volcanoes, and other natural disasters.

The Planet Earth currently supports over 5 billion humans who are thinking and creating a mass consciousness that forms an energy ring around the entire planet. Not only is it affecting nature but this large consciousness extends out into the universe and is felt by other civilizations as well. Most of the effect is here on Earth. It is the people who create it who are most affected. If we damage nature, then we are hurting the food chain that supports us, the air we breath and the water we drink. On the other hand, if through the use of the boomerang we can clean up our thinking, we could get all 5 billion people to think with balanced thoughts of love and human kindness and create a beautiful world of peace and harmony. The key to doing this is to start with yourself, and then share the process with others until we have changed mass consciousness through wisdom. Let me give you an idea of how we can do this.

Growing up in small towns in Kansas, I was always close to nature. It was a very normal thing for me to sit under a tree and talk to it like a friend, or sit by the river for hours and communicate with the energy flowing by me. All of the birds, animals, and natural vegetation around me were my friends. I had developed my own way of communicating with the universe through a little system that I would like to share with you. Meditation will teach you the basics of thought control, but the ultimate goal is spiritually bonding with the universe around you and contributing something useful.

The Steps to Spiritual Bonding

1.   Find a good spot to commune with nature. It could be a park, forest, garden, or just in your own backyard. It should be a quiet place where you won't be disturbed for a while.

2.   Calm yourself and get into a balanced state with some basic meditation methods of breath control. Become an observer and begin to become aware of everything around you. Shed any need

176

for attention, approval, or control.

3. Shift your eyes out of focus and learn to observe the aura of energy that is around everything. Notice the colors in the auras around the trees and flowers. Even rocks and stones give off energy that is perceptible.

4. Let your mind become aware that everything you see and feel is a part of the universe and is of equal importance, including yourself.

5. Pause and let the unconditional love of the universe around you present itself. Nothing in nature hates or demands anything from you. You can only receive unconditional peace and love from nature.

6. Form the idea in your mind that you equally love everything in the universe. Add respect, peace, integrity, and the feeling that you are giving freely and want nothing in return.

7. Push that idea of love out from yourself and let it bathe the whole universe. Within a few seconds the universe will respond and return the feeling of unconditional love back to you, only much stronger. Create no new thoughts and observe your energy flow out from your body and spiritually bond with everything around you.

8. You will begin to feel lighter and start losing the sensation of your body. Make no conscious thought about this.

9. Again push out your feelings of unconditional love and let it flow outward. Try to observe the energy of your thoughts as it bonds with all around you.

10. Shift your attention to the trees, pause for a few minutes, and then shift your attention to the river, and then to the flowers. Spend a few minutes with each life form within your awareness in order to become friends. Sense their energy, learn their names, and feel what they can tell you about themselves. Give each observation a few minutes. You will be surprised at what you can learn from nature.

11. Observe the knowledge, intuitions, and sensations that come into your spirit. You will be receiving answers to your questions and visions of your future. Contemplate the meaning of all of your connections in life and you will discover their meaning.

Accidents in life are only material perceptions that are understood by the spirit. Here they can all be explained.

12. Feel the level of your consciousness increase to new heights and the energy that flows into your body. You should strive to raise your level of consciousness each time you do this. It is while you are spiritually bonded with the universe that you can improve your health and increase your life span.

Peace on Earth

Man is always talking about peace on Earth. I have an idea how we can start a spiritual bonding practice that will produce peace between people. If it catches on, it could end prejudice, hate, anger, fear, and the other negative feelings that prevent peace.

Once a day sit yourself down in a public place where there are many people. A park would be a good place. Get into a comfortable position and relax yourself. Now let your eyes fall on someone that will stay in one place long enough for you to concentrate on them.

Begin your meditation concentration on this individual, using the basic power of observation that you learned in the breathing exercise. In other words, concentrate on the individual without any material thoughts of recognition. Turn off all thoughts, feelings, and preconceived ideas about what a human being is. Feel your mind move into the familiar position of balance that allows you to begin the spiritual connection.

Form the thought of unconditional love in your mind and let it flow out towards that individual. Shift your eyes out of focus and see the energy of your love actually flow around them and engulf their aura. As the concentration develops, you will no longer see a material person. Their color, size, gender, looks, and all that you normally perceive will disappear as your perception turns from the material senses to spiritual awareness. When you see another as a spiritual being, you cannot feel any hatred, anger, or prejudice. Their spirit will send energy impulses to you and the spiritual bonding that connects you together will happen. Within an instant you will feel the awareness that lets you know that you are both creatures of Creation. In this mental state you can only know love and peace for one another.

As you leave the concentration and return to your normal senses, you will bring with you the feelings of love and spiritual bonding that you felt in the concentration. There is now peace on Earth for you two spirits.

Pass it on!

The Story of Jmmanuel

Jesus Lived in India

During my stay at the Semjase Silver Star Center, I spent a lot of time reading both Billy's *Contact Notes* and several other books that I had brought with me. One of them was a book, called *Jesus Lived in India,* that was given to me by a friend before I left. It was all about the life of Jesus Christ and was centered around an investigation by a German historian named Holger Kerstein, who claimed that Jesus survived the crucifixion and lived in India for many years afterward. The book was a detailed report of years of research in Israel, Pakistan, Afghanistan, and India where he had uncovered the path taken by Jesus after the crucifixion. His story told of the search he embarked upon to find out the truth about Jesus. He followed the path that Jesus had taken after the crucifixion, which led him through several countries where he discovered old scrolls and writings that described the man and his teachings. The book ended up with evidence to support the idea that Jesus had spent his last years in a place called Srinagar, India, where he had raised a family and passed away at a very old age.

I found the book fascinating, and it was written so well, with all of his arguments so well supported, that in a court of law the author would surely win his case. Intrigued by what I read, I was anxious to find out if the Pleiadian material would either substantiate or repudiate the book. I knew that Billy had asked Semjase many questions about religion, God, and Jesus and that he was very well-informed on this subject. Since the Pleiadians have the technical ability to move in time and see history for themselves, they have the ultimate knowledge of personal experience. Whatever information they may have passed on to Billy would surely be closer to the truth than other sources. It is quite easy to say that few events in history have had the impact as the life and death of Jesus.

In our search for our identity and our role in Creation, we have created religions and different belief structures in order to explain the reason for our existence. All religions are man's attempt at explaining the "meaning of life." Throughout our history the meaning of our life

179

has been explained through the use of idols, myths, sun gods, bird gods, and countless other man-made philosophies which have reflected the understanding and intelligence of the time.

Man must learn the lessons of life step by step. He must challenge, discover, and learn for himself in order to evolve. The New Age represents a time for a new paradigm in thinking, a time for us to search out the truth for ourselves. We no longer should listen to religions and philosophers as the absolute authority, but instead perceive their words only as information to be used on our own personal path of discovery. In our new paradigm, we will learn to take responsibility for our own connection to Creation, and most importantly, we will learn to find truth for ourselves. In this era, there will be no need for a spiritual middle-man who will tell us what God wants us to do. Instead, we will all learn to discover truth for ourselves and freely share our understandings with one another. Learning to face the challenges of life and taking 100% responsibility for our actions is truly one of the greatest lessons to be learned in the coming times. The leaders of the future will teach this concept through role-modeling and example.

In ancient times gods ruled the Earth,
but today man is on his own to
discover his spiritual place
in Creation.

In the New Age, man is getting in touch with his spirit and finding out he is already part of Creation. We are becoming aware that we are more than just a material being, and that we also have a spiritual energy within us that is connected to the Creation itself. This spirit is an active part of our day-to-day existence that requires a new understanding. As we learn more about Creation, we learn that our spirit has unique powers which include telepathy, telekinesis, future vision, and most importantly, the ability to communicate directly with the Creation and other beings of higher consciousness.

This is going to require new kinds of education, new methods, and new thinking. We are asking questions that the old paradigms cannot answer. The need for a new, practical method of understanding our spiritual self and applying it to our day-to-day life is here, and religion does not have the answers.

If we look at the average man 2,000 years ago, it's not hard to see how valuable organized religion was. It was a time of chaos, when man was sadly in need of some kind of organized plan by which he could live his life. Religion provided this through the organization of a logical method of explaining God and the meaning to man's life. First we had the Ten Commandments by which man could begin to rule himself. Here were basic laws of living that everyone could understand and live by.

Then through the life and teachings of Jesus, people began to understand their connection to God and developed a reason for being and felt closer to Creation. Their lives then became richer and more meaningful. Religion was born when these teachings were put together to form the New Testament. Just like in Egypt, where the Sun God reflected the understanding of the times, religion was formed as a reflection of the understanding of its time. Now 2,000 years have past, and as we prepare to enter a New Age, a more complex and sophisticated understanding is required. Religion in its original form has outlived itself and can no longer provide the answers to our questions.

Turn inward to find answers to your
questions and you will find the
connecting link through
your spirit.

Being raised in the Episcopal Church in which my parents were very involved, I was an acolyte, an assistant to the priest, and almost had the entire Communion ceremony memorized at one time. My upbringing was very normal for the Midwest, and I was taught Christianity just like everyone else in my community. As I got older, I began to question things and wanted to know more. Business trips had led me to Japan, China, Europe, and Egypt, and I was exposed to many different views and understandings. It was my opportunity to find out that not everyone thought the same way or believed in the same thing. There are more philosophies, beliefs, and religions than there are countries. Everywhere you go, you will find a new explanation for the meaning of life. It was fascinating to learn new things, leading me to read this book about Jesus living in India, and now I had a few more questions.

The Life of Jmmanuel (Jesus Christ)
I found Billy in the kitchen having some lunch. He knew I had been reading this book for days, and I think he was just waiting for me to show up with all of my questions. I grabbed a couple of scraps of note paper off of the radio and sat down. I think my first question was about what Jesus really looked like, and Billy took it from there.

Billy started off by reminding me that Jesus was not his real name.

The man we think of as Jesus was really born with the name of Jmmanuel, which means "God with us." Throughout his lifetime he was never called Jesus Christ. This was a name given to him in the year 189 A.D. by those who were still forming Christianity. It was also during this time that the teachings of Jmmanuel were being rewritten, probably to the best of their knowledge. In early Christian writings Jmmanuel was spelled *Emmanuel,* and it still is found in many hymn books by this spelling. In the old language of the Lyrians, which is still used by the Pleiadians, the spelling was with a *J,* so Billy referred to him as Jmmanuel.

The image most of us have of Jmmanuel is that of a young man with long, blond hair, thin and small-boned. Billy had me stand up, and taking a few seconds to think about it while looking me over, said that Jmmanuel was actually about 5'11" tall and weighed around 175 pounds at the time of the crucifixion. He had black, curly hair and was large-boned with big hands. His skin was tanned and had the look of a working man who was outside in the sun a lot.

His Birth

The Pleiadians wanted to make it perfectly clear that Jmmanuel was an Earthborn human being who lived and died as all men do. His life was that of a prophet who fought for the truth about the meaning of life. He became well-educated through the wisdom of the celestial sons from the Pleiades. Through the force and wisdom of his spirit he found the will to fulfill his mission of bringing the knowledge of Creation to Earth. His birth had been caused by the Pleiadians at the request of the Plejos, the last Pleiadian leader on Earth. Plejos wanted to return to the Pleiades to live out the rest of his days, so he decided to leave behind a prophet who could carry on the teachings of Creation and the lessons of life.

There were no longer any gods ruling over Earth, so Plejos asked for permission from the Pleiadian spiritual leaders to procreate the spirit of Jmmanuel and permission was granted. In Jmmanuel's case his spirit was too highly evolved to be born to normal Earth parents, so it was decided that his father would be a more highly evolved Pleiadian man. A Pleiadian named Gabriel was chosen to be the father and a Earth woman named Mary was chosen to carry the child. She was one of the old Lyrian spirits who was living on Earth and had highly evolved genetics to support the high evolution of the incoming spirit.

We are not told the means by which Gabriel impregnated Mary, but it is said that he explained to her how important it was to help with the birth of this most special spirit-form. She agreed, and the spirit of Jmmanuel made its decision to come to Earth and entered her body.

182

Mary was betrothed to a man named Joseph, who when hearing of this special impregnation broke out in rage and would have nothing to do with it. He was planning to leave Mary and cancel their wedding plans.

Understanding how Joseph felt, Gabriel came to him and explained the importance of this event and that the god that ruled over the Earth had commanded this event to happen. Joseph was a god-fearing man and calmed down and went through with his plans to wed Mary. Jmmanuel was born in a manger just as the Bible says, for there really was no room at the Inn.

Throughout his life Jmmanuel was aware of his true father, Gabriel, who visited him on several occasions. He knew that his father was not a god, but that he had been ordered by the Pleiadian spiritual leaders who ruled over Earth at the time to bring him into life. The knowledge of the Pleiadians was that of a god, but they chose to merely observe as it was time for the people of Earth to learn self-reliance and discover their spiritual connection to Creation. There would be no more gods on Earth. When Jmmanuel tried to explain this, he discovered that the people of Earth had become accustomed to being ruled by a god, and the idea of taking responsibility for themselves would come very slowly.

By our calendar today, Jmmanuel's birthday
is really February 3rd, not December 25th

Jmmanuel's special gift was that of seeing the future. He was aware of what the future held for his teachings and how man would interpret them. He knew how his name would be changed, and how man would call him the Son of God instead of understanding that his father was a celestial son who was flesh and blood just like us. His teachings were of Creation and of the eternal spirit that is part of all humans. But he knew how man would attach his lessons to a god figure. Man still needed a god to take care of him and was not ready to be responsible for himself. Too many lessons of life had to be learned before man could properly understand the teachings of Creation that he shared with them. But still, even knowing the future, he perceived that his life was worthwhile, and his words would provide the truth which would endure for all times on Earth; eventually, his true teachings would once again surface in the future to be a guide to those who were ready to take the spiritual responsibility to lead the people of Earth into times of peace and prosperity.

Jmmanuel traveled to India at an early age, around 13, and began his studies. Here he practiced mediation and learned the lessons of life from the great thinkers of that time. The knowledge of the East had been passed down for thousands of years since the time of Atlantis, when the celestial sons and daughters from the stars populated the Earth. On several occasions he was visited by his father who guided him and instructed him in the use of the spiritual powers which would serve him well during his later life.

Truly, he was well aware of the events of the future, but felt he could do nothing to change them. He was born as a human being, and as such, he would live and fulfill his mission. The power of his spirit could easily see into the future and allowed him to know his destiny. He knew that as a human being he would suffer the fate of bodily death at the age of 115. His body would be very old then, but his spirit would be unbroken. The coming event of his crucifixion would change nothing, for the occurrence would only be bodily pain, which would be dispersed by the force of his spirit; then, he would finish his mission. All the hate levied against him did not keep him from his path. The truth was more important than the pain of the body, which passes away. He could be tortured and destroyed, but the truth and his spirit could not be harmed.

The Writings of Jmmanuel

I was interested in any teachings that Jmmanuel may have written in his lifetime that the Pleiadians may know about. Growing up as a Christian I was aware of the gospels of Matthew and Mark and how the New Testament had been centered around them, but I wanted to know why there were not any original writings by Jmmanuel himself so that we could know what his real words were.

Billy had asked these same questions of the Pleiadians and had been told that during Jmmanuel's time, there were few who could read and write, so the necessity to write down his teachings was minimal. He planned to do this after the crucifixion, returning to India where he had learned the lessons of spirit and living a long and prosperous life. At that time his teachings were written down by Judas Iscarioth who was his scribe and good friend, not his betrayer as is commonly believed.

The Pleiadians also wanted to make it clear that these teachings were merely being handed down by Jmmanuel, for he had learned them himself from his Pleiadian father Gabriel, who was his celestial father, and the learned men of India, who had taught him so well during his early years of living there. Indeed, his teachings would be written down and buried in a safe place for the future.

These teachings which were written by his scribe, Judas Iscarioth, and added to by his son, Joseph, made it through the ages so the truth

184

would endure for posterity. The people of his father, the Pleiadians, would see to it that the writings would be found in the future and become accessible to the Earth human beings. But he knew then that even 2,000 years in the future man would not be mature enough, and it would take another 200 years before the grain of truth would find a bit of nourishable soil.

Judas Was Not the Betrayer

Judas Iscarioth was not the betrayer of Jmmanuel as we have been told over the years. One of Judas' scripts was stolen so that it could be used as evidence against Jmmanuel by a Pharisee's son by the name of Juda Iharioth. He secretly took the script from the bag of Judas Iscarioth and sold it for 70 silvers to the scribes and Pharisees, who were pursuing Jmmanuel. This would enable them to accuse Jmmanuel of blasphemy. Judas Iscarioth would have to write the text another time and preserve it well to endure the times.

The father of this man Juda Iharioth, who was the real traitor, wanted to hide his son's guilt and protect the family name, and announced to the people that the traitor was the scribe of Jmmanuel named Judas Iscarioth. Because of his power and standing in the community, his words were believed. This worked well for the scribes and Pharisees as the people now would say "Look, one from his own ranks has betrayed him and surrendered him for the death on the cross. Look, realize: How can his lessons be of truth if his own followers betray him and sell him out?" It was really Juda Iharioth who hung himself in the blood acre, not Judas Ischarioth, his friend who traveled on and continued to be his scribe.

The Crucifixion

Jmmanuel came before Pontius Pilate who did not want to sentence him but left it up to the people, who yelled for his blood. He was to be crucified on the cross along with two murderers. As the crowd yelled, he was beaten badly. Most of his ribs were broken and he could barely stand. He was not even able to carry the cross but needed the help of a man called Simon. At a place called Golgatha, he was nailed to the cross, and then raised into the air for all to see. It was most unusual for anyone to be nailed to the cross, it was customary to be tied, but the crowd and the soldiers had been greatly stirred up into a frenzy of hate by the high priests.

After Jmmaneul had been left on the cross, a terrible storm started which filled the sky with blackness and lasted for 3 hours. At the end of the storm his head suddenly fell forward, and he slipped into a coma, causing the soldiers to think he was dead. A lance was used to pierce his loins to see if he was alive, and when blood mixed with water came out, the soldier felt his life was slipping away. He called out that Jmmaneul was dead.

In the crowd was Joseph of Arimathea who was a follower of Jmmanuel. He could tell that he was not dead, but had slipped into a coma brought on by the many broken bones and terrible beating he had suffered. Jmmanuel was strong in spirit, but this much damage to his body was even too much for him.

Joseph received permission from Pontius Pilate to take Jmmanuel down from the cross and bury him. He then found some friends of Jmmanuel's from India who were there, and with their help took him to the tomb that Joseph had built for himself. It had a secret entrance, so he and the men from India could come and go as they pleased without being noticed by the soldiers who had been left to guard the entrance. It took 3 days for Jmmanuels health to return to the point where he could walk again. He had been nursed well by the men from India, who had brought with them special oils and salves which helped to revive him.

After Jmmanuel had left the tomb through the secret back entrance, there was a great roar in the air and a bright light shown, out of which stepped Gabriel, his Pleiadian father. He put the soldiers to sleep, rolled back the great stone which covered the entrance and let Jmmanuel's mother, Mary, and Mary Magdalene into the tomb to see that he was gone. They were told to go into the city and tell his disciples that he had risen and to meet him on the road to Galilee, but not to tell anyone else.

Jmmanuel appeared two more times before his disciples, once in the room where they had just gathered a few days before to celebrate the Last Supper, and again on the road to Galilee. He then disappeared and was dropped off by his father in Syria and lived in Damascus without being recognized.

Jmmanuel and Saul

It was at this time that he was joined by his brother, Thomas, and his mother. His brother informed him of the terrible things that were being done to his followers by Saul. Jmmanuel told him not to worry as he would take care of it. Saul would be later known as Paul, and for the most part, he was responsible for creation of Christianity. It was his understanding of Jmmanuel's teachings which survived to help form the New Testament.

Thomas informed him that Saul had become a bitter enemy and was issuing threats against any who would believe in him. He was even

186

writing letters to the synagogues in neighboring countries to find any who would follow Jmmanuel's teachings so that he could bring them to Jerusalem for persecution.

Jmmanuel decided to take care of Saul himself and went about his plan. He knew that Saul was on his way to Damascus, so he planned to confront him on the road and teach him a lesson he would not forget. Since Saul believed him to be dead, he would think he was seeing a ghost.

Jmmanuel prepared himself with some secret things, such as powders, salves, and liquids, and left the city and hid along the road waiting for Saul. During the night he saw a group of men approaching along the road and could see Saul among them. Jmmanuel started a fire, mixed it with his special preparation, and caused a tremendous bright light which blinded the group. As the smoke covered the men on the road, Jmmanuel yelled out so that Saul could hear him. Hearing the voice of Jmmanuel, Saul thought he was hearing a ghost and became very afraid. Jmmanuel continued to speak through the smoke and telling Saul to go into the city and let his disciples teach him how to live. Jmmanuel then disappeared into the night and headed for Damascus.

Saul and all of his men thought they had heard a ghost and were frozen with fear. They could not imagine how Jmmanuel could be speaking to them from the grave. Scared and confused, they continued on to Damascus where a disciple of Jmmanuel's preached to Saul the new teachings of Jmmanuel so that he would slowly understand. Still afraid, though, Saul was slightly confused and didn't understand very much.

Saul was of the belief, as were the high priests of that time, that once you died it was possible to resurrect the dead; they did not believe in reincarnation. Because of that, when Saul heard the sound of Jmmanuel's voice and saw the light, he thought he was resurrected and began to use this in his teachings. This is where the idea originated that Jmmanuel arose from the dead and was resurrected. Saul had no idea that Jmmanuel had never died, but had only tricked him.

Jmmanuel, his brother Thomas, Judas Ischarioth, and his mother then began the long trip to India. During that time he preached in many countries and often had to flee because his speeches were so revolutionary. That is why his journey to India took several years and was connected with great hardships.

In the country which today is called West Pakistan, way up in the north near the last foothills of the Western Himalayan Mountains, his mother became very ill and died when Jmmanuel was about 38 years old. She was buried in a little town which today is called Mari, Pakistan. A

187

small stone monument marks the grave where she lies. After he lost his mother, Jmmanuel traveled to the area known as Kashmir, which crosses the northern part of India, where he continued to spread his teachings further.

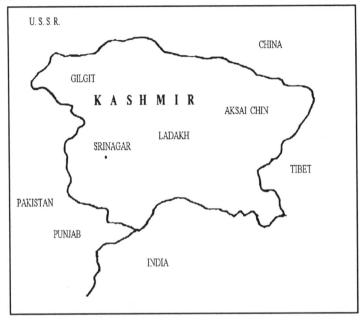

When he was about 45 years old, he married a young, pretty woman who bore him numerous offspring. As every normal head of a family, he decided to settle down and raise his family, living in Srinagar, India, which is located in the most northernmost part of the country. From there he made many journeys and kept on preaching his new teachings. At the age of about 115 he died a natural death and he was buried outside of town in an unknown grave.

Judas Ischarioth died at the age of about 90 and was buried at a place not far from Srinagar. But the first-born son of Jmmanuel, called Joseph, wrote down his father's story and left India after his death. After a three year journey he settled in Jerusalem where his father was born to live out his days. He brought with him the original scrolls of his father's teachings, and hid them in the tomb in which Jmmanuel had originally lain. He thought that this would be the safest place.

The Talmud of Jmmanuel

It wasn't until 1963 that the Pleiadians led a Greek Catholic priest named Rashid to the site where the scrolls were buried. The writings had been placed into resin and were kept in a crystal-like box given to

188

Jmmanuel by his father Gabriel when he was young, just for this purpose. Written in old Aramaic script, the scrolls were found under the flat rock where they had been hidden almost 2,000 years earlier by Jmmanuel's son Joseph.

Rashid began translating the scrolls from Aramaic into German and making copies, for he knew it would be his job to bring them to the world. The scrolls were long and contained over 120 chapters of information. So far he had only sent 36 of them to Billy in Switzerland.

Hiding out in Baghdad with his family, the good priest was being followed by assassins from both the Christian and Jewish faiths. Fleeing for his life to Lebanon, he camped there with his family in a refugee camp. But he and his family were found by the Jewish military who attacked the camp and slaughtered most of the refugees. Barely escaping the massacre with his family, he fled into the night at the cost of losing the scrolls.

Shortly afterward, the priest and his family were murdered by a terrorist gang who machine-gunned them down in hatred and anger. Only the 36 chapters which he had translated survived; the fate of the original scrolls is unknown. They have been translated into English, and today are available in a small book called *The Talmud of Jmmanuel*.

Published by Wild Flower Press in America, it also comes with a companion book called *Celestial Teachings,* written by Dr. James Deardorff, a Christian historian. This book is the result of 6 years of study on the *Talmud of Jmmanuel* to determine its validity.

The Lord's Prayer

In school and in church most of us learned the Lord's Prayer. In The *Talmud* we read it in a slightly different way. Jmmanuel was trying to teach those around him how to become aware of the spirit within us and our connection to Creation. No one understood the concept of meditation that he was trying to teach them, but instead they thought it was a prayer to God to help them. Being misunderstood, the Lord's Prayer was written down in *The Talmud* the way that Jmmanuel had first said it and taught it to his disciples. It was a meditation called *My Spirit*. Here is the Lord's prayer in its original form taken from the Talmud of Jmmanuel, the original writings of Jmmanuel. (Reprinted with permission from Wild Flower Press).

My Spirit

(Known as the Lord's Prayer)

My Spirit, you are omnipotent,
your name is Holy.
May your kingdom be incarnate in me.
May your power reveal itself within me,
on Earth and in the Heavens.
Give me today my daily bread and
thus let me recognize my sins and
I shall recognize the Truth.
Do not lead me into temptation and confusion,
but deliver me from error.
For yours is the kingdom within me and
the power and knowledge forever.

Amen. (I agree)

The Mysteries of Earth

The Pleiadian contacts in Switzerland continued for almost three years; during this time they answered many questions put to them by Billy, members of the F.I.G.U., his friends, and family members. Centered around the many unexplainable events of Earth's history, most of the answers provide an insight into our past that does not appear anywhere in our school books. I'm sure if given the opportunity, most of us would ask many of the same questions about the mysteries of Earth.

What Is the Mystery of the Bermuda Triangle ?

A mystery that has long plagued us is the strange disappearance of ships and planes in the area known as the Bermuda Triangle. Many books have been written on the subject, offering a variety of theories on the unexplainable disappearances of ships, planes, and people. It has even been suggested by some that the peculiar events surrounding the Bermuda Triangle may be caused by ET's, Satan, or some other dark force.

To the Pleiadians, the events in the Triangle are not caused by any extraterrestrial influence. As a matter of fact, even ET ships have been affected by the phenomena from time to time. As far as the Pleiadians are concerned, the events of the Bermuda Triangle are quite logically explained. Actually, there have been three different places on the Planet Earth where similar effects have occurred. Old pirate stories have done much to lend an aura of intrigue and mystery to the subject.

The area called the Bermuda Triangle is part of the old continent of Atlantis, which extended from the West Coast of Africa all the way to the east coast of South America and northward to the area where Florida is now. It is in this location that the descendants of this lost continent still live, in a base far beneath the sea. They are quite peaceful, and do not represent a threat to the surface world of Earth. They have ships capable of underwater travel and interstellar flight and have been seen entering and leaving the water on occasion. But this is not the cause of the strange disappearances.

There exists in the Triangle, as well as off the coast of Japan and Madagascar, what you might call a dimensional door to a parallel universe. In an effort to explain it, the Pleiadians took Billy into the Parallel Universe so he could see for himself. As the ship entered the dimensional door, Billy noticed that he could see our present-time Earth behind the ship, and in front of him he could see the Parallel Universe with three Earths looming into view. It was necessary to make the trip in one of the more advanced Pleiadian craft because the small Beamships would not be capable of returning.

It was explained that the dimensional doors are caused by the effect of 2 giant suns located 720 light years from our Earth. Certain high-energy radiations from these 2 giant bodies occasionally come together at certain points on our planet. When their energies cross, it forms a rip or tear in the fabric of time causing unpredictable results wherever the rip occurs. Since the Earth is moving, this radiation most commonly hits the planet in 3 different locations: The Bermuda Triangle, off the coast of Japan, and near to Madagascar. This only occurs at that time when the Earth moves into the focus of this wandering radiation. This crossing of energies serves to open a dimensional door to the Parallel Universes. This effect is erratic and unpredictable and disturbs the magnetic energy in the area for a short time. On many occasions in the past it has caused the floor of the ocean to rise up and appear as an island for an hour or so. Ships in the night have run aground, only to be pulled down when the ocean floor sinks. Airplanes have flown into this dimensional door, which acts like a cyclone, and they have found themselves displaced in time forever. In most cases ships and planes that have entered these areas slip forward in time and will probably reappear in the near future.

In the Parallel Universe, entered through the Bermuda triangle, there exists three Earths, caused by an accident 3,500 years ago when the planet Venus came too close to the Earth, disturbing the harmony of both of the dimensions and the two planets closest to the sun, Mercury and Earth. A rip or tear in time resulted and caused two different Earths from different time epochs to be pulled into the dimension of the future planet. Because of this there are three planets now existing in our Parallel Universe: The ancient prehistoric Earth, a newly formed Earth which is still covered in gas, and a third future Earth, existing as we know it in the present.

These three planets are close together, and they can be seen by the human eye at the same time. The future Earth is approximately five hundred years in advance of us. A society has developed there with space travel abilities, which has led to cities on the Moon and beyond.

The Pleiadians are careful not to let themselves be known to this future society, for they regard them as still too aggressive to get along with. It is interesting to note, though, that five hundred years into our future some form of our society does still exist. With all of the drama of survival here on Earth today, our future is certainly in question.

The prehistoric Earth is one which existed at the time of the dinosaurs. This was the state of the second planet, a prehistoric world with no signs of human life. Billy was so intrigued with the dinosaurs on the planet that he talked Semjase into letting him get out of the ship and touch one while it had been temporally paralyzed by her technology. He even took a couple of pictures which, oddly enough, shows a dinosaur with a large pyramid in the background. This seems very unusual since man did not exist on Earth when the dinosaurs roamed the Earth, so who built them?

The third planet Earth is one which is only just now forming from gas into solid matter and represents the very beginnings of our present-day planet. Not yet in solid form, it presented little or no interesting features and was not explored.

Earth has since moved out of the position where it is affected by the crossing of the strange radiations from the giant suns, so the dimensional doors should be closed forever. Because of this, we should not be plagued with any more disappearances or strange stories from this area, at least the ones caused by this strange energy. It should be noted, though, that the area of the Bermuda Triangle is known for its sudden storms that could still cause problems, but these storms do not have the capability to move objects in time or interfere with the magnetic forces of the planet.

Who Was the Warrior Called Quetzalcoatl ?

He was a very high-ranking officer of an extraterrestrial group that was exercising control over Egypt for a short time. He was wise and kind and was often sent on special missions. One of the missions took him to South America where he was praised as a god by the Aztecs. He came into contact with Huitzilopochtli, a leader of the Gizeh people, who led the Aztecs into creating the ritual of human blood sacrifices. Quetzalcoatl was against these rituals and a bitter feud developed for power. In the end Huitzilopochtli was able to drive Quetzalcoatl out, forcing his return to Egypt.

Are There ET's Living under Mount Shasta in California ?

Today, under a mountain in northern California there exists a race of extraterrestrials called Hyperboreans. This mountain is called Mt. Shasta.

The entrance to their city is high on the eastern side of the mountain and inaccessible to us. Their ships are gold in color and are sometimes seen entering or leaving the mountain. They are white-skinned people who usually have long, curly, blond hair. They sometimes come out of the mountain to local towns but are very shy toward Earth people. They are the descendants of the ancient Hyperboreans who came to Earth over 30,000 years ago.

What Is the Purpose of an Ice Age ?

Known to us as a glacial period, this is a natural event in the development of the planet. We have to accept the fact that the planet is a living entity, and it must evolve just as we must. Since it does not reach for perfection as we do or go through periods of material life and nonmaterial life (sleeping), it has its own way of evolving. This is done through an event called an ice age, or glacial period. This is a natural process covering entire regions or even the entire planet with ice. Temperatures fall and changes occur in atmospheric pressure. As a planet ages, the amount of ice subsides.

Ice Ages occur in rhythmic patterns in accordance with the size and type of planet. The time of an ice age can be determined by simple mathematics. On Earth, this cycle lasts about 700,000 years, which means that every 700,000 years a certain region of Earth will fall into an ice age and cover from 1/6 to 1/4 of the entire surface of the planet. The periods in between are interglacial periods, where from 1/10 to 1/12 of the Earth will be covered. We have had four glacial periods in the last three million years, and we are only 150,000 years away from the next interglacial period and 550,000 years from another great glacial period.

All forms of creation go through a process of waking and sleeping. The Earth is no exception. As the Earth has become more evolved, less area of the planet is covered in ice (sleeping) because this would damage some of the other life forms on it. This ice age, or sleeping period, serves as an evolution time for the plants, animals, and humans. This means that a beautiful flower changes into a still more beautiful one. Animals also evolve, for instance, the prehistoric mammoth has become the elephant.

The Ozone Problem

For many years the Pleiadians have controlled the dangerous effects we have caused by our irresponsibility toward nature. Many different chemicals are discharged into the atmosphere, including bromine gas, which slowly dissolve the ozone layer. As early as 1975 they informed us that the ozone layer is 6.38% affected and destroyed. This began 60 years earlier. It allows ultraviolet radiation into the atmosphere, affecting all creatures. There are currently three different areas where the danger exists. Bromine gas is not the only source of the problem. Our scientists are aware that explosion motors and matter-destroying processes of other sorts, including atom-splitting devices, also contribute to the problem.

Since 1945 the problem has increased greatly due to the splitting of the atom. Some governments have designed missiles that release bromine gas into the atmosphere as a weapon, stupidly thinking that such an action would be harmless to their own country. To close these ozone holes may take hundreds of years. The problem looks worse when we realize that the holes can wander.

The splitting of the atom is also a far greater danger than we realize. Setting atomic energies free through the use of nuclear plants, atomic testing, and explosion motors releases electrical energies at very high frequencies. This is not to be confused with what we think of as electricity. It is a different kind of energy that affects the ultraviolet radiation field which our scientists are not aware of yet. Normally, this energy mingles with oxygen to generate huge quantities of ozone. Normally, there is 1 part ozone to 500,000 parts air. When an explosion occurs due to atom splitting, the ozone value increases to 28 parts. These dangerous energies then destroy many varieties of microorganisms important to the preservation of all Earthly life. The ozone value then decreases very rapidly. The effects of these energies can continue for hundreds of years. Atomic explosions also affect the Van Allen belt by disturbing the electrons and photons important to the function of Earth life. The belt exists at a height of 620 miles and consists of charged particles in constant motion traveling in a spiral-like course from pole to pole. The problem is worse today, just as predicted. Try to educate yourself about this problem and make your voice heard. We are in serious danger.

Who Built the Statues on Easter Island?

The occurrences on Easter Island are connected to the city of Tiahuanaco, a pre-Incan culture that existed 300 B.C. to 900 A.D. chiefly in Peru and Bolivia. Even though they are more than 3,000 miles apart, they were ruled by the same leader and represent the last colonization of ET's in this area around 13,000 years ago. Out of this group came a semi-Ishwish leader named Viracocoha, who was very greedy for power. He conquered the 12,000 ft. high city of Tiahuanaco and then settled on a small island near Easter Island called Mot, which means bird in the old language. He and his followers were Lyrians with giant bodies around

195

thirty feet tall. They taught the local natives how to use their highly developed machines, which were then used by the natives, out of tribute, to construct the statues we see today on Easter Island.

Similar events also happened in Peru near the cities of Pisco, Nazca, and Sacsayhuaman. On lava walls on Easter Island there are reproductions of spaceships that were made by the local people who lived there. These were attempts at telling the story of Viracocoha and his reign over them. After several thousand years, the giants suddenly became ill from disease and fled Earth in their ships, taking all their technology with them. Where they landed is not known. It is presumed they died in their ships.

Many of the statues were never finished. The natives tried finishing them with primitive stones and failed. They apparently tried to get the gods back by finishing the statues with red hats made from clay from a local volcano. The Pleiadians have been able to ascertain that the giants were somehow in contact with a race of humans in Andromeda, prompting an expedition by the Andromedans to Earth 2,568 years ago. These humans from Andromeda were around 5 foot 10 inches tall. They stayed for 20 years and 7 months, building up an advanced culture. They are responsible for constructing the Nazca lines, half-tube channels that protect electrical energy centers buried in the ground. The Andromedans could not acclimate themselves to the Earthly atmosphere and were forced to leave in order to save their lives.

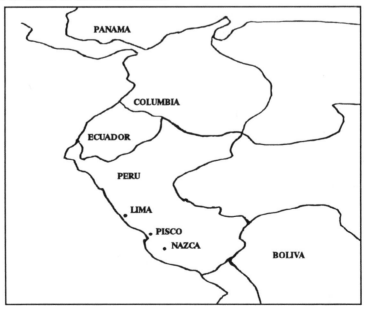

The Mysteries of Earth

Who Were the Giants and Gods of Greek Mythology ?

Over the years, many races of titans have colonized many parts of the world. Some of the ancient Lyrians who came to Earth were 25 - 35 feet tall. Many of the Greek gods were among these. Hercules was over 10 feet tall. He and many of the Greek gods were descendants of the Hyperboreans. Noah was around 12 feet tall and Adam was almost 16 feet tall. The great god from the Sumerians, Gilgamesh, was more than 24 feet tall.

Many of our ancestors were giants who, by interbreeding and adjusting to our atmosphere, have become smaller. Ancient dwarf races are likewise becoming larger as they evolve. After adjusting to their planet the present day Pleiadians, whose ancestors were also giants, are about the same size as we are.

The 3 Great Pyramids

The age of the pyramids has always puzzled the historians and scientists since the clues left behind to be examined are confusing. The Great Pyramid of Gizeh, sometimes called Cheops, stands just south of Cairo on a great plateau of land along with two other Pyramids which are smaller and built at different times by different techniques. The Great Pyramid, or Gizeh Pyramid as it is called, covers 13 acres using 6 1/2 million tons of stone, and stands 481 feet tall with its capstone in place. It was built 73,300 years prior to 1956 at a time when the star sign of Lyra stood in the sign of Cancer. At the time the Gizeh Pyramid was built, there were also two other pyramids built of the same design and for the same purpose. One of them is in China and is buried deep under the ground and may not be discovered for some time. There is also another one in South America somewhere which is just below the surface of the ground and may be discovered sometime soon.

The pyramids were built by a group of Lyrians who designed them for their own needs. When this race vanished, the Great Pyramid stood for many years uncared for and ignored. It wasn't until three hundred years before the Great Flood that once again the pyramid was of interest. By the way, the Great Flood is incorrectly thought to be around 9,000 years ago, but Pleiadian information tells us that is was really in the year 8,104 B. C. It was during this time that there lived a king named Sahluk who had a son named Saurid, who had the gift of seeing the future and often informed his father of events that would come to pass.

Saurid had a dream that a great planet would come dangerously close to the Earth, causing tremendous noise and darkness. Earth would be thrown into great upheavals of water, avalanches, and darkness. The loss

197

of life would be great. Saurid told his father of his dream and of the consequences of it. Knowing his son had a great gift of vision, the wise king counseled with his scientists to verify the time this event would happen. It was discovered that a great comet was indeed going to come very close to the Earth, causing the events of the dream to happen in about three hundred years.

It was decided to warn the people of the future by leaving a message on the Pyramid. By order of the king, the story of the dream was handed down from one king after another, who all prepared the Pyramid as a place of refuge. Lime mortar was used to cover the Pyramid so that it would be safe from the water. Once the mortar had sealed the entire Pyramid, the story of the dream was pressed into the side of the Pyramid, so the people of the future could not miss it.

When the time came and the Great Destroyer Comet was approaching Earth, the people took heed and went into the Pyramid for shelter. The events of the dream came true, for the Comet turned the Earth on its axis and caused great flooding and destruction all over the planet. The area of Egypt was flooded and was under water for several years. Most of the people of Earth were killed, and only a few managed to survive in the large underground caverns that had been hollowed out under the Pyramid. Thousands of people were able to live for many years in the subterranean world until the waters subsided. Once again the Pyramid had served a useful purpose. Historians have been misled by the material which covers the surface of the Pyramid and by documents and writings which tell of the Pyramid being built by the Egyptians. It was built by the ancient sons and daughters of the heavenly sons, the star travelers, who are the essential settlers of this world. The Egyptians have only remodeled the Pyramid on several occasions for their own needs.

The ancient heavenly sons who built the pyramids were well informed about the future of Earth, including the future which still faces us in this century. Because of their great knowledge, the Pyramid of Gizeh was built with the mathematical ability to tell us about coming events, in particular, events which will affect us from outer space. The changing position of Earth and its axis was even taken into consideration, for they felt the need to let us know about certain events to come, including the fate of the Earth. A prophecy was built into the Pyramid to warn those in the future. The exact time of the event of cosmic destruction is when the solar light of the central sun of the Milky Way, as well as the light of our own solar Sun, falls through the tube-like opening which reaches from the outside of the Gizeh Pyramid to the center in a straight, uninterrupted line and shines on one particular point. More was not told about this, for only those with the ability to unravel and figure out the math would be allowed to know the exact date of the cosmic event. The idea is that if you do not have the wisdom to solve a puzzle or riddle, then you are probably not ready to be responsible with the answer.

Are There ET's Living under the Great Pyramid ?

A group of extraterrestrials originally called the Bafath came from the far regions of the Ring Nebula. They are the ancestors of the leader Arussem, who was exiled around 3,300 years ago with 72,000 of his followers. They secretly returned to Earth and hid under the Gizeh plateau which supports the Great Cheops Pyramid. The Great Pyramid had been built by their Lyrian ancestors about 73,475 years ago. At the time, it served as the top of a small underground city where they lived.

The Bafath creatures are a wicked group who would like to rule the Earth. For almost 2,000 years they have tried to take over the Earth by controlling the minds of religious and political leaders through telepathic means.

For many years the Bafath have controlled many religious leaders, causing confusion and wars among the people. They have also caused illusions of religious saints to come into the minds of people, causing them to fall further into delusion and illogical thinking.

The Bafath caused the Waldport, Oregon incident in September of 1975, where people were giving up their worldly possessions to leave Earth in a spaceship. They were told the end of the Earth was near and that they could be saved. After the Pleiadians became aware of the interference of the Bafath and their control over the people of Waldport, they intervened and brought the incident to an end.

An American named Reinhold Schmidt was controlled telepathically by the Bafath to believe he had been in the pyramid to see the crucifixion tools. He also was fooled into thinking he had a ride in a spaceship to the Arctic. This was all illusion caused by telepathy to control the poor man. He is not lying because he actually believes it to be true. During the year 1976, 723 persons were under the telepathic control of the Bafath.

After causing many problems for the Pleiadians during their Mission to Earth, it was decided to remove the Bafath from Earth so they would not be able to cause any more problems for the people here. They were captured and placed on other worlds. One of the Pleiadian leaders named Ptaah also affected their spirit-form in some fashion, so they would not be able to reincarnate for several thousand years. This will, in effect, ensure that they can no longer interfere in the affairs of Earth.

Was Adolf Hitler Influenced by ET's ?

Adolf Hitler was born a person of very great worth. He was not spiritually advanced but was of very high intelligence. He was destined to bring great change to the world through his intellect. Through the Thule Society in Germany, the Bafath were able to seize possession of Adolf and to use him for their dark and wicked purposes, something he could not defend himself against. Many around him were also controlled.

Adolf became convinced that he was doing the right thing for Earth, and set out to create a master race that would bring the world to new heights of civilization. His out-of-control ego and desire for power made him easy prey for the implanted thoughts of the Bafath. The world came to hate him without really understanding what had happened.

Is There Really an ET Named Ashtar ?

Kamagol was a wicked leader of the Bafath. In 1937 a commander of his named Aruseak, known to some as Ashtar Sheran, fled the tyranny of his rule in his own personal effort to know the truth. He and his men left the Earth to keep away from the power of Kamagol and make a better life for themselves.

Since the Bafath are no longer on Earth and Kamagol has passed away, it has been safe for Ashtar to make contact with some of those on Earth. He sends information to the minds of many Earth people, but is not really informed of the truth himself. We must be careful with his information, since he still uses the tactics of the Bafath by appealing to those who are seeking a god to worship. Using the same methods as his former leaders, he will quite often control Earth people by pretending that Jesus is with him in his ship and is working for Earth. This is very unfortunate, for many people of Earth prefer to believe in the teachings of Jesus and are being led astray by the deceptive teachings of Ashtar. There are too many incidents were ET's take advantage of the mind-set here on Earth and find it easy to take advantage of us.

Who Are the Blue Race?

There is a blue-skinned race of people, who for many years have kept to themselves and lived in subterranean cities. This race has two underground cities, one in France and one in Asia, and rarely come to the surface. They have been seen on many occasions in India. They are very peaceful and pose no threat to our society, for they are not interested in us except for the fact that we may cause the destruction of the planet.

What Is the Destroyer Comet ?

In ancient Lyrian history they speak of a Destroyer Comet that came through their system and wiped out a large percentage of the population. This was a great setback to their civilization. That same comet led the Pleiadians into our system around 226,000 years ago. On several occasions, the comet had a dramatic effect on our planet. Earth was disturbed by the Comet passing by too closely 10,215 years ago, parting the waters of the Atlantic Ocean in the area where Atlantis had been. Again, 10,079 years ago (8104 B.C.), the comet passed by Earth and caused what is known as the Biblical Flood. At that time, the Earth day was 40 hours long and the sun did not set in the East. Egypt was flooded and covered with water for many years, forcing the inhabitants to hide under the Great Pyramid.

On two other occasions, 5984 B.C. and 4930 B.C., the comet caused tremendous storms on Earth. The cycles of the comet are rather erratic and unpredictable to a point. Sometimes it will come as quickly as 478 years and sometimes as long as 683 years, but always the average appearance figures out to be every 575 1/2 years, which is very unusual and puzzling to the Pleiadians. It is when the cycle is closer to the 575 1/2 year that it passes the closest to the planet Earth. It is expected that the comet may return again in 2255.

The Great Comet passed by Earth about 3,500 years ago and once again created a terrible storm in the Mediterranean and brought the sleeping volcano of Santorini to life. Located on the island now called Thera, just 60 miles north of Crete, the great volcano erupted with a terrible force, causing a 200 foot high tidal wave that rolled over Crete, Egypt, and Syria. At the time Crete was called Minoa; her people were the descendants of the Atlanteans. Many of them fled to safety as their homes went under water. Minoa remains standing today, but the island of Small Atlantis, which was situated close to the great volcano, slipped beneath the ocean and disappeared forever. The last passage was in 1680 which again caused great damage in the Mediterranean area.

Where Did the Moon Come From?

Millions of years ago our moon was a fragment of a destroyed planet in another system. It was caught by the immense power of the Destroyer Comet and pulled into our system. The moon was part of a planet that is 4.5 million years older than the Earth. Theories that the moon was once part of the Earth can easily be dispelled by an examination of the minerals found there which date back farther than any on Earth.

How Many People on Earth Are in Contact with the Pleiadians

In 1975 the Pleiadians stated that there are over 17,422 people on Earth in contact with Pleiadians. These are not physical contacts, even though there may be some isolated cases where they have had brief physical contacts. These contacts are the result of transmissions by the Pleiadians that can be picked up by Earth people. It is quite common to receive thoughts or ideas during sleep or daydreaming. It is part of the Pleiadian morality to not ever let the receiving party be aware of the origin of transmissions, for they feel this is interfering with our free will and our right to evolve on our own. It is also part of their decision not to interfere with a developing species. It should be noted that this information was given to us in 1975. I feel strongly that since then, many people may be aware of the origins of the transmissions and may even be in contact physically.

For those who are aware of their contact with the Pleiadians, only a few come to the public with their ideas. As we are advancing more into the New Age, perhaps more will feel the need to help out by going public with what they are learning. It is very easy in nonphysical contacts to mix your own ideas, wishes, fears, and dreams with transmitted data. The human mind is capable of manufacturing almost anything, so great care and personal integrity must be exercised before relaying any information you may have to the public.

Sometimes special people may be contacted for specific tasks that the Pleiadians have in mind. It should be noted that none of those chosen are in any way connected with the government, for this is directly against Pleiadian laws.

Where Is the Closest Planet to Earth with Human Life ?

Located just five light years from Earth on a planet called Akart by the Pleiadians, there is a human race very similar to our own. Technically, they are only around 117 years ahead of us and are in the first stages of development of space flight.

They have visited Earth on several occasions from a space station that they have out in free space. Even though they have developed space flight, they have not yet advanced to the point of breaking through to hyperspace. This means they cannot travel in time or traverse the huge distances of the universe in short periods of time. Even their trips to Earth take several years.

They suffer from body pain when they travel in space, and they use drugs to help overcome this problem. Their ships are not yet equipped with energy-protection screens of the type that can shield them from special radiations that penetrate their ships.

They mostly come to Earth for food, taking with them seeds, plants, water, and other staples of life that they may need. Their home world is greatly overpopulated and supports over twenty three billion people. Here on Earth we have built our population up from around 1.5 billion, to over 5.4 billion people just in the last one hundred years. Are we headed for the same problem of overpopulation that may send us out into space for food?

When Will Earth Have Open Contact with ET's?

The Pleiadians have been watching and observing our progress as a society and have indicated that they may instigate an open contact for the people of Earth. This may be done around the year 2000 with a race of beings not so different from ourselves.

If this plan for contact comes to fruition, we will be contacted by radio and informed that they are approaching Earth and will be here in several months. At first there may be a lot of panic and fear, for we will have no idea who they are and why they are coming here. The thought of beings from another world strikes fear into the hearts of many people on Earth.

After several more radio transmissions, people will begin to calm down and get used to the idea. Continued transmission will explain that they look similar to us but have no hair, their bodies are thinner and taller, but with hands and feet like we have. They will arrive in a ship which is very large, white in color and oval shaped, something like a large egg. The landing will be in America, for they will have ascertained that here people will be more receptive and less prone to panic and fear. It is not known for sure if the Pleiadians will continue to encourage this contact. As we approach the year 2,000, we can only wait and hope for the first radio transmission.

Did the Atom bomb Dropped on Nagasaki and Hiroshima Have any Lasting Effects on the Planet?

August 6th, 1945 saw the end of World War II between the Japanese and the United States due to an atomic bomb which was dropped on Hiroshima, followed a few days later by another atomic bomb over Nagasaki. The effects of these blasts have several lasting effects on the planet.

To begin with, the explosions had a very small, almost undetectable effect on the rotation of the planet. It has also affected the normal orbit of the planet around the sun.

Scientists have no idea of the far-reaching effects that these two actions will have on the planet. The magnetic poles of the planet have been shifted and continue to rotate. The North Pole has already moved into the Canadian Sea, and in 1,000 years it will be located on the western coast of Saudi Arabia at a point between Dschidda at the Red Sea and the Islamic town called Mecca. The South Pole is likewise shifting and is heading toward South America. The effects of these changes are not recognizable yet, except for some minor changes in weather, but over the long haul the entire planet will have been affected since entire continents will become uninhabitable as the weather changes. All of the oceans will be affected, and millions of people will have to move out of Europe as it slowly becomes the ice-covered North Pole. In Russia scientists have already discovered the shift in the poles and have properly calculated the direction of the shift and the effects on the planet.

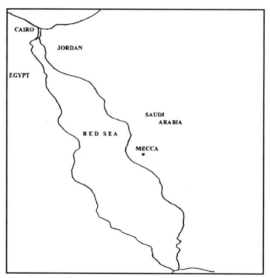

By the year 3000 the north pole will be located in Saudi Arabia near the city of Mecca.

At the time of the explosions, large amounts of very high frequency radiations were unleashed which are having disastrous effects on the ozone belt around the planet. This is not normal electrical energy, but a radiation energy detectable in the ultraviolet field that is currently unknown to the scientists of Earth. This radiation normally mixes with

204

the oxygen in the air and generates ozone. Normally 500,000 parts of air has only 1 part of ozone, but after the explosion the ozone value increased 34 times for a short time which amounted to 28 parts. Just after the blast, the ozone values decreased very fast. The consequence is that this imbalance will destroy the microorganisms, which are of enormous importance to the preservation of all Earthly life. This effect will last for hundreds of years.

The Story of St. Germain

The man known as St. Germain was born under the star sign of Aries into the family of Rakoczi in the year 1711 in Collonia, known today as Koln, in West Germany. He had the title of Count St. Germain.

He became friendly with a power group called the Rosicrucians who were interested in his ability to influence people of power such as kings and nobles. Since he was a man of few morals or scruples, he began to work for the Rosicrucians in order to gain control and power. Using illusion and deception that was not understood by many of his time, he could easily fool his followers into believing he was a man of great magic who could live for thousands of years. Being particularly good at magic and alchemy, it was easy to beguile the simple minds of the people of his time.

St. Germain never became a member of the Rosicrucians, although he claimed to have attained the high ranking of a member of the 7th Beam, which means he would be an Initiated One. In actuality, he was nothing more than a slight-of-hand artist who was good with chemicals, which allowed him to produce a glare - gold, using certain chemicals on metal.

He would hypnotize women of importance and get their secrets, then wake them up and tell them what he knew about them, causing them to marvel at his supposed abilities. They had no idea that they were being hypnotized and used so easily. He would even convince some people that he could become invisible since the people of the time had no idea of the power of hypnosis over the conscious mind.

To further enhance his image he claimed to have traveled to China, which was not true. He actually only went to Berlin to report to the Rosicrucians. This was a splinter group, for the main group was in Vienna. The Rosicrucians used alchemy to make him look younger so that people would believe that he was really timeless and would live forever. After his death at the age of 73, the Rosicrucians found people who looked like him and altered their faces to keep the myth going. The Pleiadians tracked down his spirit, and found that the man who was

205

known as St. Germain is currently reincarnated and is currently living in Germany.

Are There any Pleiadians Working with our Government.?

According to the Pleiadians in 1975, no government is in contact with ET's on a regular basis, and there are no Pleiadians working in government positions. To begin with, the Pleiadians, as well as most other races which come to Earth, have no authority to interfere with the political or power structures on Earth. The alliance of planets that they belong to forbids this. They have a policy of noninterference as long as the inhabitants of a planet are not technically advanced enough to leave their own solar system. There are, of course, some races who come to Earth or pass by who do not belong to this alliance, but they also have no interest in the affairs of our planet, and they would be discouraged by the Pleiadians and other races anyway.

The Pleiadians do not interfere or work with any governments. If they did there would be no need for secrecy. Their Mission is to help the beings of the planet, not individual organizations, self-appointed governments, or political leaders. Also, if they were involved with governments, the military would not so busy hunting for their Beamships.

It has been almost 20 years since the Pleiadians commented on this, and things are different today since the American, Russian, English and other governments have all come in contact with ET's from different systems. It is unfortunate that none of them, except the Belgium government, have decided to share what is going on with the public, but the time is rapidly approaching when the secret can no longer be kept as thousands of people all over the planet are having contacts of their own, and the truth is coming out.

Do any Earth Governments Have Beamships?

As far as the Beamships are concerned, several Earth governments have been working on their development for many years. These are not real Beamships like the Pleiadians have developed, but they are equipped with explosion-type motors, or with a kind of drive system that has a thrust effect. The first ship of this type was developed in February of 1941 in Germany under orders from Adolf Hitler. The first flight of the craft attained altitudes of over 40,000 feet, with speeds of over 1,200 miles per hour. If the Germans would have been able to perfect these craft and get them into the air, they would made a decisive difference in the outcome of the war.

At the end of World War II, the ship was destroyed so that it would not fall into the hands of the enemies, although some of the plans for certain parts of the ship were taken, and other governments started work on these flying discs after the war and still continue today. The test flights of these flying discs are sometimes seen by individuals who believe they are looking at extraterrestrial craft and are not aware that they are manmade.

The size of the Earth-made discs are normally 300 feet in diameter, and they do not fly very well. They cannot leave the atmosphere and are confined to low altitudes on Earth, and in some cases there have been emergency landings made because of faulty equipment. This has been a serious health problem in some cases, since many of the craft now being developed using atomic power and give off radiation which is harmful to those who come in close contact to it. In events where this has happened, the pilots of these craft usually seize any witnesses and threaten them with harm if they should tell anyone of the incident. Or in some cases they will say they are from other worlds, and pretend to be extraterrestrials who will kidnap them and take them away if they speak about what they have seen. Since most Earth people can be so easily controlled by fear, this method has worked well to keep their secret, and there are many Earth beings who are quick to believe that extraterrestrials are visiting Earth, and would gladly go along with this story.

While there are certain evil-minded extraterrestrials who do come to Earth and occasionally kidnap Earth beings for study and experimentation, most of the kidnappings are by Earth craft, using the people for their own devices and study. Certainly most of the sightings and observations reported are of Earth craft. It is very unfortunate that men of Earth have such little respect and love for each other, for there are many cases where Earth craft have pretended to be sent by God or that they are angels on a mission, then exercise control over Earth beings to do their will or perform certain tasks for them. In some cases the makers of these Earthly craft have tried to control public knowledge this way, by telling the Earth contactees that they are ET's and giving them information to tell the public which is not true. This is most common with religious messages. Since the Earthman is so easily controlled by the "message of God," it is easy to make him believe that he is having contact with God's own messengers, or that Jesus is on board the craft, and has chosen them to speak for him. This is very unfortunate, since the well-meaning Earth contactee does not know any better and is being used by his fellow man.

There is also no truth to the story that the Pleiadians or any other ET's have come to save the Earth and create peace. This is probably the most harmful thing to tell people, since it only builds up false hopes and serves to enslave the thinking of Earth people even more by making them think that someone else is going to save them, or create the long-awaited peace while they do nothing to create it themselves. The Pleiadians, as well as all other races that they are in contact with regarding Earth, would never do this, for it is not their responsibility to control the future of any race. They care about us like little brothers since we have common ancestry, and they love us as they do all creatures of Creation, but they will not solve our problems or control our destiny. We must follow our own path and take 100% responsibility for ourselves and our world. It can work no other way.

Life Forms in our Universe

Here on Earth there is probably no bigger question than whether or not there is life on other worlds. It challenges our belief systems and the deep question, "Are we alone?" It is probably a good idea that we have not been exposed to the answer yet, for until we reach a stage of development where we can live in harmony and use the technology necessary to get there with responsibility, we probably wouldn't properly understand what we would see anyway. The possibilities for societies of different morals, philosophies, and customs are endless, and as yet we have not even been able to get along with our neighbors here on Earth who merely look, dress, or speak differently. So, as in all things, we need to take one step at a time and get our own house in order before we go visiting someone else.

Pleiadian science, along with information that they have learned through their contacts with other races, can give us a picture of the development of human life throughout the universe. The planet Earth was one of 40,353,607 planets which naturally developed the human life form during the course of its evolution. As billions of years of evolution went by and race after race developed and spread out into the universe, proliferation of the human form began. Currently in our Galaxy alone, it is estimated that there are over 7,500,000,000 planets that support various forms of human life. The Pleiadians have come in contact with 1,800,000 of them and found 343 different variations of the human form. The differences come in the number of fingers, eyes, skin color, height, etc., but all are erect homosapiens as we would classify them on Earth. As we move out into free space and explore, we will begin to come into contact with some of these races and will discover there is a large family of man extending to the depths of the universe.

Future Visions and Pleiadian Prophecy

Billy's home, the Semjase Silver Star Center, is located up in the hills among beautiful rolling countryside with deep valleys filled with clouds misting the beautiful flowers and making everything seem fresh and alive. Taking walks in the forest around the Center was a particularly enjoyable pastime for me. There is a little road that passes by the Center and leads off into the woods where you can easily be alone for as long as I desired.

Large trees and lush shrubbery filled with nature's little creatures lend to the magical feeling that permeates the Swiss air. I had a couple of places that I liked to go that weren't too far into the woods, but distant enough to feel alone. My favorite time for forest-sitting was late in the afternoon as the sun was starting to go down. The sunlight would be breaking through the tall trees and creating dancing lights that frolicked across the ground like small children playing. I often spent an hour or two sitting in this beautiful, serene place just bonding with all around me.

I had been at the Center for a couple of months and my head was filled with new ideas for my mind to assimilate. Here in the forest was a great place to be at peace and commune with nature while working out many of the questions I had. Billy, Bruni, Silvano, and many of the other members of the F.I.G.U. had all been very kind to me over the past few weeks and shared with me their hearts and their minds. I was very thankful, and I had a lot to think about.

One of the really nice things about a forest is the great energy that it contains. It's a wonderful place for personal reflection since the energy of nature helps you raise your consciousness and spiritually bond with the universe. I was very interested in connecting with the future to see how the knowledge of what I was learning would fit into the world. The Pleiadians had made such an effort to bring us knowledge in so many areas, and I had to think that the future could be changed for the better.

Visions of the future, daydreams, and unexplained flashes of ideas were common to me as I always welcomed information from different realms. As a child I learned how to open myself up to seeing future

209

events. I believed the future was being created by the present and we could foresee what we were creating if we so desired. To me a future vision was nothing more than a glimpse of what my spirit was planning for my material self to do, and I always enjoyed watching.

My times in the Swiss forest helped me work out the meaning of what I was learning about the coming times of change for man on Earth. Besides, something rather peculiar was happening within myself. I was having vivid daytime dreams and visions that seemed to deal with what I was learning. I was very drawn to the history data. Somehow it seemed a little familiar, but not like I had been there. It just seemed to make a lot of sense to me, as if I had already known about it. My feelings were getting stronger all the time about my attachment to the Pleiadian Mission. Bruni had suggested that perhaps I was of Lyrian decent and had come to Earth many thousands of years ago as a rather violent warrior. Possible this was all true, as my visions were all very strong and vivid and seemed to occur in real time, which is indicative of future visions. They weren't fleeting daydreams of ideas of feelings, but real time remembrances, like I was there living the moment. Sometimes they would last for several days like a movie running in the background while I was doing other things.

I was using a routine of mental exercises to cause these visions that I had learned when I was a kid. It was a game I would play with my mind that would allow me to turn off the physical world and tune into other realms of consciousness. The game was my own invention and is a little childish, but it does provide results. It was certainly working for me with the Pleiadian material since I was doing more remembering than I was learning. Almost everything I would read from Billy's *Contact Notes* was easy to understand; as if I had known it before and was being reminded. Even the concepts of space travel and the structure of the universe seemed like things I had known before but had just forgotten somehow. None of the concepts seemed difficult or profound, but instead had a very strong ring of truth about them and were serving to open my mind up. I was enjoying a frenzy of learning and awareness.

I would find myself a comfortable spot in the woods out behind the Center and spend a few minutes relaxing and enjoying the scenery. My mind would start to wonder and become attached to the trees, the wind, the flowers or whatever was around. I would begin to lose awareness of my conscious, physical self and slip into a waking dream-state of observation. I begin with taking three deep breathes very slowly, holding each one in for a moment and then releasing the air very slowly. This serves to calm down the body and begin the focus of attention on the breath which is directly connected to the life force. The attention to the breath got me in touch with and let me feel my life force as it flowed in and out of me. After taking the deep breaths I would feel a calmness and tranquillity come over me which allows me to begin the move from my conscious mind to my subconscious.

This next step is a routine I developed when I was a kid. It has always worked for me, so I used it during my stay in Switzerland to tune into what I was learning. Here's how it works. It is my intention to let my mind go traveling without any interference from my physical self. I assume the role of an observer, like viewing a movie. I see myself walking into a small movie theater with just a few seats. I sit down in the front row in the middle seat. I'm the only person in the theater; its very dark and quiet just like a normal movie house. When I sit down, I notice that the movie screen is very large and white. It's only a few feet in front of me and there is a large red knob just below the screen that turns it on. I have programmed myself over the years to know that once I turn the red knob, the movie will start and I can observe whatever is playing that day. Sometimes I will just turn the screen on and watch whatever comes on, or maybe I will want to continue a movie I have seen before, or perhaps I want to know something from the past or future; it's all here.

There is a brief pause as I tell myself very firmly, "Now I will turn the red knob which will start the movie and no other thoughts may come into my mind." I put myself in the role of an observer who may only watch and not participate. This is real important because if I allow any of my own thoughts to come in or influence the movie, the information cannot be trusted. I have also discovered that if I interject my own thoughts into the movie, they will usually be thoughts that are wishful thinking, desire, fear, or ego from my conscious mind. The movie screen must become a source of information to be observed only. I take a brief pause to get ready, and then reach forward and turn the red knob. Now I sit back and enjoy the show.

Once the knob is turned and I'm in the observation mode, all attention is on the screen. No other thoughts are allowed. If I feel a thought creep in, I order it out immediately. It's important that I have strong discipline with myself if this is to work. The process of putting myself in an observation mode with no outside thoughts is very rewarding as my subconscious can then connect to outside knowledge of the past and future and create a movie for me that I have never seen. If I let my own thoughts come in it becomes daydreaming and wish fulfillment, and that's not what I'm after.

The screen is usually blank for a minute or two, but I keep my concentration on it with no thoughts. The trick is to go blank and wait. I just concentrate on the white screen with no expectations or involvement.

211

Soon the screen will start talking to me in sound and pictures, the movie is beginning. At first it may just be a flash of light or a passing image. Whenever something starts, I make sure I'm watching with that same feeling that I have when I watch a movie for the first time. I don't know what is going to happen next; I am just an observer and I am not going to get involved. If I make no attempt to add any thoughts or direction of my own, I'm in for a pleasant experience of creative thought.

As the movie begins to show itself, it may not be recognizable at first, especially if I ask myself to see something in particular, like a past life or a future vision. But I remain in my observation mode and things get better. It's very exciting as I realize that I am seeing things for the first time. My subconscious mind is actually creating images for me and drawing information from different sources including my past, my future, my higher and older self, other life forms could also be sending me an impression or two.

In my case I was interested in the Pleiadian information, so I preprogrammed myself to see anything in connection to the Pleiadian contacts. I was happy to find many new images relating to my childhood dreams of the great white-haired warrior who seemed so familiar. I had related these dreams to Billy and Bruni and was told these were the images of ancient Lyrian warriors. These dreams were common when I was a kid, and I had never made any connection to what they might mean. But here in the woods of Switzerland I was once again back in ancient times somewhere on a far away world fighting great battles with high technology. I was very tall, around 15 feet. My body was thin but well-muscled. My long white hair hung halfway down my back and served as a flag to the men who followed me, for I was always on the front line leading the charge. I could feel an attitude of invincibility as I pushed forward with no fear. My arms were covered with huge bracelets of technology that obeyed my mental commands and fired tremendous weapons of destruction upon my very thought. I moved slowly forward, burning the air and ground in front of me as another world fell under my attack. Overhead were the large flying warships that would soon land once my men had taken control of the situation. There had been many worlds succumbing to the forces of my power. I led the way for my race to dominate hundreds of worlds and control the galaxy.

Childish dreams? Perhaps. But my movies tell the story of ancient Lyra all too well. Forty years before I had ever heard of the Pleiadian contacts and read Billy's notes, I had already seen much of the Lyrian history without knowing it was connected to Lyra. Here in the Swiss forest my daydreams were connected to a past that lay deep inside of me somewhere. I had dreamed all of these thoughts years ago when I was little and they were still with me, but more vibrant and in-depth than ever before.

I returned to the forest whenever I could to create more movies. The more I did this, the more in-depth the movies would become. They were serving as a teaching mechanism to allow me to work out new ideas and concepts that I was learning. I could play them out here on my movie screen as real experiences. It's very stimulating when the movie is vivid and so many things come to you from out of nowhere. Many of my movies were seeing Billy having contacts with the Pleiadians in their Beamships. I would feel like I was eavesdropping on their conversations and sometimes wondered if I was really there. Quite often I would be concerned that Billy and Semjase might be able to sense my presence. Sometimes it seemed so real that I thought I might be able to join in the conversation.

On several occasions I would get direct images from the Pleiadians in the form of thoughts or ideas which would encompass entire concepts or ideas for me to think about. The fact that I was keeping my own input out of the movies made it exciting, for I was sure the ideas were coming from a source other than myself. The *Contact Notes* were starting to feel more and more like experiences that I had lived or experienced before. I felt no connection to the Pleiadians themselves; I have never had the idea that I may have lived on a Pleiadian world or actually had any physical contact with them. It was just that the stories, ideas, and concepts that they talked about all seemed so familiar. I must have had some involvement at some level somewhere in the past for all of this to seem so real and easy to understand.

The Future Movie

Since I was very interested in the future, many of the movies I would create were about the events that were to happen on Earth. Some of the more interesting ones were about events I saw happening over the next 20 to 50 years. Here are some of the future visions that I have had.

Community

The problems of running America will become too much for the government. They will not be able to maintain control much longer. Small communities will appear in rural areas that refuse to follow the federal system. They will make their own rules for survival reasons. These communities will produce new inventions in energy and health control that have been suppressed for years. A community system of barter will spring up as well as the issuance of a new community money

213

that becomes the denomination for this new culture. New forms of local government will be invented that really are "government by the people for the people."

Politics

The end of over 200 years of American politics is just around the corner. I see politicians fleeing the cities and even the country as Washington is overrun by angry mobs. An attempt will be made to use international troops to hold off the angry mobs, but it won't work and the government will fall. A new Constitution will have to be created so the people feel like a new day is coming. Scandal will rock the country as the public discovers how the rich have bankrupt America and taken the money abroad. Several rich and powerful people will be killed in public by angry and outraged citizens. A secret room will be discovered under the White House that will expose how the American people have been lied to over the years. It will contain the secrets of how John Wilkes Booth escaped after killing President Lincoln. Other secrets involving World War II, President Kennedy, and George Washington will be discovered and brought to the public.

Flooding

A tidal wave will hit southern California and wash over Long Beach. The wave will be several hundred feet high and will extend completely out into the desert and leave Palm Springs under water. A new waterway will be formed from the Salton Sea all the way to San Diego. Most of the water will recede and leave Los Angeles covered in mud and debris. Those who survive the flood will try to save the city and begin to clean it up. This is a bad idea since after they clean it up the city will be hit again by earthquakes.

War with Aliens

There will be a steady increase in the sightings of alien spacecraft, so many that the government can no longer hide it. There will be a mass sighting near a military base and the American Air Force will shoot down one of the alien craft. The ET's will react and wipe out most of our air bases all across the country. People will be screaming in the night as large round alien craft will be floating over the cities of America. Many people will disappear. The alien activity will not last very long because peaceful ET's like the Pleiadians will run them off.

The Islands of California

Over the next 30 years a series of floods and earthquakes will leave the southern half of California split up in several islands. The disaster will come at a time when the fragmented American government cannot help. Southern California will decide to leave the Union and be the first state to become its own Republic once again. It is soon joined by the northern part of the state and the California flag will fly over its new capitol somewhere east of San Francisco in a small town. The new Republic of California will flourish once it is on its own. New breakthroughs in energy, communications, and health, will be manufactured in the new Los Angeles built in the Mojave desert. These products will provide free energy for man and eliminate disease and increase the life expectancy to over 150 years. News of these breakthroughs will spread around the planet and change the way we live on Earth. This new Republic will be the role model for a new generation that will be the leaders of Earth by the year 2050.

Uncovering Ancient Cities

Ancient cities under the ocean will be uncovered that existed over 10,000 years ago. Written documents about our history will be discovered as well as drawings and plans for weapons that were used at the time of Atlantis. In Egypt they will discover more underground rooms under the Sphinx containing treasures and information that will tell us about life on Earth for the past 12,000 years, causing Anthropology to be rewritten. Giant tunnels will be found in South America that lead to cities which are thousands of years old that people still live in.

The End of New York

New York City is hit with a series of disasters beginning with more terrorist attacks that ruin the subway system. Earthquakes in the Atlantic will cause flooding that will roll over Manhattan Island, Queens, and Brooklyn. The city will be underwater and will have to be abandoned. Its ruins will stand for years since there is no way to reclaim the land. The tops of the Empire State Building and some of the other skyscrapers will still be sticking out of the water and will become small cities for the homeless who live by sailing small boats to shore for food.

Accidents in the Sky with Technology

During testing of high defense systems in orbit around Earth, there will be an accident that will ignite the air, causing the fire to be seen for thousands of miles. The atmosphere will be burned and unbreathable for

215

years. The infected air will float around the planet causing major loss of life and many new diseases. Other countries will be rise up in anger at the apparent stupidity of the US military.

The Food Goes Bad

The oxygen content of our atmosphere gets so low that our food no longer has any nutritional value to it. People will take to surviving off of food grown underground or in water. The process of photosynthesis will become so weak that trees and plants cannot make enough oxygen to keep us healthy. New diseases will flourish that we cannot fight, and people will be left to die where they fall because everyone is afraid to touch them. The oceans will become lifeless pools of death and cease to supply us the oxygen we need. Panic will break out as millions starve and kill each other over food.

Underground Cities

Governments and military will hide out in the huge underground cities that they have been building for years. Their plan is to ride out the difficult times and take over the surface later. This plan backfires as earthquakes destroy most of the cities. It is discovered that the "secret government" has been secretly building cities on Mars for years, but that has backfired also and almost everyone there is dead.

Giant Space Platform

Once California becomes a Republic science flourishes under the new leadership, and they launch a huge space city in orbit around Earth. By the year 2030, thousands will live there in an effort to make sure the human race survives. It is eventually decided to use the great power of the space city to stop the many wars that rage on Earth. The new government of America is still failing and Europe is ruined. Peace comes to man finally, and everyone agrees to let the Space City become the new government of Earth since they have the technology to survive. No one argues because they have no choice.

Contact with Peaceful Aliens

Around 2050 when man has survived and is rebuilding his society, we will make peaceful contact with other ET's like the Pleiadians. We will then be a planet of higher consciousness guided by spirit and love and continue our move into the New Age. The old paradigms of military and politics are gone forever and only exist in the history books.

Conclusion

I would remind you that these future visions are only my own and **do not reflect the prophecy of the Pleiadians.** All of these visions were seen by me and are more logical than they are prophetic. I would encourage you to practice the process that I use and connect yourself to the future and see for yourself. The future is only what we make it to be, so ask for enlightenment and answer how you can contribute something useful to the transition our civilization is in.

Prophecy and Predictions

During the 3 years that Billy was in contact with the Pleiadians, they put him in touch with highly advanced beings of consciousness that transmitted him prophecies about coming events on Earth. Some of the prophecies are from conversations and some are received in symbol form through spiritual telepathy. Billy also created several predictions himself that are the result of his own calculations. The transmissions from ET's and higher spiritual levels have turned out to be more accurate. Billy received them in a spiritual language of symbols and then translated them into our language.

Before going any farther, let me explain something about prophecy and predictions that Billy taught me. There is a difference between a prediction created through the use of numeric calculations and a prophecy, which is a vision of the future created by one event leading to another that has originated from a certain point.

Predictions are future events which are computed with cabalistic calculations that lead to very exacting results. Correctly done predictions come to pass with absolute accuracy since they are based on established fact and proceed to a certain effect that must take place.

Prophecies are different, though, and are generally a warning function and only show the end effect which would result from certain facts if no change were initiated in time. If there is no change then the prophecy becomes a prediction and will surely come to pass. Prophecy is also variable according to the free will of man and so consequently is not nearly as accurate as a prediction. Therefore, it is not certain that a prophesied event will take place since it will always come out a little different because of the intervention of man. This means that prophecy only demonstrates one possibility and generally is nothing more than a warning.

When it come to prophecy involving specific people, you must be very careful. Prophecies should never be clearly revealed to an individual because then they will make changes in their actions to avoid

217

certain events and cause their evolution to be faulty. This means that a person's evolution must happen without any knowledge of prophetic events so that their evolution will run its course naturally. Also certain events of a prophecy must be kept secret so as not to cause fear, hate, or disfavor, etc. Those who offer prophecy should be careful because their knowledge of events may be inaccurate, causing unnecessary fear and distress for the individual.

In the case of prophecy for individuals certain information within the prophecy should be vague, so the person receiving the prophetic information will have to struggle to understand it. Billy does not make any attempt to explain the prophecies in any more detail, for he believes only a person who can understand the truth himself when it is given to him in hidden form is able to bear and tolerate the consequences of the knowledge. Just as the stomach can only digest digestible foods, the human understanding can only take in and comprehend that which is digestible; otherwise, it is overpowered and becomes insane or delirious.

We all have the ability
to create our own
future

Remember the future is not fixed but is only a projection from a fixed point. The purpose of future predictions is to warn us of the future we are causing to happen; it does not have to happen this way. Once we quit waiting for someone else to create our future for us, once we stop relying on a god, a myth, or some religious leader to save us and learn to take 100% responsibility for ourselves and our future, we can create the kind of peace we all want. It won't come any other way.

Pleiadian Prophecy
The following section is prophecy based on information given to Billy by the Pleiadians and other highly advanced spiritual beings for the people of Earth. Remember, they are only prophecies and their outcome can be affected by the free will of man. Billy's book called *The Prophecies* is over 100 pages long and deals with many subjects including the Antichrist, earthquakes, and politics. It is only available in German and can be purchased by writing to Billy in Switzerland.

President Reagan
The Pleiadians said that President Reagan would be the man who,

through his deeds, will accomplish everything in a way that the old prophecies of the Bible will come to pass and bring us closer to the next war. He will be too aggressive and bent on solving everything through military force and rearmament. Remember, these forecasts were made and documented in 1975. President Clinton may well be the last president elected in our normal manner.

The Volcano Vesuvius

In Italy the volcano Vesuvius will erupt. This event will be a signal that the Third World War is imminent and hard to avert. The eruption will be caused by all of the negative energy in Rome. No where else on the planet is there as much negative and hostile energy as there is in the Vatican state. The Earth people should know that even though the papacy talks of peace, they have been the major cause of death and suffering on the planet for two thousand years. Even though the volcano Vesuvius is closer to Naples, the main activity of the volcano is very deep under the city of Rome.

The Antichrist Already Lives.

Billy first reminded me that the prophecies of the Bible are like any other future vision and are not fixed events. Prophecy of the future can be changed and never actually happens exactly as it is predicted, so it is only a projection based on events that are happening at the time the prophecy is made. A prophecy is only a warning of things that could happen. They are meant to warn man so he can do something to change the future so that it does not happen. This is why prophecies are usually always negative events; they are the ones that need to be changed. In the case of the Antichrist, the problem is that man is doing nothing to control his future or change the events of the future, so the Biblical prophecy still has a very high probability of happening.

To begin with, the man who will be known as the Antichrist will be born to a devoted woman of God in an inconspicuous place around sunrise, during the 7th hour, and brought to the East where he is to starve to death. He will be saved and taken in by an evil one who knows who he really is.

He will come into his own personal power at the age of 11, and surround himself with like-minded people for the next eight years. At first it will appear as if he is a follower of Jesus Christ, but he will soon place himself above God. His reign of terror will last for 27 years, at a loss of 2/3 of the life on our planet.

During the 27 years of war, most of Europe will perish and many new diseases caused by the decaying bodies will flourish. We will see the end of the British Empire as we know it, and China will invade and take over India.

As the Antichrist invades Italy, the Pope will go into hiding for years, and Christianity all but disappears. He will be the 266th Pope and will be the last one. The Antichrist will not be responsible for causing the war, but will be a spokesperson for an organization that is. All of the names he will be called and his organization will numerically be connected to the numbers of 666.

Billy then closed his comments by telling me that the world organization that will be involved with the Antichrist has something to do with the initials W.U.V. This is not an acronym for the name of the organization but has something to do with it. I have never figured out what these initials mean. By the way, Billy also commented that the Antichrist is alive now. So our future is racing towards us and will probably occur just as the prophecies say if we do not do something about it.

Natural Disasters

Volcanoes such as we have never seen, from the very core of the planet, will erupt and fill our atmosphere with smoke and debris, making it very difficult to live in many parts of the planet. Deep in the Peruvian jungles, giant warriors who were the old enemies of the Incas will appear from their hiding place, a deep tunnel in the Earth. They have been living underground for thousands of years, but will surface and raid villages for food and hide back in their underground tunnels.

In Peru there will be a severe earthquake in Udine from deep within the Earth's core. America and its Islands are areas named as suffering from the great smoke from the planets core. There will be great fires in Japan, Arabia, China, and India. The prophecies state that much of the earthquake activity is caused by our atomic explosions and the robbing of the planets oil and gases. There are many of us who are aware of how we are ruining our planet and must make an even greater effort to motivate others to do their part to save our planet before its too late. If we are to avert some of the planetary disasters, we must stop the underground testing and the robbing of our natural resources.

Large tidal waves will sweep over the east coast of America and cause tremendous loss of life. The waves will continue across the Atlantic and roll over England and plunge deep into northern Europe before they stop. This is one of the main reasons Billy lives high up in the hills.

The Great California Earthquake

Not all of the events of the future were predictions or prophecy. On March 18, 1978 Billy was brought aboard a Pleiadian Beamship by the base commander, Quetzal, for the purpose of fulfilling a request from Billy to see some events in the future. Quetzal had consented and arranged for a special Beamship that was capable of moving in time. The normal Beamships do not have this ability, so he had to obtain a suitable craft that was capable of taking Billy on this excursion.

Once onboard the Beamship Billy asked Quetzal to take him into the future to see the next great earthquake in California. He had never before seen an event like this while it was happening, and was very anxious to watch.

After setting some instruments, Quetzal informed him that they would leave immediately for a future time in California. The Beamship that they were in would be able to make the shift in time and put them in a position so that Billy could see the event take place. Quetzal warned, though, that they would only be able to stay in the future for about 30 minutes. He gave no explanation for this and Billy didn't press for one since his interest in science was minimal.

The Pleiadian craft left the Earth and instantaneously was high above the planet, leaving Earth looking as small as a basketball. Then just as quickly as it had left, the craft rushed back down to the surface. As they raced back into the atmosphere, the spacecraft had moved several years into the future to a time around the end of the 20th Century. It is not possible to know the exact date, and it would not make any difference anyway since it would be inaccurate. The earthquake had been traced to a specific time through the use of what is called an *event clock,* a technology that follows the path of events to a certain point in time. If they returned here every day, the date of the earthquake would be slightly different each time, for the future is not a fixed thing but merely a projection of events based on the present and affected by the free will of man.

As the Beamship moved down close to the ground, it was explained that they were in California somewhere over the San Andreas fault line and the earthquake would start in just a few minutes. It was about 180 miles south of San Francisco when the earthquake started. At first the ground started moving slightly and then with a jerk it seemed to split and break apart. There was a tremendous noise as the fault line looked like a snake writhing across the ground. The quake would be greater than any in current history and would take a great toll on California. To the south the city of San Diego would suffer from flooding, but it would survive. On the other hand, San Francisco would hardest hit, suffering greater

221

damage.

The Beamship moved to a point southeast of San Franciso where the quake was still shaking the ground. Most of the city was on fire and covered with a blanket of smoke. The Golden Gate Bridge was broken in half and was laying in the water. The Transamerica building was the tallest building standing, and it was broken in half. Most of the city was in rubble, with a tremendous loss of life. Since the 30 minutes was almost used up, it was time to leave. The great amount of destruction was devastating.

Remember, nothing is ever as
bad as it seems

The Death of Semjase

At the Center there is a hallway off of the kitchen that leads to a large bathroom/shower for those working at the farm. On the wall is a color drawing of Semjase walking away from her ship to meet Billy. It's not a real picture, but a beautiful lifelike representation created by artist Jim Nichols. It's so good that you have to look twice to see that it is not a real photograph. I stopped to look at it everyday and let my mind ruminate a little on what it would have been like to have been there.

To Billy it is a very important picture, for it reminds him of the lady from the Pleiades that had such an impact on his life. He had spent almost two years of his life meeting with her and working out the problems of getting the Pleiadian message out to the public. I had heard several rumors that she had died or was killed as her ship flew into a sun. Something had happened that caused the Pleiadians to end the contacts, and I was curious to know if Billy felt like talking about it. When I brought it up, he told me the whole, sad story of how one small accidental event had changed the course of events of the Pleiadian Mission.

The Story of Semjase

Billy said that his contacts with Semjase had started in January of 1975, and that they had continued almost weekly for about 2 years. Most of these meetings with the off-world visitor had been inside of her Beamship hovering somewhere in the Swiss mountains. On their ninety-fourth contact, however, she had come to Billy's home for a meeting that would have significant impact on future events for both of them.

It was December 15th, 1977 on a cold, snowy night, and Billy was entertaining Semjase in the meditation room located just about thirty meters from the main farmhouse. The family and resident F.I.G.U. members were all gathered around the kitchen table discussing how exciting it was that Semjase was so close by. Perhaps they might even be

223

lucky enough to see her leaving, or better yet, maybe there would be a chance to meet her. After all, she had allowed most of them to see her ship on one occasion or another, so the idea of meeting her at last didn't seem too far-fetched. Hanging on the wall was their schedule for meditation which listed the names of all the members. But no one would be using the meditation room tonight.

Jakobus was sitting quietly, keeping his thoughts to himself. Billy had told all of them that Semjase was coming tonight and to stay clear of the meditation room so as to not make her uncomfortable. Her senses were quite good and she would probably be able to detect anyone nosing around the little building. Her Beamship was hovering somewhere directly above the Center shielded from view by the energy screens. Jakobus couldn't help wondering what she really looked like in person. Billy had, of course, described her to everyone. He had even taken a picture of her once but was forced to promise Semjase that he would not show it to anyone. Jakobus was just thinking to himself, what's the big deal, what harm could it cause to just peek through the window and have a look. He wasn't thinking of barging in or anything, he just wanted to see the mysterious lady from the Pleiades.

The meditation room was very comfortable as you might imagine from its name. It was an important place on the farm because it was the center for all of the F.I.G.U. members to meet in. It had become a monument to the rising consciousness of this little group as they studied the lessons given to them by Semjase. Most all of them had participated in the building of the room and could imagine just where she would probably be sitting, right next to the little space heater which warmed the cold Swiss air that could chill you to the bone. It was a real honor that tonight the meditation room was being visited by the very person who had inspired it. Her being there somehow gave them all a feeling of approval and acceptance.

Inside of the meditation room Billy and Semjase were very comfortably seated. Billy was listening intently; Semjase had met him here on some matter of importance that couldn't wait. She was just about to tell Billy the purpose of her visit when suddenly she stopped, held very still, and looked around as if something was wrong. She thought she heard someone knock on the door, and she asked Billy if he heard anything. Billy cocked his ear and tried to listen for what she had heard, but could detect nothing. He remarked that she must be mistaken, but Semjase said she was sure someone was at the door and rose to leave. As she stood up and moved away from her chair she accidentally caught her foot on the table leg and tripped over the small space heater sitting on the floor. Billy quickly turned around in time to see her fall and hit her head against the wall just as her hand had pressed the small apparatus around her waist that caused her to dematerialize and return to her ship.

Billy was disturbed by this and being left alone in the room, he moved to the door to see if someone was actually there. Semjase had seemed so sure of herself but he had heard nothing. But there he was, Jakobus was hiding just outside the door in hopes of catching a glimpse of the star lady. Billy was very upset with Jakobus because he had embarrassed himself and ruined the meeting. Jakobus said he was sorry, he only wanted to have a look, he didn't mean any harm. He had hoped no one would detect him and he could just steal his look and be gone. But instead, Semjase was gone.

It wasn't until two days later that Billy was visited by a worried looking Quetzal, the base commander for the underground complex in Switzerland. His pale lime-white expression caused Billy to inquire about his health. But it wasn't *his* health that was on his mind. He asked Billy to explain what had happened on the evening of the 15th when Semjase had been present in the meditation room. The manner of his speech and his attitude gave Billy a little start, something was wrong, he was sure of it. For two days the whole affair had bothered him. He was concerned about Jakobus messing things up, and then there was the nagging feeling that something might be wrong with Semjase. He had seen her hit her head on the wall, but then she still dematerialized and returned to her ship.

Billy did the best he could to recount the evening to Quetzal. He told him how Jakobus had hidden outside the door, hoping to see Semjase, and that she had become alarmed and left the room. As he was explaining how he had seen her hit her head against the wall, a sudden wave of anxiety came over him because now he knew why Quetzal had such a sick look on his face. Semjase must have been hurt much worse than he had thought. This would explain why he hadn't heard from her in two days after leaving so quickly. She had come to talk about something important; it only made sense that she would have contacted him soon afterward.

Quetzal had been waiting for Semjase to return to the base two nights ago, for he knew she was having a meeting with Billy in the meditation room. He was the base commander and watched over Semjase like she was his own child. When she didn't come back or send a message, he had gone looking for her, only to discover her lying in her ship which was still hovering undetected above the farm. She had a broken arm and a heavy fracture at the base of her skull. She was in a coma and close to death. Quetzal immediately transported her body into his ship and took off for their home planet of Erra for medical attention. She had been

225

lying in her ship for hours with serious brain damage and was still seven hours away from help on her home planet in the Pleiades.

Upon arriving on Erra, Semjase was taken directly to their scientists who, unfortunately, could do nothing. There was too much damage to the brain, and she had been without medical help for many hours. They had done their best to take out the damaged brain tissue but were powerless to do anymore.

Once her situation had been stabilized, Semjase was frozen. Her father, Ptaah, had made a desperate call to their friend, Asket, who was the representative for a highly evolved race of being called *Timers* who were from a neighboring universe the Pleiadians referred to as the *Dal Universe*. Technically they were far more advanced than the Pleiadians and might have a way of saving her that was beyond the science of Erra. It was soon discovered that she and her people could not do anything either, but encouraged everyone to not give up. They had an idea that might work to save Semjase's life. There was a race of people called *Sonas* who had an understanding of life far beyond Asket's people. If they could some how get in touch with them, perhaps they could come to her aid.

Asket was successful in reaching the Sonas, and within a short time several beings called Sonas suddenly appeared in the medical room on Erra where Semjase's body lay. They had not traveled by ship but just seemed to appear, as if they had projected themselves across the far reaches of a universe by the sheer power of their own minds. Their medical methods were unusual to say the least, for they offered no explanations and set to work immediately, needing no help from the scientists of Erra. After making sure the dead parts of Semjase's brain had been removed, they took the frozen brain acids from her body and inserted it into some kind of artificially produced plasma proton that they had brought with them. This was put inside of her skull which was then closed up.

Within minutes Semjase returned to consciousness with no memory of the last 42 hours or of what had happened to her. She simply opened her eyes and brought a sigh of relief to everyone in the room, and the life force raced through her body and let everyone know she was going to be all right. Semjase was back from the dead and the men from Sona disappeared as quietly as they had come, returning to their home world somewhere far off in another universe.

It was a week, a very long week for Billy, before he once again heard from Quetzal. He had been informed by the Pleiadians that Semjase was dead, but he somehow wasn't going to feel comfortable until he heard it from Quetzal. He waited patiently at the location that he had been led to by the telepathic impulses from Quetzal and watched for the familiar silver disk that would soon dash out of the sky. Soon he noticed the birds begin to rustle in the trees and take flight, and within a few moments his old friend from the Pleiades had arrived; it was sort of like a family reunion.

Quetzal quickly reassured Billy that Semjase was well. He apologized for taking a whole week to make it back to Earth, but he was delayed from the many things that he had to do in consequence of Semjase's accident. One of these was the replacement for Semjase at the base in Switzerland. This would be a man named Isados who would be here for about 6 or 7 months helping out. He was unfamiliar with Earth and with the work that Semjase was doing with Billy, so it had been decided that Billy would not have any contacts with him and that he, Quetzal, and two ladies named Menara and Pleja would continue on with the task of instructing Billy until such time as Semjase may again be ready to take up her duties. This change would cause some problems for Billy, for he had been working with Semjase on several problems concerning certain members of the group which would now come to a halt because Quetzal had no knowledge of these things. Billy was even more let down to find out that when Semjase did return, she probably would not be able to resume all of her duties, for part of her recovery was to take it easy and not challenge her brain too much. She would need some time for the implanted plasma to heal the brain and was to rest and relax as much as possible. It had been decided that she should not engage in any work that would be too mentally challenging. Even though the Soneans were very advanced, the transformation of the artificial protoplasm would take 3 or 4 years before it would become a natural part of her brain.

The brain is the central steering of the human, and because of this the brain needs attendance and a special energy supply. This energy supply is the cosmic-electrical energy of life which nourishes and feeds the brain material as well as the spirit. It should be made clear that this life force provides nourishment but no impulses for healing or regeneration. Because of this, if the brain becomes sick or hurt it is not capable of regenerating or healing itself. Semjase's brain now contains the artificial plasma put there by the Soneans which has restored the use of her brain and allowed the life force to flow once again through her. Part of the programming of this artificial plasma is to heal the brain by transforming the plasma into real brain matter which will be accepted by the cosmic electrical life force, and become part of her natural brain material within 3 to 4 years before the body rejects the foreign material. A rather amazing feat of engineering, indeed.

227

Until this tragic event the Pleiadians had no knowledge of the existence of the Soneans, so little was known except these few details which they had learned in the past few days. They are from the Dal Universe, which is adjacent to our universe. Their average life span is around 2,360 years. They grow to be about 68 inches tall and have skulls approximately 50% greater in size than our own. The name *Sonas* comes from some language which was completely unknown, and their spiritual development is 4,000 years in advance of the Pleiadians. Their knowledge of time and space was quite impressive also, for they were able to project themselves through the universe with out the need of flight machines, only the force of their minds. This really impressed Quetzal, for this was far beyond anything the Pleiadians were capable of.

The recent demonstration of the Soneans ability to control the flow of the cosmic life force and to heal Semjase's brain brought up the idea that they might be able to live forever, but even though this may be possible for several thousand years, at some point the material body can last no longer and gives up. The spirit will run out of energy and go to sleep, causing the individual to fall into the death cycle. It is a natural part of the Creational logic that dictates that the spirit must have its sleep at some point in order to regain its energy and to cogitate what it has experienced throughout the material life, and add those experiences to the accumulated wisdom that will be carried forward to the next life. It is unnatural for man to tamper with this process beyond a certain point.

The prognosis for Semjase looked good. She was told to stay home for a few months and rest her mind and not engage in new mental challenges. Her brain would need time to heal and it would not be good for her to endure any undue stress or anxiety for awhile. Consequently she would not be able to continue her contacts with Billy on Earth.

This was very sad news for Billy, for he had developed very close feelings for Semjase over the years and felt responsible for her accident because of Jakobus. He had been trying so hard to control all of the egos, jealousy, and petty arguments that were continually going on among the F.I.G.U. members, whereas he also was a father, contactee, and prophet. But many of the members were very headstrong and difficult to deal with. The stress on Billy was becoming too much for him and showed in his health. He was losing too much sleep and letting himself get run down.

Is It Time to Stop the Contacts?
The Pleiadian Council had been watching Billy very closely and could see that he was having a lot of leadership problems with the F.I.G.U. members that were affecting the Mission. Now that Semjase would not

be able to continue the contacts, they were very concerned that it could be time to stop them. They instructed Quetzal to have a contact with Billy to explain the situation.

It was very difficult for Quetzal to tell Billy that it may be time to stop the contacts. He had grown very fond of him and could tell by the look on Billy's face that he was hurt. He knew he would miss Billy, and there was the problem of the Pleiadian Mission. The Pleiadians had hoped that through educating Billy and making their presence known to the public through the photos he had taken that they could help change Earth's future to a more peaceful and happy outcome. The dark times that would come around the turn of this century could be avoided if mass consciousness could be affected in the right way, and they were putting their hopes in Billy. Now it seemed that most of their work may have been for nothing, for Billy had not made the *Contact Notes* easily accessible to the public. In addition, he had not followed through with his promise to give more public speeches as he had been asked, and several of the F.I.G.U. members had become such a problem that they were jeopardizing the Mission. Things were not working out as well as they hoped, and with Semjase out of the picture the prospects for the future did not look very good.

As Quetzal continued to explain the Pleiadian's viewpoint, Billy agreed that certain members of the F.I.G.U. who were angry and jealous would have to go. Quetzal would help Billy by monitoring the thoughts of these individuals in order to help him better understand them. Billy agreed to cut back on his work and take care of his health and delegate more responsibility to others. The contacts would continue for awhile with Quetzal until they found out if Semjase could return.

For the next couple of months things seemed to be going well. Quetzal had made suggestions to Billy to ask certain people to leave the F.I.G.U. and to change his own work habits. The Pleiadian Council went along with Quetzal and left the decision up to him for awhile, but they made it clear that if the F.I.G.U. could not get their egos in line, the contacts must stop.

For Billy and Quetzal things were developing nicely. The relationship between the two had developed into a good friendship, and Quetzal had taken time for several contacts which were very beneficial to Billy. His easy-going manner and rather obvious intellect were proving to be a great stimulator for Billy. But not everything was going well. The Council back on Erra had been monitoring the thoughts of the F.I.G.U. members and found that instead of getting better, the attitudes were deteriorating and becoming even more harmful to the Pleiadian Mission. Billy seemed to be lacking in leadership abilities, and some of the people in the F.I.G.U. had become so emotionally unbalanced that they served no purpose to the Mission and were becoming destructive to themselves. It was on Monday, April 10th, 1978 when Quetzal informed Billy that the group was failing and future contacts would be limited to telepathic transmissions to Billy only. The F.I.G.U. was on probation. If they could not get their thinking straightened out, the group would have to dissolved and could no longer take part in the Mission.

Reunited with Semjase

It was only a few weeks later on May 20, 1978 that Billy felt the familiar presence of Semjase in his thoughts. She and Pleja, her sister, were coming to see Billy. She was feeling better and wanted to see her old friend whom she missed so much. Billy quickly dropped what he was doing and raced out of the house to meet her. She lead him to a remote spot not far away and picked him up into the ship. Billy was flush with excitement as he saw her again. He had really missed her. But here she was just as before with that pretty face and long red hair and that gentle manner that always made Billy feel so comfortable and loved. She was back and seemed healthy. He was hoping she would never leave.

Semjase gave Billy a hug that seemed to last forever. It had been 5 months since they had seen each other and they were making up for it all at once. Billy suddenly noticed Pleja was there and broke up the hug to say hello. He had not seen her for over a year, when he taught her how to ride his moped one afternoon in the forest. Everyone was happy and smiling and remarking how nice it was to see each other again. It was a great reunion for all of them.

Semjase had been recuperating for months and seemed healthy enough. The Soneans and their technology had seemed to work wonders. Her brain was slowly repairing itself and while she had trouble remembering some things, she seemed pretty much herself. Life at home had been very calming for her and had given her plenty of time to relax and catch up on her home life.

She had spoken with the Pleiadian Council about Billy and the group before coming here, for they were concerned about her ability to return to work. Unfortunately, she had to inform them that she would not be able to continue with the contacts or her other work; the doctors had informed her that her brain was healing slower than anticipated, and she should continue to take it easy. Billy was sad to hear this because he was hoping that she would be able to resume their contacts. Although he was really finding a helpful friend in Quetzal, he certainly missed her.

Once the Council was told that Semjase would not be able to

continue, they had consulted with Quetzal about the progress of the
F.I.G.U. members and were told that things were getting worse. Several
of them were openly trying to cause Billy trouble. They were making up
untrue stories about Billy to hurt his feelings and causing other problems
that rendered the group dysfunctional. None of the F.I.G.U. members
were taking the spiritual teachings seriously and were questioning Billy's
authority so much that he had no control anymore. It had been decided
that the group was on probation for 7 months. They would have to take
their commitment of personal development more seriously and work to
help Billy or they would no longer be allowed to help him with the
Mission. Quetzal would continue having contacts with Billy, but the
Contact Notes he would write would no longer be available to the
members.

Billy had to agree, things were beyond him. He was very worried
about the state of affairs. He had tried his best to help everyone get
along, but there were some pretty head strong people in the F.I.G.U.,
and the seriousness of the pressure that was on them to help with the
contacts and to be responsible for getting the Pleiadian information out to
the world was proving to be too much for some of them. They had
developed elitist attitudes, believing that they were better than other
people, and fought among themselves like cats and dogs. The rivalry
over self-importance was bringing the whole group down, and the
Pleiadians would have no more of it. The Mission to help the people of
Earth through the understanding of higher consciousness could not be
accomplished by this kind of thinking.

Breakdown

The following weeks were very difficult for Billy. He couldn't sleep
or get any work done. There was so much pressure on him from
everyone around him that he was unable to think straight. He was
beginning to feel like he had failed the Planet Earth. In his mind he was
responsible for the future of Earth and he was letting everyone down. He
had tried so hard to perform his mission as well as he could, but things
were out of control. He did not possess the leadership qualities to control
the F.I.G.U., and the pressure he felt to keep the contacts going was too
much for him.

It was on Monday, July 17th, 1978 while on his way to meet Quetzal
for a contact that Billy's health failed him. He was in the forest waiting
for Quetzal to meet him when suddenly he collapsed and fell to the
ground. His health had given out and he was having a nervous
breakdown. He blanked out, losing consciousness and lay flat on his
back in a small gully near the contact site.

It was just a few minutes before the alert mind of Quetzal picked up on Billy's condition and raced to his aid. He was not surprised that Billy had collapsed. He had been warning him for weeks to protect his health. Now it was too late. Quetzal sensed that Billy was suffering a breakdown of his nervous system and quickly brought him up into the ship.

Billy was still unconscious as Quetzal quickly examined his body and internal organs. He was right, Billy was having a nervous breakdown caused by exhaustion and anxiety. Fortunately Pleiadian science is far beyond our current understanding and Quetzal immediately knew what to do. As Billy slowly regained consciousness, he looked up at Quetzal who quickly told him not to speak yet, just relax and he would be okay in a moment. He was passing some small device over Billy's body which was reviving the nervous system and restoring his health. Within minutes Billy seemed much better and was able to sit up and talk. He almost felt normal. The device had somehow repaired the nervous system and balanced the cells of the body, relieving the stress, and pumped energy into his body. Billy felt pretty good, actually, and wasn't even aware of what had happened until it was explained to him.

Quetzal informed him that he had suffered a nervous breakdown brought on by the problems at the Center. It would take 12 to 14 days for the nerves to completely regenerate themselves, but he would be okay. Quetzal moved his ship close to the Center and materialized Billy's body into his own bed so he could relax and get some rest. The highly developed consciousness of Quetzal caused Billy to fall into a deep sleep without worry and anxiety so his old friend could heal himself. Quetzal was very concerned because this was a strong indication that Billy could no longer control himself or the F.I.G.U..

The Contacts End!

Once Billy's health had returned, there were only a couple of more contacts with Quetzal and then on Thursday, October 19th, 1978 the final meeting took place. There had been 115 contacts so far, and Billy had accumulated over 1,800 pages of *Contact Notes* for the people of Earth to learn from. He had done his best, but it had not been good enough. He had to agree with the Council that it was time to end the contacts. He no longer had the strength to deal with all of the problems, and he had not turned out to be a good enough leader to keep the F.I.G.U. in line. Billy left the ship that day for the last time. There would look in on him from time to time to see how he was, but the contacts were over.

A New Vision for Earth

My summer with Billy had opened up my mind to many things. But most importantly it made me aware of how we need to work together to create our own future. It's one thing for the Pleiadians to come to Earth to help us out, but this is our planet and we have to take care of things for ourselves.

I hope from what I have written in this book, you can find in yourself the need to help make the world a better place. We need to do something with all of this information. We need to study it and find ways to make it useful for our people and our planet. Peace is only going to come to Earth when we address the problems of our lives with spiritual understanding. It is time for us all to discover the spiritual bonding that connects all living things together with the Creation. Once you can feel this bonding, you are in touch with power that can change anything. Imagine if for just 1 hour, everyone on Earth bonded together and allowed their spirits to connect in love and understanding. In just that one hour we could solve all of the problems that we have.

This last chapter is for you and me. Perhaps here in the next few pages I can spark your thinking, and we can come together and find ways to rebuild our world and move into the next century as a peaceful and loving planet where we all can live to our fullest potential. Who knows, we might even get the neighbors to come and visit.

Coming Together

In the Smithsonian Institute in Washington D.C. there is a small glass case containing a rock from the moon. Each year millions of people crowd around the case and stare at the rock, taking pictures and spending hours in conversation about the excitement of outer space. This simple little piece of rock is not more than two inches long and looks no different from any small stone you would find in your back yard, but it's from the moon and carries with it all of the dreams and mystery of the biggest event in our history, contact with outer space.

233

Those dreams are coming face to face with reality, for our contact with the Pleiadians provides us with new mind food to deal with. We have been given an opportunity to see ourselves through their eyes, a view of Earth as we really are, not as we think we are. But what do we do with all of these new ideas? How can we integrate what we are learning into our own society and help with the transition into the New Age?

Nothing is more important than to educate the minds of Earth about the material and the spiritual realm. People must learn to understand that they are more than just physical beings. We must help everyone get in touch with their spiritual self and feel the love of Creation. This is the way we will break down the material forces of hatred, prejudice, and other forms of illogical thinking that put so much stress on our world. For us to make any progress in our quest toward a more enlightened planet, we must educate and wake everyone up to the spiritual side of life; only then can we accomplish the transition into the New Age with a level of higher consciousness.

The Pleiadians and other races see us as spiritual beings in material bodies. They listen, observe, and study us as spiritual beings. If we are to take our place in the family of man throughout the universe, we have to clean up our thoughts and create a collective consciousness here on Earth of peace and love. If we continue to project thoughts of anger, jealousy, prejudice, hate, and other negative feelings, it will not be possible for us to communicate with the races of higher consciousness such as the Pleiadians.

Time is running out for Earth, for our technology is pushing us out into space and right into the backyards of other races who are far more developed. We won't be able to take our systems of economics, religion, education, and government with us, for they will no longer be adequate in a more advanced universal community. The Pleiadians tell us that they can no longer defend us once we are capable of leaving our system under our own power; that time is rapidly approaching. What are we going to do when more advanced races come to Earth who might like to conquer us, coerce our leaders into aligning with them for darker purposes, or worse yet, wipe us out and take the planet for themselves?

The Earth will soon have its opportunity to align itself with peaceful races like the Pleiadians or with immoral races that would offer power and control to a handful of men on Earth to rule us. The people of Earth must come together with a common vision in order to make Earth a peaceful and loving planet as we move into the New Age. We must overpower the greedy few who currently rule the planet with money and power and begin the transition from a material society to a more spiritual

234

one. In order to do this, we must come together in a state of higher consciousness and align the power of our spirits with a common view of a New Vision for Earth. By directing the spiritual power of thousands, even millions, of Earth people on a common vision, that thought can become a force of energy that can change the world toward peace.

Meditate on the following peaceful vision of Earth and put power into it. Explain the vision to others and ask them to help out. If enough of us concentrate on the vision, our thoughts will create energy and cause the material world to give way to our force, and the planet will start to change. Remember, always start little things in motion to cause the big things to happen. Just like the Creation, which started with a thought and created a universe, we can start with a thought and create a new world. Our future is up to us!

A Vision for Earth

Blue, Blue Earth, Your light is bright
Shining through the Milky Way tonight
Sending out a beam of love
and riding high on a consciousness, of
living in the Creation way,
harmony with nature, in every way
a world of peace where everyone
can win a dream and love someone
And now you've moved through time and space
to join the family of the human race
your life is rich, your spirit bright
and now forever you'll live in light

The Lightworkers of the New Age

Earth is currently a planet of over 170 nations with as many different ideologies, philosophies, and social customs. The leaders of the New Age must find ways to bring these many different concepts and theories together and find the common denominator that will allow us to live together in peace. To begin with, we must learn to understand each other with an open mind that allows acceptance of other viewpoints without anger and value judgments.

This is a time of education for Earth. If you find yourself able to share knowledge with others who are on a quest of enlightenment, here are some suggestions that may help you communicate and be of help to others.

Find Your Own Truth. Don't ask people to blindly accept your ideas or your information. Remind them that one man's knowledge is just another man's information. We must all earn knowledge for ourselves by experiencing it and making it part of our lives. Guide people to find truth for themselves. As questions are asked, try to answer only what is needed at the time. It is better for people to start with small bits of information and earn the next question through learning. All of life is a school, a spiritual experience of learning and growing. Knowledge is most useful if it comes at the right time. Try to promote the idea of an open mind; not only is it a sign of intelligence, but it is the way to faster and more accurate learning.

Promote Integrity. Acceptance of new ideas comes from respect for those who offer them. If you project integrity and sincerity instead of ego or vanity, you will not only be of more help to others, but you will feel better about yourself. Don't exaggerate or say things to get attention or gain importance. Your spirit knows when you are being untruthful; you can't lie to yourself. The New Age is an exciting time filled with lots of new information and experiences, but we must be careful to be honest with each other and ourselves. There is no better way of feeling good about yourself than giving freely without expecting anything in return. If you want to fill your heart with love, simply give some to another, and it will come back to you.

Role Model. Our heroes in the last century have been captains of industry, movies stars, adventurers, athletes, musicians, and war heroes. There have been many fine people among those heroes, to be sure. But the attraction is usually that we see in these people that which we want for ourselves, a role model for how we would like to be. People learn by studying others. In happy homes little boys want to be like their dads, and little girls want to grow up to be just like their moms. Role-modeling is very important to our young and needs to be taken very seriously. In the New Age our heroes need to be of a different type. We need role-modeling which projects wisdom, integrity, intelligence, and love. Let's use our schools, movies, books, and television to create heroes who are rich in value and honesty. The very fabric of our society is based on the integrity we instill in our young, for they create the future we will live in.

Project Equality, and Universal Love. Not enough can be said about the need for Universal Love in our thinking. Learn to see each other as spiritual beings on a path of growth and education and sense the spiritual bonding that ties us all together. It is the material side of us that we find so much fault with. We are imperfect as material beings, but we are all logical and loving as spirits. If we are to eliminate prejudice, hate, and anger, we must educate everyone about the real meaning of life and the power of the spirit. If you share with each other as spiritual beings, your material heart will swell with love for one another. Learn to give of your heart and ask nothing in return, and you will gain the greatest gift one human can give another, the gift of love.

The Planet. It is time to consider the planet we live with as an equal part of Creation. Although it does not have a consciousness as we do, it is comprised of particles of matter that have a life force. All matter in the universe is composed of energy generated from the evolution of Creation and should be respected as such. Get yourself on good terms with the planet and nature. Start by learning more about the planet itself. As a hobby you might want to study about the oceans, the forests, or volcanoes. Spend an afternoon watching birds build a nest or sit down by a stream and talk to it. There are life forces in nature that you can communicate with. Sometimes called elementals, these beings of nature will let themselves be seen by humans if you are of the right consciousness. You can feel their presence and commune with them. It is a good idea to go for a walk everyday for about 30 minutes with your shoes off. Not only can you feel the planet, but the pressure on the bottoms of your feet will stimulate the organs of your body and provide for your health. It is an age-old practice called reflexology and can be a valuable part of your health care, so take a Saturday and learn about it. Keep pieces of rock, crystal, plants, and beautiful pictures of Earth around you. Give them names and make them your friends. Live with the planet, not on it.

Study Spirit. Study about spiritual consciousness and share it with others. Read books, go to conferences, expos, and fill your mind with an inventory of information that can help you discover yourself. You might want to join or start a study group with others of like mind and experience and learn together. Practice mediation as much as you can, for it's the gateway into your spirit and your older/higher self. Through meditation you can develop more balanced thinking and make life more enjoyable. You can also try out your ideas and learn about the different levels of consciousness and how your mind works. Listen to those who have gone before you and then find your own path and develop your own wisdom. Your life is your own journey and must be walked alone, but you can use the footsteps of another as a guide and make your own discoveries. Get in touch with Creation and experience the spiritual bonding that we all share, and your material life will be forever easier and more fruitful. Then share it with another!

Help Educate the Young. At any age we are nothing more than the accumulated experiences that have gotten us to where we are now. And the experiences of our youth are the formative years that create our adulthood. Too many people are having difficulty with adult life because of childhood experiences that control their thinking. We must learn to educate our young better and eliminate child abuse. Over 50% of the children in America today are abused either mentally or physically by parents who don't love them or understand them. We are creating a nation of unhappy people who are not capable of offering anything to anyone else because of the hurt they carry around inside of themselves. Spend some time with children and help them with your love and understanding. If you can, adopt a child or be a big brother; you can certainly donate some time at a local park or school. Children respond very well to love and understanding, and so will you.

Be Creative. Creative thinking keeps you young and alert. It stimulates your brain and makes your spirit happy. The personal satisfaction that comes from being creative is a doorway to sharing your love with others. A beautiful picture you paint, a song, or a poem can project the love of your spirit to thousands of others and really make the world a better place. Art in any form should be promoted for everyone. Make it a regular part of your life. It's not important how good you are at it; the satisfaction comes from the process of creation, not the adulation of others. Shed the need for approval from others and express yourself in art that brings out your unique qualities and helps you understand yourself better. You should at least keep your environment filled with music, paintings, beautiful crystals, books, and stimulating objects which challenge and stimulate your senses. Every now and then buy some object of technology that is beyond your present understanding, and just keep it around until you figure it out. It is important to teach your mind to constantly be learning and trying to grow to new levels of understanding. Remember life is a school, enroll now!

Who Speaks for Earth

As we think, our thoughts move through space. If millions of us combine our thoughts, we can communicate with other worlds and develop relationships with more advanced beings. In this way we can create alliances for Earth with peaceful races. This is very important, for the American government as well as other 1st and 2nd world nations are all anxious to make connections with other worlds in order to gain power, weapons, and control over other nations. The dangerous game of "King on the Mountain," played by the world powers, can lead us to alliances with nonhuman races who will offer technology and power in exchange for our lives.

It is already happening in America, and certain "above the law" elements of our government have created alliances with a nonhuman race of ET's from a twin star system called Zeta Reticuli. It began in 1947 when one of their space ships crashed in New Mexico. The bodies of small nonhuman beings were discovered in the wreckage and gave our government a serious problem. Not knowing how to handle the sudden appearance of visitors from another world, especially nonhuman ones, and fearful of a panic, they decided to keep it quiet. A wise decision at the time, but within a short time more ships came and the administration was confronted with having to make a deal with these visitors, and decided to provide bases for them in exchange for technology.

These small nonhuman beings, who are called *Greys,* have no emotional concern for us, and look at us as lab experiments. The Pleiadians have confirmed their existence, stating that they are a highly scientific race, more interested in the planet than in us, but on some occasions take Earth people for experiments. Over the years many Earth people have been contacted by these little Greys but have learned very little about them.

Earth is being contacted by the Pleiadians, the Greys, and several other races. Millions of people all over the world have seen their ships and have had contacts of various kinds. It is no longer a question of whether or not it is real, but a question of whether or not you know about it. The people of Earth need to make contact with the Pleiadians and other peaceful races so we can be involved in how Earth becomes aligned with beings from other worlds.

I feel that nothing is more important right now than educating everyone about their spiritual selves and creating a large mass of humanity that can come together on the higher planes of consciousness and communicate with the Pleiadians and other peaceful races. The thoughts of Earth are being monitored all the time by many races. If they begin to detect a growing mass of people coming together spiritually, I believe they will come to our aid. Lets send "Greetings" from the people of Earth, and not from any special branch of the government.

Peace on Earth

It takes nothing more than watching the evening news to see how much trouble we are in as a planet. There are wars raging everywhere. The leaders of our planet are making no attempt to create peace since they stay in power through turmoil. No government wants to relinquish their own authority and blend in with other countries. This is why we have no real power in the United Nations. It is up to us, the people, to find a way to bring the nations of the world together in spite of the governments.

Imagine if you could form a group of spiritually-minded people who understand and live by the principle of unconditional love, and visit different countries around the world. You could go to each major city and put on a spiritual education expo where everyone shares and listens to one another and talks about our different customs, philosophies, and ideologies. By sharing we can find the common ground between us and blend our heritages together in a common goal for our planet. We can carry the message of spiritual bonding all around the world.

An educated mass of people can do far more than any government. There is nothing more powerful than 100 million people with common thinking and common goals. Look for ways to communicate and make this happen. You might want to join a computer bulletin board service and make friends around the world; it's the modern day pen pal. Talk to people at embassies and send newsletters to organizations in different countries. Record audio and video tapes of your ideas and make them available to radio and television in other countries. Write, or better yet, read a book about another culture. Find ways to communicate and understand people in other countries so that we can come together as a planet. People do not have trouble getting along, only politicians have that problem.

A Constitution for Earth

As the nations of Earth do start coming together, we don't want it to be at the hands of the bankers, politicians, and military leaders who are in power now. If they have their way, economic oppression will only get worse and we will continue on our run-a-way path of material greed. How about if we get together with a few million of our neighbors in other countries and write up a constitution for Earth and create a new plan for our future.

In May of 1787, seventy-four Americans got together in Philadelphia and spent the summer creating the Constitution of the United States. The public had no idea what they were doing until long after it was done. It was a bold move that brought the thirteen colonies together because of its simple logic and fairness for all.

How about if we send a group of spiritual minded people to each country and promote the idea of creating a Constitution for the planet? In other words, let's get the people of Earth mobilized and start bringing the world together in a more spiritual fashion before the material powers have their way. Once we have a Constitution for Earth that has been created by people from all the countries of the world, we will have accomplished a great deal in the way of understanding one another. Perhaps we could start with our own Constitutional Congress in Philadelphia and invite representatives from every country to participate. If we came up with a framework for creating a peaceful future for our planet that was beneficial for everyone, we would have a big jump on the politicians who are trying to form a one-world government based on money and power. The Constitution for the People of Earth could be the first step towards coming together as a people and governing ourselves. If we want to communicate and have commerce with other worlds, we will need to start getting along and demonstrating that we can live as peaceful spiritual beings.

It is time for us to turn the emphasis of our lives from finance and money to the development of the individual and the quality of life and begin to live as one planet with one people. Here are some ideas to start you thinking:

The Constitution
of the People of Earth

PREAMBLE

We, the people of Earth, in order to form a more harmonious union of nations and to protect the human rights of all people, to insure for the common defense, create spiritual growth, promote the education of all citizens, to protect and preserve the planet we live on and all creatures of nature, to establish protocols for communications with beings from other worlds, and to provide for the equal and fair distribution of all resources of our planet, do ordain and establish this Constitution for the People of Earth.

Article 1

All powers granted herein shall be vested in a General Assembly of the People of Earth, which shall consist of a membership of all nations and a Directorship comprised of 7 leaders.

The General Assembly

The General Assembly shall be the legislative body of government and shall consist of representatives from every country on Earth. Each country shall send 1 representative for every 50 million people of its population, or a minimum of 2 per country. Representatives shall be elected for a term of 6 years in their country of origin. All representatives shall be born in the country they represent and be a minimum of 25 years of age. Compensation to representatives shall be in the amount of the average salary of Earth; no other compensations are allowed. Representatives are citizens of Earth and are subject to all laws of Earth without special privileges.

The Directorship

The Directorship shall be comprised of 7 members and shall serve as the Executive Leadership for the planet. Each one of the 7 directors shall first have been an Assembly Representative for 2 sessions and must be voted into office by a two thirds vote of the General Assembly. Directors shall serve for one term of 10 years, and then may volunteer to serve in an advisory capacity.

Article 2

The General Assembly shall make its home in the country of Greenland which has donated 1,000 square miles for this purpose. The Assembly shall be required to meet four times a year for 45 days at a time to conduct business. Any citizen of Earth has the right to address the General Assembly either on appointed days or in writing. All citizens have the right to be heard.

Article 3

The People of Earth shall have free speech and free thought. The written and spoken word can be freely expressed in any format without fear of reprisal. Free thinking is also protected, and it is not allowed to use electronic, psychic, or other means to listen or interpret the thoughts of others without their consent. No one may be persecuted or denied their rights because of any spoken word or thought.

Article 4

An individual is considered a material being 21 days after conception and shall be given all the rights of life. Since a spirit enters the material world and makes its decision for life at this time, he or she will be considered alive in the material world and shall be defended by the laws and consciousness of the universe. It is a violation of Creation to kill any living being in material form.

Article 5

All citizens may move freely to any part of the planet Earth or other planets without hindrance. National borders are for mapping and historic reasons only, for all people are citizens of Earth and can move freely in any manner.

Article 6

The General Assembly shall issue the "Earth dollar" to all citizens and be responsible for its issuance. The Earth dollar shall be the monetary exchange for all countries and no other money shall be used. Each country shall receive Earth dollars in accordance with its gross national product and in consideration for its contribution to the general welfare of the planet. Developing countries shall receive extra compensation until they are at a level equal to other countries. The Earth dollar will be in paper form or in electronic form, citizens may choose either, and it is honored everywhere on Earth. The General Assembly shall have the right to issue Earth dollars in any amount to protect the welfare of all Earth citizens. Any citizen is entitled to Earth dollars in accordance with his contribution to society. The Earth dollar is based on the value of all products created on Earth. The intention is to raise the quality of life by providing goods and services of highest quality to all citizens, and to not be hampered in any way by an economic system that is used as a weapon against them.

Jobs are provided to any citizen capable of work, so everyone can contribute to his community and care for himself and his family. Compensation is related to the value of your position and its contribution to society. Wisdom, integrity, teaching, role-modeling, counseling, and service to community are among the most rewarded.

Article 7

There shall be no credit system of any kind since it leads to one man having control over another. A system of Time Payments for large purchases such as homes can be arranged, but there is no interest. A more complex system of economics is not encouraged, for the purpose of life is not to acquire material possessions or to create control over another through debt.

Article 8

The General Assembly shall form committees for Education, Economics, Spiritual Education, Off Planet Relations, Human Rights, Science and Technology, Social Development, and Agriculture in order to fairly distribute the resources of Earth to all citizens. All citizens have the right to a full education, a home of their own, proper health care, and legal representation. It is the duty of the General Assembly to ensure these rights.

Article 9

Local governments shall not make any laws that conflict with the Constitution of the People of Earth or the Natural Law of Nature.

Article 10

Spiritual education shall be offered to all who seek it in order to raise the level of consciousness of all citizens of Earth. A council of the highest minds will be maintained to guide us all towards higher consciousness. The council will be comprised of learned spiritual leaders capable of creating high levels of logical thinking and spiritual bonding that others can tap into. This high level of loving and neutral energy will be "on" at all times to heal the Earth and its citizens. At any time, citizens are encouraged to add their energy to this bonding force to make it stronger. As the people of Earth evolve, there will be a gradual increase in the intensity of this connecting band of energy. This can be used to stabilize the health of all the creatures of Earth and communicate with higher life forms on other worlds.

Article 11

No law may be passed which endangers any species of life or harms the essence of nature, including the oceans, rivers, forests, and atmosphere of Earth. Any citizen of Earth who violates the planet or nature shall be educated until he understands the importance of living in harmony with nature and Creation.

Article 12

The General Assembly shall be responsible for speaking on behalf of the people of Earth and representing them to all races, alliances, and councils from other worlds. A special city in Greenland shall be built to accommodate visitors from other worlds and to make them comfortable. Special rules and laws for visitors will be in force in this city only.

Article 13

The General Assembly shall maintain a Peace Force comprised of members of all nations. Each citizen of Earth between the ages of 18 and 25 shall serve 2 years in the Peace Force. During this time each citizen shall have the opportunity to serve in different capacities which shall allow him to visit and work with several different cultures. The Peace Force shall maintain the defense of the planet Earth, work in communication networks that make all information available to anyone on the planet, serve as local enforcement aids, work as teachers in education centers, plus a variety of other community tasks which offer the opportunity for education and service to community. Each citizen may select the type of service he would like to be involved in. It is desirable to promote the idea that we all should give to our community and not expect something in return. No other armies shall exist.

A New Vision for Earth

Article 14

The General Assembly shall provide for schools which allow any citizen to attend at no charge for as long as he wishes. The purpose is to raise the intelligence standard of all people of Earth. All levels of education, including the supersciences, are available to any citizen. No citizens shall be denied access to an education. School teachers shall be regarded among the highest rewarded in our society, for they mold the minds of our young who create our future. No society can be stronger then the people it raises.

Article 15

All citizens shall learn the English language, and it shall become the international language of choice. All local languages may be continued as a second language.

Article 16

The human population of Earth shall be reduced to under 1 billion, and not less than 500 million, in order to live more closely in harmony with nature and Creation and to relieve stress on the eco, social, and agriculture system. The population of the animal kingdom shall also be regulated in accordance.

Article 17

All citizens may barter any goods or services without the transfer of Earth dollars since there is no taxation.

Article 18

Hospitals shall be maintained in all cities on Earth. Doctors may use any remedy they choose, so long as they have been educated in its use. Natural remedies, such as sound, light, consciousness, and food will be highly promoted because they are the natural form in nature and do not pollute the body. Toxic chemicals are not allowed except in special cases.

A public panel shall be open at all times to inventors and developers of health remedies. All health remedies are freely available to all citizens. Contributions by citizens to the health of all is considered to be among the highest of gifts and is to be rewarded with Earth dollars for life.

Article 19

No form of energy shall be used on Earth that damages the atmosphere, oceans, or forests of nature. No energy shall be used that damages the thinking or health of Earth citizens. All energies shall be free to citizens and regulated by a public committee. No chemicals or toxins of any kind are to be used as energy sources unless completely harmless to life. Field generators, solar power, and tachyon energy converters shall be the primary source of energy on Earth, for they are free, safe, and come in unlimited supply from the universe. A public panel will be open at all times that encourages any citizens to come forth with inventions or ideas which can better the quality of life on Earth through energy. A contribution of such great importance by any citizen would be highly rewarded with Earth dollars for life.

Article 20

Rehabilitation cities shall be maintained in Greenland to be used for the reeducation of those who break the laws. Those who are found guilty of a crime shall work and study in cities designed to educate them within the areas of their crime until they are ready to reenter society. The utmost care, attention, love, and understanding shall be given to those who are having trouble with their lives, so they may reenter society and live a more meaningful and rewarding existence.

Those guilty of violent crimes and who cannot be rehabilitated due to mental problems will live in special cities and kept away from society. They shall be cared for with the greatest of human understanding, in the hopes that by the end of their lives they can reach a better level of thinking so as not to impair the next life.

Article 21

Public communications systems cannot be used in any manner that displays human conduct that is not in line with the excepted role modeling for life. No form of violence, sexual explicit or illogical materials can be transmitted in any form using public systems.

Public forums shall be maintained by all communication systems to keep the voice of the public heard. Any citizen of any age has the right to be heard over public communication networks. All citizens are encouraged to take an active part in the development of community and planet

Article 22

A citizen is allowed all freedoms in his home that are not harmful or disruptive to others. Alcohol, drugs or other narcotics of any type cannot be used in any public area. A personal license will be granted to any citizen for the use of such products in his home. The license requires annual meetings with counselors on the use of these intoxicants.

Summary

This is just a rough framework for a Constitution that should be started and worked out among us all. The idea is that the people must take part in the development of our future, and not leave it up to a handful of men who dictate how we should live because of some economic standard that is designed to keep them rich. We should take control of our world and live to our highest level of achievement based on wisdom and intelligence, not money. Our current system of economic control over the planet will have no use in the future, so we should evolve our system and prepare to move out into the family of man in the universe.

If you have any ideas or suggestions about The Constitution for the People of Earth, write and let me know. With enough of us putting our thoughts into creating a new future perhaps we can make it happen.

The Pleiadians and other races are awakening us to who we are and to our potential as beings, but we should remember that Earth is our responsibility, not theirs. While we thank them for their help and their concern, it is time for all citizens of Earth to assume their part of the responsibility of creating the kind of future we want for ourselves, and complete the *Pleiadian Mission.*

See you in Philadelphia!

Epilog

I want to express my thanks to Billy and his family for extending me their courtesy and friendship during my 3 trips to their home. Even though they have endured so many hardships and difficult times over the years, they still had time to make me feel welcome. My thanks to Silvano, Bruni, Billy, Popi, and the other members of the FIGU, for providing me with the spiritual food to help me along the path of my own discovery.

I hope that the information I have made available here in this book has in some way contributed to the ongoing efforts of the Pleiadian Mission and is of benefit to mankind.

I have no plans to return to Switzerland, but instead hope that the experiences of my travels can be of some benefit to other seekers of truth.

Saalome,

Randolph Winters

Glossary

7 Sisters   A term used to by the Kiowa Indians to describe 7 Indian maidens who were put in the heavens by the Great Spirit to escape the advancement of a bear. The 7 sisters became known as the star cluster called the Pleiades.

Absolutum   A term to describe a large body of Creational energy that contains billions of universes. Ours is one of them.

Adam   In the old language of Lyra it means "Earth human being." A Lyrian scientist named Semjasa created an "Adam," or Earth human, through genetic engineering which started the story of Adam and Eve.

Age of Aquarius   A time period of 2,155 years as the Earth moves through the constellation of Aquarius, one of the 12 constellations. Also called the Age of the Water Bearer.

Age of Waterman   The same as the Age of Aquarius. Used to describe the period that the Earth passes through the constellation of Aquarius.

Agharta   An ancient underground city built in the Gobi desert under the gigantic city of Mu around 33,000 years ago.   There were two cities called Agharta Alpha and Agharta Beta and were connected by an underground tunnel. Mu was destroyed, but Agharta still exists today.

akashic   In Eastern philosophy the term akashic means the same as etheric and refers to the unseen energy of thought that is stored in a ring around the planet. The akashic is a store-house of thoughts from the past that can be accessed through meditation.   In India it is regarded as including material and nonmaterial entities in a common medium. Sometimes referred to as the akashic records.

android   A synthetic or artificial creation made to resemble the human form. It is used for the purpose of serving man in many different forms.

Andromeda Galaxy   A large spiral galaxy that can be seen from Earth. It is similar in shape and form to the Milky Way Galaxy that we live in. It is 2.2 million light years from Earth and is 160,000 light years wide. It is the home of a very advanced race of beings that provide advice to the Pleiadians and other races.

Andromeda   A constellation in the Milky Way that supports human life as we know it. Beings from there have visited Earth on occasion.

Arahat Athersata   A spiritual entity that no longer exists in material form but exists in pure spiritual form and is comprised of 7 different spirits. The teacher of Jesus Christ that also telepathically sent information to

Earth at the request of the Pleiadians to Billy Meier in the 1970's.

Arahat Mountain   A very large mountain in eastern Turkey. Believed to be the resting place of Noah's Ark, this religious mountain has special meaning to many religions and belief systems.

Aramaic   The language that was spoken in the days of Jesus Christ. His teachings were written down in Aramaic and were discovered in 1963 by a Greek minister.

Armenia   An ancient culture who originally lived in the region known as Armenia in northeastern Turkey. Today most Armenians live in Russia.

Armus people   In the year 8104 B.C. the great war between Atlantis and Mu left the world largely uninhabited. One of the three surviving tribes were the descendants of the people who lived in an area known as Armenia 33,000 years ago, and were called the Armus people.

aura   A field of energy that surrounds a human being. It is magnetic in nature and can be seen using kirlian photography. It appears in colors which reflect the thinking of the human mind.

Bafath   A race of extraterrestrials who are the descendants of ancient Lyrians. They were forced to leave Earth over 10,000 years ago, but returned and hid under the Great Pyramid of Gizeh in Egypt and fought to gain control of Earth. The Pleiadians removed them from Earth and they are no longer a threat to us.

Barnard Star   Located just 4.4 light years from Earth, this star has two planets in orbit around it that have supported human life in the past and possibly still does.

barter   A form of trade that does not require money. Before our current system of money most of the world engaged in trading their products and services in this system called barter.

beamdrive   One of the two drive systems used on a Pleiadian Beamship to propel it. A beamdrive is a system that creates energy by converting light into power. It is an older system and is no longer being manufactured.

Beamship   On Earth we call round flying discs from other worlds flying saucers. The Pleiadians call their ships Beamships after the drive system that powers them.

Beta Centauri   Located only 4.3 light years from Earth the planets around this star have been home to human races in the past.

big bang   Many Earth scientist believe the universe we live in was created by a big bang of energy that exploded and pushed itself out, creating the formation of the galaxies that currently exist.

Boomerang   When we create thoughts in our mind, the, speed out into the universe. At a certain distance they change polarity and return to the sender. This process is called the boomerang.

Capricorn   One of the 12 constellations that the Earth passes through every 25, 860 years. We are now in the Age of Aquarius; Capricorn is next.

Caspian Sea   The world's largest inland sea. It lies between Europe and Asia. The south coast belongs to Iran while the rest of the sea is surrounded by the territory of the USSR.

central sun   In the center of our galaxy there is a large ball of energy that provides life-giving rays to the entire galaxy. It is called the central, or universal, sun by many.

Central Universe   The Pleiadians are aware of 3 types of universes that are evolving within the Original Creation which is called the Absolutum. A Central Universe is the highest order that they have discovered, but its function is still a mystery to them.

Changing Belt   One of the 7 belts of energy that divide up our universe. The Changing Belt is a nonmaterial area that is responsible for the conversion of energy into other forms.

channeling   The process of entering a meditative trance in order to call forth other entities which may use your body to speak.

Cheops   Cheops was a pharaoh in Egypt and is sometimes thought of as the builder of the Great Pyramid. It is also called the Great Pyramid of Gizeh which refers to the Gizeh plateau on which it is built.

coarse-matter   Energy that is in the solid state of matter, as opposed to fine-matter which is energy in nonmaterial form such as thought.

codex   The codex is a form of karmic debt that many Earth people live under because of their previous lives as Lyrians who ravaged the Earth. It is the spiritual awareness of owing a debt to humanity for atrocities done in previous lives.

cognition   When knowledge becomes part of the individual it is called a cognition.

coherent   That which is logically connected; consistent as a coherent argument.

Consciousness   The formation of rational thoughts. The human being has a material consciousness and a subconsciousness which are both capable of producing a collection of thoughts we call consciousness.

constellation   The Earth and all of our solar system travels in a large oval pattern which takes 25,860 years to complete.   This time period is divided into 12 sections which are called constellations as in Virgo, Aquarius, Capricorn, etc.

Creation   This is the spiritual energy that had the idea to create the universe that we live in.   It is a spiritual form that contains the eternal energy of life and knowledge that rules all things.

Creational Universe   This is a type of universe that creates a material belt of planets, stars, and life forms in order to evolve.   The universe we live in is a Creational one.

cuneiform   This is an ancient form of writing that was used by the Babylonians, Persians, and others.   Its characters are in the form of wedges, and are slim, triangular shapes that form into a language.

Dal Universe   This is the universe that is right next to ours.   It is a Creational Universe as ours is and supports human life.   The Pleiadians are in touch with a race of humans from there called Timers.

Dead Sea Scrolls   A collection of ancient manuscripts discovered in caves in the cliffs at Qumran, Jordan in 1947.   The writings date back to 200 B.C. and largely reconstruct the Old Testament and the long-lost books of the Apocrypha, and the books of Enoch, Jubilees, the Testaments of the Twelve Patriarchs.

dematerialize   The Pleiadians have a high technology which allows them to convert their ships into a nonmaterial form.   The process is called dematerializing.

depolarize   The process of reversing the magnetic pole of something; for instance, you can depolarize a magnet by changing the polarity of its poles from positive to negative and vice versa.

Destroyer Comet   A large comet that passes by Earth approximately every 575 years. It has been the cause of much destruction on Earth as well as many other worlds.   It was the cause of the Biblical Flood in 8104 B.C.

Devils Tower   Located in Wyoming this large mound of Earth is a sacred site of historical importance to the Indians.   They believe that 7 Kiowa Indian maidens were being chased by a bear.   The bear tried to catch the maidens and left his claw marks on the side of the tower which is evident when you see it.   The great spirit intervened and put the 7 maidens up in the sky as stars which are called the Pleiades.

DNA   Deoxyribonucleic Acid.   The main carrier of genetic information in all living organisms except viruses, that contain ribonucleic acid.

Easter Island   Located 300 miles off the coast of South America this island is covered with strange monuments carved in stone. The monuments were images created of extraterrestrials led by a man named Viracocoha who supplied the tools to the local people to make the statues.

ego The "I" or self of any person. Egotism or conceit or self-importance.

etheric In India etheric is used to describe the unseen energy and thoughts of humans. It comes from the word *ether*. It is sometimes also called the akashic.

Eva This is a Lyrian word which means "Earth female." It is used in reference to the Earth female that was coupled with the "Adam" or "Earth human being," that created the story of Adam and Eve.

fauna The animals of a given region or period considered as a whole.

F.I.G.U. A German acronym for Free Community of Interest of Border and Spiritual Scientists and Ufologists. The F.I.G.U. is a special group of people who have banded together to help Billy Meier disseminate his Pleiadian information to the world.

fine-matter Energy in nonmaterial form such as thought.

flashing Refers to the flashing of the mind as impulses are sent from the conscious mind to the subconscious in order to create a thought. The rapid process occurs millions of times per second and is called flashing.

flora The plant life of a region or period. Refers to the food kingdom of Earth.

fluffy matter During the evolution of energy into matter, fluffy matter is the term used to describe the state of evolution between thought and gas.

Gabriel Gabriel was a Pleiadian man who was the father of Jmmanuel, who was known as Jesus Christ.

gemut The sensory connection to creation that is within all of us that connects our spiritual self to the infinite Creational energy.

genetics The science of heredity. Dealing with the resemblance and differences of related organisms resulting from the interaction of their genes and the environment.

Gizeh Pyramid Sometimes called the Great Pyramid or Pyramid of Cheops, the Gizeh Pyramid was built on what is called the Gizeh plateau which is just outside of Cairo in Egypt.

Gobi Desert A large desert located in Mongolia. It was the home of the great city of Mu which was built around 33,000 years ago.

greattime   A unit of time measurement which describes the complete cycle of a creation from the time it has the idea to create a universe, the creation of one, and then the collapse back into itself to sleep.   One greattime amounts to 311,040,000,000,000 years by our calendar.

Hebrews   A band of people who survived the great holocaust of 8104 B.C.. They were known as gypsies, spies, murderers and were thought to be the dregs of society of their time. a.k.a. Hebrons.

Hesperides   This planet was a refuge for human life that escaped the great wars in Lyra.

Higher self   As life forms we are both material and spiritual beings. Higher self refers to the consciousness of our spiritual self that is generally more knowledgeable than our material consciousness.   It is higher in wisdom, intelligence, etc.

Homo Sapiens   The species of bipedal primates to which humans belong.

Hyades   A planet which supports human life forms who escaped from the great wars on Lyra and made it their own home.   It is not known if life still exists there.

Hyperborea   A colony founded on Earth over 15,000 years ago in the area that is now called Florida.   Hyperboreans live underground and are believed to be now living under Mt. Shasta in northern California.

hyperspace   One of the dimensions of our universe that is outside of the 3-dimensional existence we live in that makes travel at high speeds possible.   Pleiadian Beamships enter hyperspace to cross the large distances of the universe in part of a second.

Ideologies   The body of doctrine, myth, belief, etc. that guides an individual, social movement, or group.

Ishrish   A female who has become a King of Wisdom.   To have obtained total knowledge of the material existence of the human being.

Ishwish   A male who has become a King of Wisdom.   To have obtained total knowledge of the material existence of the human being.

Jmmanuel   A great prophet of his time who taught the lessons of Creation.   His father was a Pleiadian man named Gabriel, and his mother, Mary, was of Lyrian decent.   His teachings were adopted by the Catholic Church who changed his name to Jesus Christ in the year 189 A.D.

karmic   Taken from the word *karma*.   Thought of as bringing upon oneself inevitable results, good or bad, either in this life or in a reincarnation.

Kashmir   A large valley which stretches across the northern tip of India, the valley of Kashmir is administered partly by India, partly by Pakistan, and partly by China. Considered to be a spiritual area for many religious leaders.

kilometer   A unit of measure.   One Kilometer equals .6 of a mile.   100 kilometers equals 62 miles.

Kiowa   A race of Indians who inhabited the area of North Dakota until around 1800. It is believed that 7 Kiowa Indian maidens were put into the sky and became the star cluster known as the Pleiades.

Lahson   A small planet of unknown position in the cosmos.   It is the home of an ancient spirit-form that was brought to Earth by the Pleiadians to assist with their Mission to help man.

light year   A unit of measure to indicate the distance that light travels in one year's time.   Light travels at 186,000 miles in a second, and 5,865,696,000,000 miles in a year.

lotus position   A sitting position where the individual crosses his legs during meditation.

Lyra   The home of the human race that populated Earth. Lyra is a star constellation.

Madagascar   A large island located off the south west coast of Africa. This area has the same mysterious effects as the Bermuda triangle.

Mayan Calendar   An ancient prophetic calendar left by a race of people called Mayans who lived in central Mexico. Their predictions have been preserved down through the ages on what is called the Mayan calendar. The Pleiadians believe that the information on this calendar is very accurate.

Mecca   Located on the Red Sea this town is the spiritual capital of the Muslim empire. Every day millions of Muslims get down on their knees and face the city of Mecca and say their prayers.

Milky Way   A name given to the galaxy that we live in. If you up in the sky on a clear night towards the direction of the center of our galaxy you can see millions of stars that appear in a milky cloud like formation which has led to the name The Milky Way.

Milona   The ancient ancestors of Lyra founded colonies on 3 planets in our solar system, Earth, Mars, and Milona, a planet that was in orbit past Mars. A violent war destroyed Milona and all that is left is the debris that we now call the asteroid belt.

Mothership   A large spacecraft built by the Pleiadians. It houses over 140,000 passengers and provides them with all the comforts of a planet.

Smaller ships can dock in it when visiting and hitch a ride to other parts of the universe.

Mt. Shasta   Located in northern California, Mt. Shasta is the home of the descendants of a race of people called Hyperboreans.   Their ships are gold in color and can be seen sometimes entering the mountain on the northeast side.

Mu   An ancient city which was founded in the Gobi Desert around 33,000 years ago.   Its founder was a man names Muras who was the father-in-law of Atlant who founded Atlantis.   Mu became an empire with satellite cities all over Earth.   The empire was sometimes called Lemuria.

Nazca   Located in South America high up in the Andes Mountains this area has large lines dug into the ground that have mystified science. Under the lines are electronic sensors planted there thousands of years ago.

New Age   A term used to describe the time period which signifies the beginning of the Age of Aquarius which started February 3rd, 1937.

nisel bodies   Small organelles in the human body which contain the spiritual self of the human being.

null-time   Outside of the 3-dimensional world we live in is an area of the universe where time is almost nonexistent.   This area is referred to as null-time, meaning no time exists there.   It is also referred to as hyperspace.

Orion   A constellation located 444 light years from Earth.   It is also the home of human life that descended from ancient Lyra.

oscillations   All matter is made up of particles that are constantly in a spinning motion called oscillating.

Other Side   The Pleiadians refer to the "other side" as a place where spirits go after the material life is over.   It is a band of energy which surrounds the Earth and is commonly referred to as heaven.

overkill beams   A term used to describe the awesome power used by the Beamships of Atlantis.   These beams of energy were capable of dissolving matter and leaving no trace.

paradigms   A phrase used to describe a set form of knowledge that serves as a model or pattern.   A model of thinking.

part second   A phrase to describe a small unit of time.   The Pleiadians refer to time as being pulses of energy that cause the rotation, movement, and animation of matter.   One second of time is divided into millions of small parts.   Part second, then, is an

256

expression meaning one small pulse of time in a second.

Petale   The highest form of consciousness before becoming one with the Creation.   The Petale level is a collection of many consciousness that no longer have individual awareness.

Pharaoh   In Egyptian the word means "Great House" or royal palace. Also used to designate the reining king of Egypt.

pictographic   An old form of language used by the Babylonians, Persians and others to leave behind their story in picture form.

Pisces   One of the 12 constellations that Earth passes through.   We have just left the Age of Pisces and are now in the Age of Aquarius.

Pleja System   The original home of the Pleiadians was called the Asael System after its founder.   His daughter's name was Pleja and assumed power after his death.   From then on the system was called the Plejas.

Pleiades   A small cluster of stars located in the constellation of Taurus the Bull.   It is 500 light years from Earth and is the home of a race of humans who frequently visit the Earth.   We have common ancestry with them.

procreated   A translation of a Pleiadian word which means to cause someone to be born, as in procreating their spirit into material life.

psychic   Pertaining to the human soul or mind.   Mental, not physical. Outside of natural or scientific knowledge.   Sometimes used to refer to a person who is allegedly sensitive to psychic influences or forces.

Push Belt   The outer edge of a universe that serves as a protective shield. It blocks out energies from other universes and protects us.

Real Time Vision   A thought that come into your mind from an outside source that is indistinguishable from reality.   The vision occurs in real time meaning that a 10 minute idea takes 10 minutes to come into your mind.

rematerialize   A high technology of the Pleiadians to cause the material form of their Beamships to become coarse-matter, or solid.   The process of returning from dematerialization.   They can dematerialize their ships and then rematerialize them at will.

Ring Nebulae of Lyra   Located in the constellation of Lyra there is a large ring in space which is the remains of a sun that was exploded during a violent war there.   It can be seen by astronomers through powerful telescopes.

Rosicrucians   A secret society started in the 17th century.   They claim to have various forms of occult knowledge and power and profess esoteric principles of religion.

Sanskrit scrolls   Ancient writings of the Indians in India dating back 10,000 years which carry the truth about life and creation. To modern science they only date back to around 1200 B.C.

Sirius   The Dog Star. It is the brightest appearing star in the heavens and is located in the constellation Canis Major.   Human life from there migrated to Earth around 33,000 years ago.   It is believed that Sirius is the home of the black-skinned race.

Sohar   When the universe was being formed, there was a great blast of energy which established the area where the universe would form.   This blast of spiritual energy is called the Sohar.

Sol System   Refers to a sun that has planets orbiting around it.

spacers   The Pleiadians sometimes refer to their large space craft as great spacers or simply spacers.   These are generally ships that can carry at least a 1,000 passengers.

spirit   The same as the soul.   The Pleiadians refer to our souls as spirit-forms since the are formed from the original Creational energy of the Creation which they called spirit energy.   We are spirit-forms from that energy.

spirit-form   The same as a spirit or soul.   Creation is the ultimate source of spiritual energy that is referred to as spirit.   Humans are a form of spirit that are still connected to Creation but have their own consciousness called spirits or spirit-forms.

Srinagar   A town in India that was the home of Jmmanuel after the Crucifixion. He lived there until he died and is buried outside of town on the side of a hill somewhere.   Srinagar is located in the very north of India in the area that passes through the Valley of Kashmir.

supernova   When a sun reaches old age, it suddenly becomes thousands of times brighter and then gradually fades to its original intensity.

synagogues   Places of worship for the Jewish people.

tachyons   A small particle that travels faster than light.   It can be detected in our own 3-dimensional world.

Taygeta   One of the 7 stars of the Pleiades and is the solar sun for the Pleiadians who live on the 4 planets that are in orbit around it.

telekinesis   A spiritual power that enables you to move objects with the power of your own spirit.

telemeter ship   Small reconnaissance ships built by the Pleiadians which are used to gather information on Earth.   They can be as small as a basketball or up to 9 feet in diameter.

telepathy   The power of the human spirit to receive and send thoughts to another human.   The material mind as well as the spiritual self both have methods of telepathy.

thought-form   Means the same as a thought.

Timeless   A part of our universe that does not contain the energy of time.   Pleiadian Beamships commonly use this timeless area to speed through light years while time stands still in normal space.

Timers   A race of human life that is in contact with the Pleiadians in order to help the human races.   Their home is in an adjacent universe called the Dal Universe.

Ur   This is the first and primary spiritual force of the Original Creation and is responsible for creating timelessness in new creations.

Ur Universe   An Ur Universe is one that creates Creational Universes.   It has no Material Belt, but is all spiritual energy.   It evolves into a Central Universe.

Van Allen belt   Either of two regions of high energy-charged particles surrounding the Earth.   The inner region has an altitude of 2,000 miles while the outer region is between 9,000 to 12,000 miles.

Vega   A star that is the home for some of the descendants of the ancient Lyrians.

we-form   Refers to a special sense within all human life that is the sensor for the ability of telepathy.   There is a material we-form and a spiritual we-form.

Zeta Reticuli   A twin, or binary, star system that is the home of small nonhuman beings that visit the Earth.   We call these visitors "little Greys' or "Zetas."   They sometimes abduct humans for experiments and have no emotional attachment for us.

Zeus   The mythical Greek god that ruled over the heavens.

References and Suggested Reading

UFO - Contact From the Pleiades. Genesis III Publishing, Inc. Box 25962 Munds Park, Arizona 86017

Messages From the Pleiades Wendelle Stevens UFO Photo Archives P.O. Box 17206, Tucson, AZ 85710

Colliers Encyclopedia

Atlas Maps of the World

Random House New English Dictionary - 2nd Edition

Semjase Reports Eduard A. Meier Semjase Silver Star Center. CH 8499 Hinterschmidruiti, ZH Switzerland German language

The Psyche Eduard A. Meier Semjase Silver Star Center. CH 8499 Hinterschmidruiti, ZH Switzerland German language

The Prophecies Eduard A. Meier Semjase Silver Star Center. CH 8499 Hinterschmidruiti, ZH Switzerland German language

The Meditation Eduard A. Meier Semjase Silver Star Center. CH 8499 Hinterschmidruiti, ZH Switzerland German language

Celestial Teachings James Deardorff Wild Flower Press P.O. Box Box 726. Newburg, Oregon 97132 ISBN: 0-926524-11-9

The Talmud Jmmanuel Eduard A. Meier Wild Flower Press P.O. Box 726. Newburg, Oregon 97132 ISBN: 0-926524-12-7

Jesus Lived in India Holger Kirsten. Element Book Ltd. Longmead, Shaftesbury, Dorset England

The Problems of New Testament Gospel Origins. James Deardorff. Published by Edwin Mellen Press. Box 450, Lewiston, NY 14092.

For more information please contact the:

Semjase Silver Star Center
8499 Hinterschmidruti, ZH
Switzerland

The Pleiadian California Study Group
P.O. Box 5108
Chatsworth, CA 91311

Art by James Nichols

CONTACT FROM THE PLEIADES

BILLY MEIER AND "SEMJASE"
Full Color Print Now Available
11x14 $15.00 - 8x10 $10.00

To order please specify size and amount plus $2.00 for postage and handling per print of BILLY MEIER AND "SEMJASE". For a complete brochure of UFO Art by James Nichols include additional $6.00. Send orders to: James Nichols, 4040 E. Ft. Lowell #20, Tucson, AZ 85712

THE PLEIADIAN CONNECTION

A classic video covering the extraterrestrial contacts of Eduard Billy Meier with the Pleiadians. This one hour tape made for television presents an overview of the Pleiadian Mission to Earth. **Includes over 100 pictures of the Pleiadian Beamships**

$39.95

UFO - THE PLEIADIAN CONTACTS

A complete 16 tape set plus a book of drawings and diagrams covering information from over 115 contacts from the Pleiades as given to Billy Meier for the people of earth. Narrated by Randolph Winters these tapes include lessons on meditation, the psyche, spiritual growth, the science of space travel, future prophecies for Earth, life on other planets, the history of man, time travel, ancient mysteries on earth and life in the Pleiades. Here is the complete Pleiadian UFO contact story containing never before published information.

16 audio tapes and a set of drawings and notes covering the Pleiadian Contacts

$139.95

THE PLEIADES PROJECT
P.O. BOX 386
ATWOOD, CA 92601
(714) 528-1218